Le Queer Impérial

Francopolyphonies

Collection dirigée par / Series Editors

Kathleen Gyssels
Christa Stevens

VOLUME 24

The titles published in this series are listed at *brill.com/fpph*

Le Queer Impérial

*Male homoerotic desire in francophone
colonial and postcolonial literature*

By

Julin Everett

BRILL

RODOPI

LEIDEN | BOSTON

Cover illustration: photography of the Senegalese dancer Feral Benga by Lucien Walery (1863–1935), Paris, c. 1930.

The Library of Congress Cataloging-in-Publication Data is available online at http://catalog.loc.gov
LC record available at http://lccn.loc.gov/2017029868

Library of Congress Cataloging-in-Publication Data

Names: Everett, Julin, author.
Title: Le queer imperial : male homoerotic desire in Francophone colonial and
    postcolonial literature / by Julin Everett.
Description: Leiden ; Boston : Brill-Rodopi, 2018. | Series:
    Francopolyphonies ; 24 | Includes bibliographical references and index.
Identifiers: LCCN 2018024146 (print) | LCCN 2018024408 (ebook) |
    ISBN 9789004365544 (E-book) | ISBN 9789004365537 (hardback : alk. paper)
Subjects: LCSH: French literature—French-speaking countries—History and
    criticism. | Homosexuality in literature. | Race in literature. | Colonies
    in literature. | Postcolonialism in literature.
Classification: LCC PQ3897 (ebook) | LCC PQ3897 .E94 2018 (print) |
    DDC 840.9/896—dc23
LC record available at https://lccn.loc.gov/2018024146

Typeface for the Latin, Greek, and Cyrillic scripts: "Brill". See and download: brill.com/brill-typeface.

ISSN 1574-2032
ISBN 978-90-04-36553-7 (hardback)
ISBN 978-90-04-36554-4 (e-book)

Printed by Printforce, the Netherlands

Contents

Acknowledgements

I am most grateful for the generous support of The Department of French and Francophone Studies at UCLA where this project began. Much love to the UC system, for its commitment to its doctoral students. My work was supported by the Eugene Cota Robles Fellowship, the Graduate Summer Mentorship Scholarship, the Alice Belkin Memorial Scholarship and by a UCLA Dissertation Year Fellowship. I have been blessed with amazing mentors. Dominic Thomas' Seminar on Immigration Literature inspired me to think about power relations in the colonization of black Africa. Portions of the paper I wrote for his course appear in Chapter Five of this book: "Is Looking Merely the Opposite of Doing? Rape and Representation in *Le Docker noir*". I cannot overstate my appreciation for Dominic's kindness and encouragement. Françoise Lionnet's works on identity and representation helped me to develop my own modes of analysis and showed me what it means to write elegantly. The feminist underpinnings of this work owe much to both her *Autobiographical Voices* (1989) and her *Postcolonial Representations* (1995). My work on the project at UCLA was also aided by Steven Nelson and Alain Mabanckou, by Laure Murat, who encouraged me to provide more nuanced analyses, and by Andrea Loselle, whose amazing courses on Surrealism and postmodern theories allowed me to spread my analytical wings.

My year as a Visiting Assistant Professor in the Department of French and Italian at Miami University gave me an opportunity to refine my ideas among distinguished senior colleagues producing excellent research. I am also grateful to Appalachian State University, where I wrote a good half of this book, especially to then-Dean Anthony G. Calamai, for his support of my research. Additionally, my colleague Nancy Love generously offered me her template for writing a book prospectus. My scholarship has also been enthusiastically supported by Ursinus College, especially by former Interim Dean, April Edwards, for whose mentorship I remain grateful.

My thanks to *Research in African Literatures* for generously giving permission to reprint, as Chapter Nine of this book, "Must *la victime* be Feminine? Postcolonial Violence, Gender Ambiguity and the Postcolonial State in *Je soussigné cardiaque*," first published in the journal in 2013. Special thanks Colette Trout for pointing me towards Rodopi/Brill, and to Christa Stevens, Debbie de Wit and Kathleen Gyssels for their efforts in bringing this project to fruition.

I thank my friends Magda Konieczna, who gave me thoughtful advice on my book prospectus and Sheri Ann Cowie, who inspired me to pursue a doctorate.

The earliest draft of this work was patiently read by J.C. Jaress, who also encouraged my brainstorming and created a space for me to work. Several chapter drafts were read by my colleague and *copine*, Leslie Barnes.

My love and gratitude to my family: Jacque Houston, Judith Scott, Ricky Green, Chris Violette and to Tartine. Finally, my love to my darling Lola, who, though she could not read, was by my side for much of the writing of *Le Queer Impérial*. This book is dedicated to her.

Introduction

Passages à l'acte: Political and Textual Violence in Francophone Colonial and Postcolonial Literatures

> ... their very violence, display of destructive power, is to be conceived as the mode of appearance of its very opposite – if anything, they are exemplary cases of the impotent *passage à l'acte*.
>
> SLAVOJ ŽIŽEK, "Some politically incorrect reflections on violence in France"[1]

∴

In the midst of the polarizing debate in France over same-sex marriage, the anonymous political caricaturist l'Arlequin expressed a view of Christiane Taubira held by many who oppose two laws which bear her name: the 2013 Taubira Law giving same-sex couples the right to both marry and jointly adopt; and the 2001 Taubira Law recognizing slavery as a crime against humanity. L'Arlequin, whose work is featured on web sites such as that of the ultra-conservative Ligue Francilienne, portrays France's first black Minister of Justice as a menacing giant standing atop a diminutive white French family composed of one woman, one man and a small boy who clings to his mother in terror. The couple too attempts to hold onto each other despite the efforts of the giant Taubira to pull them apart. L'Arlequin dresses Giant Taubira in her signature pink Yves Saint Laurent jacket, and bestows on her a protruding forehead and bulbous lips. In her hand l'Arlequin places a spear aimed at the chest of the white mother, whose face is streaked with tears. On the dark brown shaft of the spear is written: "Mariage Homo".[2]

L'Arlequin has filled his drawing with all-too obvious tropes: firstly, Christiane Taubira as the harbinger of doom for the French family, itself essentially heterosexual and white; secondly the trope of blacks as ape-like, violent spear-chuckers; and finally, that of gay marriage as social and physical death,

---

1 Slavoj Žižek, "Some politically incorrect reflections on violence in France," *Multitudes: revue politique, artistique, philosophique*. Nov. 21, 2005, accessed April 24, 2010, http://multitudes .samizdat.net/Some-politically-incorecct.html.

2 L'Arlequin: Caricaturiste, "Untitled," accessed May 9, 2013. https://www.egaliteetreconcilia tion.fr/Les-dessins-de-la-semaine-18511.html.

a dangerous, non-productive use of the phallus, here embodied by the spear. Though this drawing explicitly targets the 2013 Taubira Law on gay marriage, its racialized nature also expresses hostility towards the 2001 Taubira Law. This hotly-contested legislation, proposed by Taubira, a descendant of those whose bodies were once the property of the French Empire, was opposed by social conservatives advocating a revisionist history which, romanticizing French imperialism, would tout the benefits of colonization. And so, by representing a spear aimed at a white French family as a nod to Taubira's African ancestry, to Taubira as a constant reminder of France's lost empire, as well as to the perceived phallic danger on the Marriage-For-All Law, L'Arlequin skillfully fuses two issues which plague the contemporary French psyche: France's dread of queerness and its fear of blacks seeking retribution for their once-enslaved ancestors. The drawing thus represents an intersection of a discomfort long felt in France towards the subjects of homosexuality and imperialism. *Le Queer Impérial* presents the confluence of these timely issues by challenging heterosexist imperial and post-imperial mythologies espoused by those nostalgic for a lost empire, but who fail to acknowledge the racial, gendered and sexual economies of French expansionism.

The *queer impérial* refers to political and cultural ways of being in which queer, Othered bodies represent erotically-tempting objects of domination. But more than ways of being, the *queer impérial* is also a person: a soldier, a colonialist, a writer or a reader of colonial fiction, for whom contact with taboo sexualities constitutes crucial aspects of conquest and empire-building. The *queer impérial* relies on the racialized, gendered and sexual mythologies about marginalized populations to both justify socio-political inequalities and to deflect attention from the erotic obsessions of colonizing forces. The loss of a physical empire does not deter the *queer impérial*, which imposes itself not only on land, but also on bodies and in minds.

One felt the presence of the *queer impérial* at the Maison Française at Colombia University during a visit from the late Tzvetan Todorov. The incident is described in a 2005 article penned by Alec Hargreaves which provides examples of the deployment of colonial rhetoric by contemporary French intellectuals such as Todorov, who weighed in on the causes of the violent unrest amongst youth in France. Todorov, a literary theorist who emigrated from Bulgaria to France in 1963, had once recounted in an episode of the television program *Apostrophes* entitled "Le Choc des cultures," that he had arrived in Paris as a young Linguistics student and had been taken in and financially supported for a year by an aunt who was already living in the country. Though Todorov is Caucasian, he commented in the same interview that despite their geographic location Bulgarians did not feel like real Europeans.[3] However, by the time of the 2005 riots and Hargreaves' article, Todorov had become part of France's established intelligentsia and unquestionably authentically European.

Hargreaves describes a moment at the conference at the Maison Française when:

> Tzvetan Todorov said the riots were caused by the dysfunctional sexuality of Muslim youths obsessed with behaving in a "macho" way. Skeptical members of the audience observed that non-Muslim CRS police officers and Interior Minister Nicolas Sarkozy seemed equally macho in their behavior and asked Todorov to provide evidence in support of his assertion that there was something specifically Islamic causing rioters to take to the streets. By way of a reply, Todorov simply smiled and refused to elaborate further.[4]

Todorov assumes that all the protestors were Muslim – read violent, non-white and non-French. Secondly, he links "Muslim," with all its implications in contemporary France, to machismo and sexual dysfunction, the latter term connoting abnormality and impotence. Todorov clearly suggests that the riots were a reaction to sexual impotence in young "Muslim" men living in France. Finally, he fails to see this same sexual dysfunction in some French politicians and in members of French law enforcement who he implies are by default non-Muslim. As much *Le Queer Impérial* will show, Todorov's relation of violence to hypermasculinity and sexuality is not without merit. To be sure, much critical work has been undertaken on the subject in the field of masculinity studies by Groth and Burgess and Abdullah-Khan; in feminist theories from Susan Brownmiller and Jacquelyn Dowd Hall; and by scholars such as Penelope Harvey and Peter Gow, Frank Graziano and Achille Mbembe.[5] However, while

---

3 Bernard Pivot, "Le Choc des Cultures," *Apostrophes*, accessed April 24, 2010, http://www.ina .fr/video/CPB89002559/le-choch-des-cultures-video.html.

4 Alec Hargreaves, "An Emperor with no clothes?" *Riots in France*, Social Science Research Council. (Nov. 28, 2005), accessed April 24, 2010, http://riotsfrance.ssrc.org/Hargreaves/.

5 A.N. Groth and A.W. Burgess, "Male Rape: Offenders and victims," *American Journal of Psychiatry* 137.7 (July 1980): 806–810; Noreen Abdullah-Khan, *Male Rape: The Emergence of a Social and Legal Issue* (New York: Palgrave Macmillan, 2008); Susan Brownmiller, *Against Our Will: Men, Women, and Rape* (New York: Simon and Schuster, 1975); Jacquelyn Dowd Hall, "'The Mind that Burns in Each Body': Women, Rape and Racial Violence," in *Powers of Desire: The Politics of Sexuality*, eds Ann Snitow, Christine Stansell and Sharon Thompson (New York: Monthly Press Review, 1983), 328–349; Penelope Harvey and Peter Gow, "Introduction," in *Sex*

it might be fair to connect the violence of the rioters to a frustrated sexual and masculine agency, Todorov's comment effectively castrates the rioters while displaying his own sexual power as a man *not* affected by sexual dysfunction and thus possessing a lucidity which allows him to discern it in others. His unexplained assumptions about a "dysfunctional" sexuality and, by extension, his implied claims to a "normal" sexuality are troubling. More so is his omission of the CRS Police and Nicolas Sarkozy from his sweeping but underdeveloped theory of sexuality and violence.

Hargreaves' description of the scene suggests that Todorov may have been surprised by the challenges he faced from the audience, that he might have assumed that within the walls of the Maison Française – as it is so often within the borders of France – his declarations would be taken for common fact. Instead of finding support in the creation of an in-group mythology at the Maison Française, Todorov's comments were called out by an audience which recognized them for what they were. Members of the public heard in Todorov's declarations echoes of the xenophobic discourse which fueled European colonial expansion, and in which insidious myths created around the race and sexuality of the African were part and parcel of imperial domination. Like much of the discourse produced during the colonization of Africa, his remarks employ racial, religious and sexual stereotypes which sidestep issues of racism and oppression. While Todorov's comments represent a perpetuation of the myth of an abnormal African sexuality, the questions put to him by his audience in New York and his telling silence when unable to produce any empirical evidence reveal a challenge – at least outside of France – to the politically motivated stereotyping which has too often insinuated itself into French critical and literary discourses.[6] Further, this questioning of Todorov's theory moves him into an uncomfortable space in which he is literally silenced after being exposed as the deployer of an erotic *passage à l'acte*, an acting-out of erotic violence. Todorov's unwillingness to speak reflects Eve Sedgwick's notion of a performance of 'Closetedness' in which an uncomfortable muteness hints

---

and Violence: Issues in Representation and Experience, eds Penelope Harvey and Peter Gow (New York: Routledge, 1994), 1–17; Frank Graziano, *Divine Violence: Spectacle, Psychosexuality & Radical Christianity in the Argentine "Dirty War"* (San Francisco: Westview Press, 1992); Achille Mbembe, *On the Postcolony* (Los Angeles: University of California Press, 2001).

6 See Léon-François Hoffmann, *Le Nègre romantique: personnage littéraire et obsession collective* (Paris: Payot, 1973); Léon Fanoudh-Siefer, *Le Mythe du Nègre et de l'Afrique noire dans la littérature française (de 1800 à la 2e Guerre Mondiale)* (Paris: Librairie C. Klincksieck, 1968); Serge Bilé, *La Légende du sexe surdimensionné des Noirs* (Monaco: Éditions du Rocher, 2005); Odile Tobner, *Du racisme français: quatre siècles de négrophobie* (Paris: Editions des Arènes, 2007).

at the shame of homoeroticism[7]. This is not to make any assumption about Todorov's sexuality in general, but to refer to a specific moment when he is made speechless by the unvoiced realization of his interest in the sexuality of African men. Further, in this moment of misdirection between the smile and the refusal to speak, Todorov himself becomes a sexual curiosity whose own erotic and political motivations might then be questioned.

Le Queer Impérial follows a trajectory similar to this reading of the incident at the Maison Française, examining instances of erotically motivated passages à l'acte in colonial and postcolonial Francophone narratives while also considering the political stakes for the sources of those texts, both the authors who produce them and the societies to which and for which these authors write. As such, I focus on narratives which deal with homoeroticism between white Europeans and black Africans and which are written both by white European and black African authors. As a book which addresses both the literary and the political, Le Queer Impérial relies on both close readings and on the metatextual examination of narrative strategies which allow for displays of male homoerotic desire and domination. It asks how male homoerotic desire and domination motivate authors who explicitly and implicitly treat homoeroticism as a component of the colonial and postcolonial relationship between Francophone Europe and Francophone black Africa.

Like Hargreaves' interrogation of the convictions Todorov expressed at the Maison Française, Le Queer Impérial considers how colonial and postcolonial Francophone discourses allow us to understand both race and male homoerotic desire as underpinning the imperial projects of France and Belgium. The book does so through readings of literary texts from and about black Africa and by asking questions which have long been met with critical silence. Firstly, if the domination and colonization of black Africa by white Europeans was a primarily homosocial activity in a space which "was definitely a man's world" and in which "women were not allowed to play any meaningful role except as petty traders and farmers"[8], why then do we traditionally refer to this symbolic rape of Africa in heterosexual terms? When colonial texts feature erotic descriptions of black men, and postcolonial texts by black Africans allude to homosexuality as a vice of the white European, what do they tell us about the black African colony as a space of interracial male homoeroticism? How do African

7   Eve Kosofsky Sedgwick, Epistemology of the Closet (Los Angeles: University of California Press, 1990), 3.

8   A. Adu Boahen, African Perspectives on Colonialism (Baltimore: Johns Hopkins University Press, 1987), 107. See also Ch. Didier Gondola, The History of Congo (Westport, CT: Greenwood Publishing Group, 2002).

and European women figure into a male homoerotic dynamic? What are the sources of critical and literary discomfort elicited by narratives of black-white male homoeroticism? What tactics have been employed by literary authors to either avoid or confront this discomfort?

By asking these questions *Le Queer Impérial* argues for a new approach to reading male homoerotic desire and domination in Francophone colonial and postcolonial texts from and about black Africa. In this book, I interrogate the literary acting-out of political, racial and erotic violence in Francophone works of colonial fiction by Pierre Mille, André Demaison and Herman Grégoire and in postcolonial fiction by Ousmane Sembene, Saïdou Bokoum, Williams Sassine and Sony Labou Tansi. Closely linked to sadism, erotic violence is physical and psychic aggression which leads to sexual fulfillment. However, unlike sadism, which skews towards the individual and the interpersonal, erotic violence holds the potential of "an emblem for institutionalized violence".[9] Readings of erotic violence in *Le Queer Impérial* add original interpretive approaches to an already-rich corpus of critical works which view violence as an integral component in some of the narratives presented here. In other instances, the book provides innovative approaches to thinking about texts which have yet to be understood for their inclusion of gendered, racialized and sexual violence. Additionally, by treating the themes of race, gender and sexuality, *Le Queer Impérial* approaches each text as a political document connected to the French and Belgian colonization and neo-colonization of black Africa and parallel to black-African immigration to Europe.

The subject of male homoeroticism in colonial texts has been widely explored in the field of Anglophone literary studies by critics such as Eve Kosofsky Sedgwick, Kaja Silverman and Christopher Lane and in both colonial and postcolonial texts by Hema Chari.[10] Maria Davidis and Marc Epprecht examine homoeroticism in Anglophone colonial literature in the black African

---

9   Madeleine Monson-Rosen, "The Most primeval of passions: Incest in the service of women in Angela Carter's *The Magic Toyshop*," in *Straight Writ Queer: Non-Normative Expressions of Heterosexuality in Literature*, ed. Richard Fantina (Jefferson, NC: McFarland and Company, 2006), 240.

10   Eve Kosofsky Sedgwick, *Between Men: English Literature and Male Homosocial Desire* (New York: Columbia University Press, 1985); Kaja Silverman, "White Skin, Brown Masks: With Lawrence in Arabia," *Differences*, no. 3 (1989): 3–54; Christopher Lane, *The Ruling Passion: British Colonial Allegory and the Paradox of Homosexual Desire* (Durham: Duke University Press, 1995); Hema Chari, "Colonial Fantasies and Postcolonial Identities: Elaboration of Postcolonial Masculinity and Homoerotic Desire," in *Postcolonial, Queer: Theoretical Intersections*, ed. John C. Hawley (Albany: State University of New York Press, 2001), 277–304.

context.[11] Jarrod Hayes explores queer diasporas with an interdisciplinary study of African-American, Caribbean and black African writers in both French and English.[12] The treatment of male homoeroticism in Francophone colonial texts has historically been limited to interrogations of André Gide's narratives set in North Africa by Emily Apter and Michael Lucey.[13] Joseph Boone has written about homoeroticism in North Africa in Gide's *L'Immoraliste* and Gustave Flaubert's epistemological writings.[14] Brett A. Berliner examines Gide's travels in West Africa and his homoerotic gaze in *Voyage au Congo*.[15] Indeed, literary and cultural critiques of male homoeroticism in the francophone-African colonial context have tended to focus on homoerotic encounters between white Frenchmen and North African men or boys with a stunning silence regarding homoerotic relations between the black African and the white European.

This absence becomes all the more noteworthy when one recognizes the enormity of colonial texts which treat the sexuality of black African men, though their erotic displays are generally heterosexual or suggest a physically superb asexuality. In the first chapter of this book, a reading of Herman Grégoire's *Makako singe d'Afrique* / *Makako, African Monkey* and of Pierre Mille and André Demaison's *La Femme et l'Homme nu* / *The Woman and the Naked Man* presents examples of colonial narratives which place particular emphasis on the representation of the sexuality of the black African male.[16] Grégoire's novel, like other colonial works of fiction such as Félix Léonnec's *La Loi de la brousse* / *The Law of the Bush* portrays a black African ravishing a European

11 Maria Davidis, "'Unarm, Eros!': Adventure, Homoeroticism, and Divine Order in *Prester John*," in *Imperial Desire: Dissident Sexualities and Colonial Literature*, eds Philip Holden and Richard J. Ruppel (Minneapolis: University of Minnesota Press, 2003), 223–240; Marc Epprecht, *Heterosexual Africa?: The History of an Idea from the Age of Exploration to the Age of AIDS* (Athens, OH: Ohio University Press, 2008).

12 Jarrod Hayes, *Queer Roots for the Diaspora: Ghosts in the Family Tree* (Ann Arbor: University of Michigan Press, 2006).

13 Emily Apter, *Gide and the Codes of Homotextuality* (Saratoga, CA: Anma Libri, 1987); Michael Lucey, *Gide's Bent: Sexuality, Politics, Writing* (New York: Oxford University Press, 1995).

14 Joseph Boone, "Vacation Cruises; or, The Homoerotics of Orientalism," *PMLA* 110.1 (Jan. 1995): 89–107; Joseph A. Boone, *The Homoerotics of Orientalism* (NYC: Columbia University Press, 2014); André Gide, *Voyage au Congo* (Paris: Éditions Gallimard, 1927).

15 Brett A. Berliner, *Ambivalent Desire: The Exotic Black Other in Jazz-Age France* (Amherst: University of Massachusetts Press, 2002).

16 Pierre Mille and André Demaison, *La Femme et l'Homme nu* (Paris: Les Éditions de France, 1924).

woman.[17] Still other colonial novels contain passages describing black male bodies, their "muscles saillants"/ bulging muscles,[18] "nus et brillants de sueur" / naked and glistening with sweat.[19] Such textual representations, while not overtly homoerotic, might point to a homoerotic voyeurism which allows a predominantly European male authorship and readership access to a covert and indirect erotic engagement with black male bodies.

So, while Francophone colonial authors writing on black Africa rarely employed explicit illustrations of male homoerotic desire, many of these texts, like their Anglophone counterparts, provide opportunities to be read for expressions of homoeroticism through violence, objectification and voyeurism. The absence of this subject in critical texts likely results from a taboo that is both sexual and racial. Alan Sheridan hints at the reluctance to display relations between black men and white men within French colonial literature when noting André Gide's self-censorship in editing his travel journals for the publication of *Voyage au Congo*.[20] Sheridan tells of Gide's admission to his acquaintance Jean Amrouche: "[I am] very attracted, if I might dare to say, in a sensual way as well, by the negro race".[21] Additionally, Sheridan notes the circumstances which brought about Gide's self-censorship:

> Gide [...] had 'adventures'. Later in the year, while writing up his travel notes, he read extracts to the Petite Dame [Maria Van Rysselberghe] who [later] commented: 'On the few occasions when he referred to an adventure with one of the boys, he broke off and said: "Would you leave that in? You don't think it will discredit the rest ...? Oh well, too bad. It all happened so naturally, so easily. It would be puerile to cut it out."'[22]
> In the end, he did take a more cautious line: there are no such explicit

---

17   Herman Grégoire, *Makako, singe d'Afrique* (Paris: La Renaissance du Livre, 1921); Pierre
      Mille and André Demaison, *La Femme et l'Homme nu* (Paris: Les Éditions de France, 1924).
18   Jacques Weulersse, *Noirs et Blancs: A travers l'Afrique nouvelle: de Dakar au Cap* (Paris:
      Librairie Armand Colin, 1931), 34; Robert Randau, *Des blancs dans la cité des noirs* (Paris:
      Albin Michel, 1935), 88.
19   Marcel Sauvage, *Les Secrets de l'Afrique noire* (Paris: Éditions Denoël, 1937), 140.
20   Alan Sheridan, *André Gide: Life in the Present* (London: Hamish Hamilton, 1999); André
      Gide, *Voyage au Congo* (Paris: Éditions Gallimard, 1927).
21   Alan Sheridan, *André Gide: Life in the Present* (London: Hamish Hamilton, 1999), 401.
22   Sheridan cites Maria Van Rysselberghe, *Les Cahiers de la petite dame, Tome I (1918–1929)*
      (Paris: Gallimard, 1973); Maria Van Rysselberghe, *Les Cahiers de la petite dame, Tome II
      (1929–1937)* (Paris: Gallimard, 1974); Maria Van Rysselberghe, *Les Cahiers de la petite dame,
      Tome III (1937–1945)* (Paris: Gallimard, 1975); Maria Van Rysselberghe, *Les Cahiers de la
      petite dame, Tome IV (1945–1951)* (Paris: Gallimard, 1977).

references in the public version, though the description of his feelings for Adoum [a black-African servant] may be taken to imply a liaison.[23]

While textual clues in the published version of *Voyage au Congo* do indeed suggest that Gide had in fact engaged in a sexual relationship with his male servant, had the author included the explicit details of his homoerotic adventures, the travel narrative would have represented something quite different from what it currently does. Rather than anthropological observations of colonial life replete with descriptions of African peoples often undifferentiated from those of flora and fauna, *Voyage au Congo* might acknowledge the human and sensual connections of black Africans and white Europeans. Or, in a more pessimistic conception of Gide's censored desires, rather than simply providing sympathetic descriptions of oppressed races, the travel journal might inadvertently comment upon homoerotic exploitation as it figures into the colonial project. The exclusion of those censored passages exposes the discomfort Gide anticipated within a European readership which might accept his pederast lifestyle when reflected, for example, in reference to ancient Greece in *Corydon* or to North Africa in *L'Immoraliste*, but which would – at least in Gide's mind – balk at descriptions of him making love to a black man. Robert Aldrich makes this very observation in his essay on *Voyage au Congo*, noting the "differences between European reactions to North and Sub-Saharan Africa, the dissonance between political and sensual sentiments, and the difficulty of jettisoning colonial attitudes".[24]

Indeed, studies on eroticism in Africanist Francophone colonial fiction tend rather to concentrate on the problematic but less taboo heterosexual relations of the European male and the African concubine or on relations between African men and white women.[25] Alan Ruscio and Pierre Halen treat both *Blanche-Noir* and *Blanc-Noire* couples, with Halen's work focusing squarely on Belgian colonial literature.[26] This is also the case in critical texts about

23   Alan Sheridan, *André Gide: Life in the Present* (London: Hamish Hamilton, 1999), 406.

24   Robert Aldrich, "Colonial Man," in *French Masculinities: History, Culture and Politics*, eds Christopher E. Forth and Bertrand Taithe (New York: Macmillan, 2007), 344.

25   Ada Martinkus-Zemp, *Le Blanc et le Noir* (Paris: A.G. Nizet, 1975); Roger Little, "Blanche et Noir aux années vingt," in *Regards sur les littératures coloniales, Afrique Francophone: Tome II, Approfondissements*, ed. Jean-François Durand (Paris: L'Harmattan, 1999), 7–50; Roger Little, *Between Totem and Taboo: Black Man, White Woman in Francographic Literature* (Exeter: University of Exeter Press, 2001).

26   Alain Ruscio, *Amours coloniales: Aventures et fantasmes exotiques, de Claire de Duras à Georges Simenon* (Brussels: Collection Bibliothèque Complexe, 1996); Pierre Halen, "Les fictions amoureuses et l'idéologie coloniale au Congo belge," in *L'Exotisme*, eds Alain

postcolonial Francophone literatures, with the exception of Jarrod Hayes writing on the Maghreb.[27] While we can find important volumes on heterosexual relations between black Africans and white Europeans, critical explorations of postcolonial inter-racial homoeroticism has remained limited. Notable exceptions are articles by Daniel Vignal, Chris Dunton and Chantal Zabus, which expose male homoeroticism in both Anglophone and Francophone literatures from black Africa, and Zabus' informative monograph on Francophone and Anglophone Sub-Saharan cultures.[28] *Le Queer Impérial* builds upon these initial forays, but seeks to expand on these studies, firstly by exploring the textual and cultural relationship between colonial and postcolonial Francophone literatures and secondly, by performing in-depth analyses of each text as it relates to gender, sexuality, race and class.

By including both colonial and postcolonial Francophone texts, *Le Queer Impérial* illustrates the antiphonal relationship between works of fiction from both traditions, highlights postcolonial literature as reacting to and growing out of colonial literature, and proposes that colonial literature be read anew in light of the poetic and political expressions of black African authors. This strategy follows the work of János Riesz, who believes that "il faut voir la littérature coloniale à partir de la littérature africaine qui lui fait concurrence et qui lui succède" / We must conceive of colonial literature in relation to African literature which competes with it and which ultimately follows it.[29] To further stress the hypertextuality linking colonial and postcolonial Francophone literatures, Riesz reminds us that:

Buisine and Norbert Dodille (Saint-Denis, Île de la Réunion: Cahiers C.R.L.H, 1988); Pierre Halen, *Le Petit Belge avait vu grand: une littérature coloniale* (Brussels: Éditions Labor, 1993).

27   Jarrod Hayes, *Queer Nations: Marginalities in the Maghreb* (Chicago: University of Chicago Press, 2000).

28   Daniel Vignal, "Homophilie dans le roman négro-africain d'expression anglaise et française," *Peuple noir, peuple africain*, no. 33 (May-June 1983): 63–81; Chris Dunton, "'Wheything be Dat?' The Treatment of homosexuality in African literature," *Research in African Literatures*, 20. 3 (Autumn 1989): 422–448; Chantal Zabus, " 'Out' in Africa," *Gboungboun: The Ponal magazine*, 1 (2) (November 2007), accessed February 11, 2009, http://www.projectponal.com/newsletter/commentary/commentaryZabus; Chantal Zabus, *Out in Africa: Same-Sex Desire in Sub-Saharan Literatures and Cultures* (Suffolk, GB : James Curry, 2013).

29   János Riesz, *De la littérature coloniale à la littérature africaine: Prétextes, Contextes, Intertextes* (Paris: Éditions Karthala, 2007), 43.

[L]a plupart des textes africains des années 1920, 1930, 1940 et 1950 n'acquièrent leur pleine signification, tant au niveau idéologique qu'au niveau strictement littéraire (intertextuel, interdiscursif) que devant la toile de fond de la littérature coloniale. Pour les contemporains, les inté-ressés eux-mêmes, cela ne faisait pas de doute: pour les historiens et les théoriciens de la littérature coloniale [...] les premiers auteurs africains étaient des auteurs coloniaux indigènes.[30]

Most African texts from the 1920s, 1930s, 1940s and 1950s only acquire their full meaning, be it ideological or strictly literary (intertextually, interdis-cursively), when considered against the backdrop of colonial literature. For those writers, this was clear: for literary historians and theorists who study colonial literature [...] the first African authors were indigenous colonial authors.

Approaches similar to Riesz's reconceptualization of the colonial author as non-white have been employed by Christopher Miller who presents texts on the French-African slave trade written by African, French and Afro-French authors, and by Dominic Thomas whose work on postcolonial literatures by black writers mediates the relationship between the geographic spaces of liter-ary creation and narrative setting, while considering the varied origins of these authors.[31]

Although *Le Queer Impérial* maintains the nominal and political distinction of colonial and postcolonial genres, qualifying the postcolonial as "'post contact': that is, as a condition that exists within, and thus contests and resists, the colonial moment itself with its ideology and domination",[32] reading male homoeroticism in the texts explored in this book naturally implies the notion of hypertextuality espoused by Riesz, especially in light of the common methodology utilized in this venture. However, while Riesz's methodology is instructive, I read these texts transnationally, in terms of their literary and political congruencies so as not to fall into the trap of reading postcolonial

---

30 Ibid., 45.
31 Christopher L Miller, *The French Atlantic Triangle: Literature and Culture of the Slave Trade* (Durham: Duke University Press, 2008); Dominic Thomas, *Black France: Colonialism, Immigration and Transnationalism* (Bloomington: Indiana University Press, 2007).
32 Françoise Lionnet, *Postcolonial Representations: Women, Literature, Identity* (Ithaca: Cornell University Press, 1995), 4.

African writers through a European center.[33] In *Minor Transnationalism* Françoise Lionnet and Shu-mei Shih argue that "minor cultures as we know them are products of transmigrations and multiple encounters, which imply that they are always already mixed, hybrid and relational".[34] This description of minor cultures could be applied not only to postcolonial works by black authors, but also to the European colonial novels in this book which once occupied an important place in Francophone literary culture. For example, Pierre Mille was once known for his critically and commercially successful *Barnavaux* series. In a 1923 publication Roland Lebel declared: "Pierre Mille est notre grand écrivain colonial. Ses savoureuses histoires de *Barnavaux*, pleines de sens profond, sont connues de tous et unanimement appréciées. Il a créé un type de colonial qui restera dans la littérature" / Pierre Mille is our great colonial author. His delightful stories of Barnavaux, full of deep meaning, are known by all and unanimously appreciated. He has created the universal colonial man, an archetype that will carry on in literature.[35] Florian-Parmentier provides this comparison of Pierre Mille and Rudyard Kipling: "Entre coloniaux on se rencontre: le monde est petit. Kipling et Mille ont bu le soleil à la même coupe, observé les mêmes hommes, avec le même amour de la vie. Et Mille aime Kipling, non point parce qu'il s'est modelé sur lui, mais parce qu'en lui il se reconnaît." / Colonials find each other: the world is so small. Kipling and Mille have drunk from the same sun-filled cup, observed the same men, with the same love of life. And Mille loves Kipling, not at all because he has modeled himself off the latter, but because he recognizes himself in Kipling.[36] Robert Lejeune makes a similar comparison: "De cette conception de la vie amère et salubre, il sort une leçon d'énergie, tout autant que des livres de Kipling, tant vanté à cet égard." / From this bitter and healthy conception of life comes a lesson of energy, just as much so as from the novels of Kipling, so lauded in this regard.[37] Contemporary texts devoted to Mille have been offered by Alec Hargreaves, who examines the relationship between Mille's politics and his *Barnavaux* series, and Alain Ruscio, who presents excerpts of

33   Françoise Lionnet and Shu-me Shih, "Introduction: Thinking through the Minor, Transnationally," in *Minor Transnationalism*, eds Françoise Lionnet and Shu-mei Shih (Durham: Duke UP, 2005), 5.

34   Ibid., 10.

35   Roland Lebel, *Le Livre du pays noir: Anthologie de littérature africaine* (Paris: Éditions du Monde Moderne, 1923), 109.

36   Florian-Parmentier, *Pierre Mille* (Paris: Les Éditions G. Crès et Cie., 1923), 67.

37   Robert Lejeune, "M. Pierre Mille, écrivain de droite," *Revue critique des idées et des livres* 36. 220 (Jan. 25. 1924): 15.

La Femme et l'Homme nu.[38] Unfortunately, Ruscio's presentation of the text provides no critical analysis. Brett Berliner and Roger Little have presented important, contemporary analyses of *La Femme et l'Homme nu.*[39] Finally Serge Bilé provides historical context for the publication of *La Femme et l'Homme nu.*[40] These texts represent perhaps the sole attention given to Milles' writing partner André Demaison in recent critical writing, although both he and Mille are included in Ada Martinkus-Zemp's 1975 study.[41] As for Belgian author Herman Grégoire, neither the recent volume *Histoire de la littérature belge francophone 1830–2000*, nor Pierre Halen's informative 1988 article on colonial fiction situated in the Belgian Congo mention the author.[42] Grégoire does however figure into Halen's 1993 work, though no profound analysis is devoted to the text.[43] Once lauded by literary critics, many of these texts are now rarely treated in critical works and are often long out of print. As such, they represent the minor and the marginal. Francophone colonial literature has become marginal, not because of the quality of the subgenre's narratives, but because of the unpleasant reminders of colonial domination in the pages of texts which were once a major form of entertainment in France and Belgium. While, in their initial popularity, these texts might have been compared to the medium of the *feuilleton*, so well exploited in the Francophone context by Honoré de Balzac and Émile Zola, unlike the works of these authors, most Francophone colonial texts have not aged well. They have not been legitimized within the Francophone canon and cannot boast the readerships of Balzac and Zola. Even the most famous of Francophone colonial authors, Pierre

38   Alec Hargreaves, *The Colonial Experience in French Fiction: A Study of Pierre Loti, Ernest Psichari and Pierre Mille* (London: The Macmillan Press, Ltd., 1981); Alain Ruscio, *Amours coloniales. Aventures et Fantasmes exotiques, de Claire de Duras à Georges Simenon* (Brussels: Collection Bibliothèque Complexe, 1996).

39   Roger Little, "Blanche et Noir aux années vingt," in *Regards sur les littératures coloniales, Afrique francophone: Approfondissements*, ed. Jean-François Durand (Paris: L'Harmattan, 1999); Brett A Berliner, *Ambivalent Desire: The Exotic Black Other in Jazz-Age France* (Amherst: University of Massachusetts Press, 2002).

40   Serge Bilé, *La Légende du sexe surdimensionné des Noirs* (Monaco: Éditions du Rocher, 2005).

41   Ada Martinkus-Zemp, *Le Blanc et le Noir* (Paris: A.G. Nizet, 1975).

42   Jean-Pierre Bertrand, et al., eds, *Histoire de la littérature belge francophone 1830–2000* (Paris: Fayard, 2003); Pierre Halen, "Les fictions amoureuse et l'idéologie coloniale au Congo belge," in *L'Exotisme*, eds Alain Buisine and Norbert Dodille (Saint-Denis, Île de la Réunion : Cahiers C.R.L.H, 1988).

43   Pierre Halen, *Le Petit Belge avait vu grand: Une Littérature coloniale* (Brussels: Éditions Labor, 1993).

Loti and Ernest Psichari, still today the subjects of critical texts, cannot rival their British counterparts Rudyard Kipling and Joseph Conrad in terms of popularity. Francophone colonial literature is a minor literature, published, read and commented upon far less than most of the texts by black African authors interrogated here.

Le Queer Impérial also represents a marginal literature, a marginal mode of inquiry that poses questions which have formerly gone unasked and thus unanswered. It dares to expose the erotic entanglements of white men and black men in Francophone contexts, and claims that male homoerotic desire is an integral aspect of French Imperialism in black Africa.

The use of the term "homoerotic desire", which I distinguish from "homosocial desire" and "homosexuality", relies on the work of queer theorists such as David M. Halperin, Janet E. Halley, Gayle S. Rubin, and Ana Maria Alonso and Teresa Koreck.[44] This distinction takes into consideration notions of genital relations, self-identification, community formation and political participation, as well as specific cultural labeling.

Wayne Dynes' conception of sexual orientation presents the term "homosexual" as genital relations and thus involving physical expressions of desire between members of the same sex. This source proposes "homophile" as a term "broader in scope" which "includes nongenital as well as genital relations."[45] However, while "homophile" might potentially describe instances of romantic friendship, the term cannot be used in a general description of the erotic relations exposed in *Le Queer Impérial* as its scope is limited to "affectional"[46] interactions within a same-sex partnership.

---

44   David Halperin, *One Hundred Years of Homosexuality: And other Essays on Greek Love* (New York: Manchester University Press, 1990); David Halperin, *How to Do the History of Homosexuality* (Chicago: University of Chicago Press, 2002); Janet E. Halley, "The Construction of Heterosexuality," in *Fear of a Queer Planet: Queer Politics and Social Theory*, ed. Michael Warner (Minneapolis: University of Minnesota Press, 1993), 82–104; Gayle S. Rubin, "Coconuts: Aspects of Male/Female Relationships in New Guinea," (unpublished Ms., 1974); Gayle S. Rubin, "Thinking Sex: Notes for a Radical Theory of the Politics of Sexuality," in *The Lesbian and Gay Studies Reader*, eds Henry Abelove, Michèle Aina Barale, David M. Halperin (New York: Routledge, 1993 [1984]), 3–44; Ana Maria Alonso and Maria Teresa Koreck, "Silences: 'Hispanics,' AIDS, and Sexual Practices," in *The Lesbian and Gay Studies Reader*, eds Henry Abelove, Michèle Aina Barale, David M. Halperin (New York: Routledge, 1993), 110–126.

45   Dynes, Wayne R., "Orientation," in *Encyclopedia of Homosexuality Vol. II*, ed. Wayne R. Dynes (Shrewsbury, MA: Garland), 552.

46   Ibid., 552.

Some instances of contact between black Africans and white Europeans presented here qualify as homosocial, that is, as the societal interaction of men, usually in traditionally exclusive male domains (the military, commerce, the clergy and athletics). Despite the usefulness of the word "homosocial" for speaking about colonial and postcolonial interactions, the term is inappropriate for indicating the erotically charged motivations of masculine congregation. Eve Kosofsky Sedgwick conceived of "homosocial desire" as a continuum which included "male friendship, mentorship, entitlement, rivalry, and hetero- and homosexuality".[47] While all of these mechanisms inform the texts treated in Le Queer Impérial, the term "homosocial desire" does not necessarily imply the erotic, as it may only indicate a non-sexual desire to interact with those of the same sex, and thus does not acknowledge the sexual tension so crucial to this work. Further, the usefulness of describing the relationship between white Europeans and black Africans as homosocial is limited, as the term also implies a social cohabitation based on political and economic equality. As Todorov's comments at the Maison Française remind us, Imperial and post-Imperial cultures struggle to implement equal or nearly equal access to expressions of masculinity and to patriarchal power. And so, though "homosocial" in a male context effectively expresses the exclusion of women from spheres inhabited by both black and white men, we must be aware of the continually contested entry of black men into these spheres, a political reality which "homosocial" does not aptly express.

While neither "homophilia" nor "homosocial" are viable terms to describe the general focus of Le Queer Impérial, scholarly definitions of "homosexuality" suggest it too would not be accurate for this study. David Halperin presents a more intricate "modern" definition of the word based on an "unstable conjunction" of three components:

> (1) a psychiatric notion [...] that applies to the inner life of the individual and does not necessarily presume same-sex sexual behavior; (2) a psychoanalytic notion of same-sex *sexual object-choice* or desire ... which is a category of erotic intentionality and does not necessarily imply a permanent sexual orientation ... and (3) a sociological notion of sexually deviant behavior ... which focuses on non-standard sexual practice and does not necessarily refer to erotic psychology or sexual orientation

---

47   Eve Kosofsky Sedgwick, *Between Men: English Literature and Male Homosocial Desire* (New York: Columbia University Press, 1985), 1.

(since same-sex sexual behavior, as Kinsey showed, is not the exclusive property of those with a homosexual orientation [...]).[48]

To be sure, portions of Halperin's definition make the use of the term *homosexuality* seem viable for addressing the questions posed in *Le Queer Impérial*, especially since the men discussed are, for the most part, self-identified heterosexuals, and since desire in some of the texts might remain unfulfilled. Still, Halperin's definition proves problematic, particularly because of a breadth of meaning that seems to remove the "finite" from the definition. We see this in the distinctions which arise between the terms *homosexuality* – as a state of being – *homosexual* – as an individual – and *homosexual* – as a qualifier. Because *homosexuality* is a state of being, and thus possibly subject to changes in individual identity, Halperin rightly insists that the term is unstable. This unstable notion of sexual identity seems to be supported by Janet E. Halley's contention that "the difference *between* the categories homosexual and heterosexual is systematically related to differences *within* the category heterosexual".[49] Both modes of reasoning imply that one could move from one state of being to another and that we could perhaps even dispense with the labels all together. However, because of the popular and critical use of these terms, we cannot avoid attempts at more precise definitions. Additionally, if we speak of *homosexual* as a noun, we engage a term which, because of its politicized usage and because of its requirements for self-identification, leaves little room for the notion of ephemeral states of being and implies a permanent sexual orientation and/or lifestyle choice.

   Le Queer Impérial requires the use of *homosexuality* and *homosexual* to describe instances in which literary characters are self-identified homosexuals. However, the book declines the use of the adjective *homosexual* as a possible qualifier for the term *desire*. Were I only to conceive of the word as "related to homosexuality" then I might – based upon Halperin's loose definition – permit its use here. However, if I define the term as "related to the homosexual," using this adjective here implies the description of a chosen socio-political identity and thus becomes problematic. I also reject the use of either term (*homosexual* or *homosexuality*) in cases where same-sex genital relations or the desire for such relations are in question because the sexual or sexualized acts presented

---

48   David Halperin, *How to Do the History of Homosexuality* (Chicago: University of Chicago Press, 2002), 131.

49   Janet E Halley, "The Construction of Heterosexuality", in *Fear of a Queer Planet: Queer Politics and Social Theory*, ed. Michael Warner (Minneapolis: University of Minnesota Press, 1993), 83.

here often reproduce the inflexible penetrator-penetrated dynamic which defines heterosexual associations. Sexual penetration between same-sex agents does not necessarily imply homosexuality. Of course, this distinction does not infer a negation of the existence of homosexual desire between the African and the European. Though not the main focus of the book, homosexual desire does figure into some of the analyses presented here.

More clarity on the matter of terminology comes from the work of Gayle S. Rubin, who underlines the problematic nature of this word group by providing examples of behaviors which might seem to qualify their agents as homosexuals, but which she claims are not in fact proof of homosexuality.[50] Rubin's distinction of homoeroticism and homosexuality may seem odd, as many dictionaries treat the terms as synonyms, often omitting a definition of *homoerotic*, and simply referring us to the definition of *homosexual*. She does, however, make her case by providing two examples of homoeroticism which preclude homosexuality: the 17th-century European sodomite and the modern-day New Guinea man, neither of whom can securely be identified as homosexuals. She furthers her theory with a description of sexual encounters between the men of New Guinea:

> In some New Guinea societies, for example, homosexual activities are obligatory for all males. Homosexual acts are considered utterly masculine, roles are based on age, and partners are determined by kinship status. Although these men engage in extensive homosexual and pedophile behavior, they are neither homosexuals nor pederasts.[51]

Though Rubin uses the adjective "homosexual," she carefully distinguishes between homosexual behavior and homosexuality. Also, these behaviors suggest the establishment of a ritualistic and politically informed group dogma whose exercise of desire and power can be compared to the hypermasculinity and homoeroticism which underpin empire building.

In her presentation of non-Western sexual practices, Rubin allows for specification of what she believes constitutes contemporary notions of homosexuality:

---

50   Gayle S. Rubin, "Thinking Sex: Notes for a Radical Theory of the Politics of Sexuality," in *The Lesbian and Gay Studies Reader*, eds Henry Abelove, Michèle Aina Barale, David M. Halperin (New York: Routledge, 1993 [1984]), 3–44.

51   Ibid., 17.

The New Guinea bachelor and the sodomite nobleman are only tangen-
tially related to a modern gay man, who may migrate from rural Colorado
to San Francisco in order to live in a gay neighborhood, work in a gay
business, and participate in an elaborate experience that includes a self-
conscious identity, group solidarity, a literature, a press, and a high level
of political activity. In modern, Western, industrial societies, homosexuality has acquired much of the institutional structure of an ethnic group.[52]

Rubin's political conception of homosexuality implies self-identification and
the creation of a community or communities structured around a set of constantly developing sexual values and behaviors. Whereas the sexual acts of
New Guinea men occupy an important place in New Guinea society – in kinship associations, for example – the existence of the community does not depend upon those specific sexual acts.

Rubin refuses the term *homosexuality* in defining relations between
modern New Guinea men and between 17th-century European sodomites.
However, she does allow for the word *homoerotic* to bridge what she views
as a gap between these two circumstances and the modern, Western world:
"The relocation of homoerotics into these quasi-ethnic, nucleated, sexually
constituted communities is to some extent a consequence of the transfers of
population brought about by industrialization."[53] Rubin seems to conceive
of the homoerotic as already existing and ultimately transformed by Western
society into "the homosexual." Her usage of both terms gives credence to
the notion that the existence of the former preceded the invention of the
latter. However, though Rubin uses "homoerotic" and "homosexual activity"
interchangeably, this book avoids confusion by distinguishing the two.

Of course, defining homoeroticism becomes problematic when one is faced
with postmodern notions of gender which refuse an anchoring in strict male
or female roles. Thus, one could object that desire cannot be considered homoerotic or "hetero-erotic" if labels which require a solidly defined gender cannot rely upon a subject being purely masculine or feminine. To address this
matter, I pay close attention to the work of Luce Irigaray (1977), Judith Butler
(1993), Teresa De Lauretis (1993) and Monique Wittig (1993) who acknowledge
the social construction of both gender and sexuality.[54] However, the liberty to

52   Ibid., 17.
53   Ibid., 17.
54   Luce Irigaray, *This Sex Which is Not One*, trans. Catherine Porter (Ithaca: Cornell University
      Press, 1985), Judith Butler, "Imitation and Gender Insubordination," in *The Lesbian and
      Gay Studies Reader*, eds Henry Abelove, Michèle Aina Barale, David M. Halperin (New

assume that the narrators of the texts are operating within a social system with clearly defined gender roles will be important to my analyses and to my use of the term *male homoerotic desire*.

Because in *Le Queer Impérial* I wish to illustrate how the thematics of male homoeroticism, race and masculinity traverse colonial and postcolonial Francophone literatures, and to show how these issues are treated during the distinct colonial, post-imperial and postcolonial periods, I present the works here chronologically within three discrete sections, the first dedicated to Colonial Literature written by Europeans, the second to Postcolonial Literature written by African authors and set in post-imperial France and finally a third section on Postcolonial and Neocolonial Literature written again by African authors but set in black Africa. Further, each section examines two works, first comparatively, in order to establish overarching themes and theories related to the period and provenance of its sub-genre, and then individually, focusing specifically on how each text contributes to theories of race, gender and sexuality. The result is what I hope will chart innovative paths for reexamining colonial and postcolonial texts.

Section One of *Le Queer Impérial* includes Chapters One to Three, which present two colonial novels in which racialized colonial masculinities allow us to think about the power dynamics of imperial homoeroticism. Readings of these texts also take on the portrayal of two major female characters, both of whom engage in sexual relations with black Africans, as negative feminine personas. Chapter One, "Colonial Sexting: Homoerotic Voyeurism in *La Femme et l'Homme nu* by Pierre Mille and André Demaison, and *Makako, singe d'Afrique* by Herman Grégoire" presents evidence of male homoerotic economies in two colonial Francophone texts. It focuses on the male homoeroticism at play in the voyeuristic activity implicit in writing, not only about colonized and racialized Others, but also about the European colonizer, who himself becomes a special type observed through the lens of colonial fiction. The chapter also examines the place of white female desire in the black-African colonial context. Chapter Two, "'Entre hommes et sous l'équateur': Colonial Masculinity, Race and Desire in *Makako, singe d'Afrique*" exposes constructions of masculinity and hyper-masculinity as well as racial identity as crucial to the creation of

York: Routledge, 1993), 307–320; Judith Butler, *Bodies that Matter: On the Discursive Limits of "Sex"* (New York: Routledge, 1993); Teresa De Lauretis, "Sexual Indifference and Lesbian Representation," in *The Lesbian and Gay Studies Reader*, eds Henry Abelove, Michèle Aina Barale and David M. Halperin (New York: Routledge, 1993), 141–158; Monique Wittig, "One Is Not Born Woman," in *The Lesbian and Gay Studies Reader*, eds Henry Abelove, Michèle Aina Barale, David M. Halperin (New York: Routledge, 1993),103–109.

homoerotic "in groups" and "out groups." Chapter Three, "Nothing but a Thing:
The African Male as Fetishist and Fetish in *La Femme et l'Homme nu*" shows
how the novel establishes a causal relationship between the animist religion
of its black protagonist and his sexual appetites, and how his desire for power
influences his self-objectification.

Section Two of the book is comprised of Chapters Four to Six and deals specifically with the themes of male rape and homophobia. The location of the narratives in metropolitan imperial and post-imperial France and the status of the
protagonists as immigrants are crucial in speaking of rape as related to the violation of both geographic borders and individual bodies. Chapter Four, "Loving
the Alien: Rape of the African Immigré in Ousmane Sembene's *Le Docker noir*
and Saïdou Bokoum's *Chaîne*" explores the role of homoerotic desire in the
representation of rape and of racialized group identities. In my reading of both
novels I reflect on the representation of racialized masculinity which opposes
a decadent European sexuality to a heteronormative African sexuality as key to
both expressions of homoerotism and homophobia. Chapter Five, "Is Looking
Merely the Opposite of Doing? Rape and Representation in *Le Docker noir*"
examines the fact and fantasy of rape in Ousmane Sembene's novel by underlining the deployment of specifically male-generated discourses designed to
penetrate the physicality and sexuality of the protagonist by imagining the immigrant as a rapist of a white woman. The chapter explores how the narrative
uses an accusation of heterosexual rape to illustrate the homoerotic tensions
within a male-dominated public sphere, and to suggest that the truly significant rape in the narrative is a homoerotic violation of the African immigrant.
Chapter Six, "L'homme de couleur et le blanc: Interracial Desire and the Fear
of the Queer in *Chaîne*" shows how the narrative portrays manifestations of
male homoerotic desire in an African immigrant living in post-imperial France
as the result of his presence in the *métropole* and his abandonment of a black
identity. The chapter considers how the novel's re-integration of its hero into
black-African society "frees" him from his psychological complexes and from
homoerotic desire.

The third Section of the *Le Queer Impérial*, containing Chapters Seven to
Nine, focuses on homoeroticism in postcolonial and neocolonial relationships.
In the case of the fictional postcolonial states of Sony Labou Tansi's *Je soussigné cardiaque* and Williams Sassine's *Mémoire d'une peau*, the postcolony
as a failed or unrealized state becomes the location of sexual and racial dissimulation and shame. In addition to treating homoeroticism and masculinity,
this final section also explores racial *métissage*, gender-bending, bisexuality
and sexual and political exploitation in the postcolonial space. Chapter Seven,
"Civil Servant Whores and Neocolonial Slum-Johns in Sony Labou Tansi's *Je*

soussigné cardiaque and Williams Sassine's *Mémoire d'une peau"* studies the link between prostitution and political selling-out in postcolonial fiction. I examine how, despite a portrayal of gendered activities: women selling their bodies and men selling their influence, the fusion of prostitution and corruption in these two texts expresses the male protagonists' homoerotic panic. Further, I observe the phenomenon of what I call "neocolonial slum johns," individuals from former colonizing societies who find sexual gratification in the most abject aspects of the postcolony. In Chapter Eight, "The Space Between: Bisexuality, Intersexuality, Albinism and the Postcolonial State in *Mémoire d'une peau"* I explore the concept of the postcolonial space, whose geopolitical indeterminacy I compare to equivocal expressions of homoerotic desire. Sassine's novel presents singular postcolonial encounters, framed by ambiguous race, gender and sexuality and invites us to consider representations of the in-between space of the postcolony as a location of gender-bending, of ambiguous eroticism, and of uncertain racial and national identities. Finally, Chapter Nine, "Must *la victime* Be Feminine? Postcolonial Violence, Gender Ambiguity, and Homoerotic Desire in Sony Labou Tansi's *Je soussigné cardiaque"* provides an exploration of male homoerotic elements disguised as heterosexual economies. In my analysis of a play in which men display political capital through gender-bending, I consider feminist discourses on gender as well as the specific queer Kongo context expressed in Labou Tansi's treatment of the gendered body.

Because in addition to treating male homoerotic desire and domination in Francophone colonial and postcolonial literatures *Le Queer Impérial* deals with the complexities of race and gender, notions of the physical, of seeing and being seen are crucial to my analyses throughout. For example, in my reading of *La Femme et l'Homme nu* I point to the colonial text as a voyeuristic exercise which observes the sexuality of the black African male and puts it on display for its readers. But the novel also depicts the black African male as participating in this exhibition, yearning for recognition from the white males he encounters and putting himself on display so that they might recognize his masculinity as being equal to theirs. My reading of *Le Docker noir* and *Chaîne* in Chapter Five deals with the congruencies of rape, the gaze of both victims and their attackers, and the violence of photographic reproduction. In Chapter Eight I posit that an important aspect of *Mémoire d'une peau* is the characters' drive to hide their identities as they are related to race, gender and sexuality. They strive rather to blend into normative roles, in essence, to be misrecognized.

The theme of blindness runs through all the texts treated in *Le Queer Impérial* in that their narratives all fail in some way to question the ideologies they present. The colonial novels in the first section may be likened to propaganda for the European colonial project in Africa. Of the two texts, Herman Grégoire's *Makako* perhaps most strongly exemplifies the creation of a colonial mythology that makes heroes of white men who kill African men. And although in *La femme et l'Homme nu* Pierre Mille and André Demaison attempt to humanize their African protagonist, they at times portray him as a superstitious and vain child. Further, the failed *Blanche-Noir* relationships in both narratives point to a refusal to see beyond the colonial fear of racial mixing and beyond the notion of white women as the exclusive property of white men.

In Chapter 5, I interrogate how *Le Docker noir* accuses white French society of blindness as it persists in an inability to perceive the African protagonist as anything other than savage, and in an unwillingness to accept Africans who do not present themselves as docile and accepting of colonial domination. My analysis of *Chaîne* in Chapter Six considers the ignorance of the novel's protagonist, whose psychological bondage is the result of his internalization of hundreds of years of Western discourse which denigrates and emasculates black men. But blindness also reveals itself in the homophobic ideology presented by both Ousmane Sembene and Saïdou Bokoum which equates blackness and heterosexuality, and which internalizes Western value systems related to race, gender and sexuality.

The blindness presented in Section Three of the book is most aptly described as a refusal to both see and question misogynistic violence. The section also explores the impercipience of postcolonial and post-imperial subjects to their racial, sexual and political states. Further, these chapters consider the blindness imposed upon the reader of texts set in fictional and thus unidentifiable postcolonial states. The imaginary nation of *Je soussigné cardiaque* (Lebango) and the unnamed postcolonial state of *Mémoire d'une peau* throw readers into a state of disorientation, preventing us from fixing and defining African states on our own terms. But this lack of a knowable postcolonial state may also help us to acknowledge the shift in consciousness, the throwing-off of hegemonic entitlements of vision; an act which allows for a clearer understanding of the postcolonial. Blindness in these texts thus stands to reveal the blind spots of Western discourses which read Africa and Africans "through exclusively Western or ethnocentrist critical paradigms."[55]

---

55   Dominic Thomas, *Nation-Building, Propaganda, and Literature in Francophone Africa* (Bloomington: Indiana University Press, 2002), 15. Arguably there are practical political reasons for which postcolonial African authors use fictional states in their narratives. Sometimes in exile, sometimes living under, working within and writing against oppressive regimes, fictional place-names and invented but sometimes transparent names of leaders are often necessary for the safety of the writer and as way of getting past

Calling out blindness is also at the heart of what inspires *Le Queer Impérial*. Todorov's statement regarding the dysfunctional sexuality of the Muslim male can be likened to a myopia symptomatic of a French society which fails to see and understand non-whites because it keeps them at a distance both physically and culturally. One might also argue that the French riots of 2005, like those of November 2007, and those of July 2009 were a reaction to this blindness, that they were expressions of a desire to be seen and recognized as French, but also as men. The violence of the *banlieue* riots, like the violence of the political and theoretical discourses which sought to racially and sexually define those who took to the streets, without first recognizing their place in a common humanity, is echoed in the chapters of *Le Queer Impérial*. The transhistorical texts I have gathered all invoke in some way a desire to see the masculine Other and to be seen by him. In this book seeing and its tangential forms of recognition – misrecognition and blindness – are all functions of violence and the erotic.

By exposing the blindness, misrecognition and the refusal to see which defines many of the homoerotic encounters in these texts, *Le Queer Impérial* also challenges the critical silence vis-à-vis black-white homoerotic desire in colonial and postcolonial Francophone literatures. It is this very silence which so resonated at the Maison Française; the discomfort which Todorov seemed to experience after exposing his interest in the sexuality of masculine Others. This book confronts literary discourses which are echoed in Todorov's theories and which treat the black male as hypersexual and/or rigidly heterosexual. I also challenge the silences which follow declarations of a knowable, simplistic black male sexuality. As such the book seeks to understand the role played by violence and sexuality in the imperial project and in postcolonial and post-imperial states, uncovering how the acting-out of erotic violence within these political realities is reflected in the passages treated here.

---

government censorship. Also, fictitious place names allow for a pan-Africanist conception of the postcolony and a consideration of the troubles which haunt a large portion of the African continent. For further treatments of this issue see Achille Mbembe, *On the Postcolony* (Los Angeles: University of California Press, 2001).

Colonial Sexting: Homoerotic Voyeurism in *La Femme et l'Homme nu* by Pierre Mille and André Demaison, and *Makako, singe d'Afrique* by Herman Grégoire

> En effet comment continuer à assurer la suprématie blanche si l'indigène est lui-même l'époux d'une Française?
>
> JEAN-YVES LE NAOUR, *La Honte noire: l'Allemagne et les troupes coloniales françaises, 1914–1945*[1]

∵

At the end of World War I, Alphonse Séché, a French commander of West African troops, published *Les Noirs* (1919), a commentary on the contributions of the *tirailleurs* stationed in France, with a laudatory emphasis on their loyalty and obedience. In the latter sections of the text, Séché describes one of the French hospitals which welcomed injured African soldiers and the relationships these childlike men established with their doting nurses from the Red Cross:

> Le tutoiement, dont on a coutume d'user avec les noirs, facilitait encore le rôle maternel de ces dames. Les femmes seront toujours sentimentales, et c'est heureux, car nous gagnons à cela des gardes-malades incomparables.[2]

---

1 Jean-Yves Le Naour, *La Honte noire: L'Allemagne et les troupes coloniales françaises, 1914–1945* (Paris: Hachette Littérature, 2004), 42.

2 Alphonse Séché, *Les Noirs (d'après des documents officiels)* (Paris: Payot & Cie, 1919), 235–236. For more on the *marraine de guerre* see Pascal Blanchard and Nicolas Bancel, "Quelques réflexions sur les représentations du corps des tirailleurs sénégalais (1880–1918) *Africultures*, 25 (Feb. 2000): 41; Pascal Blanchard et al., *Le Paris Noir* (Paris: Hazan, 2001).

The familiarity which one customarily uses with blacks, facilitated even more so the maternal role of these women. Women will always be sentimental, and that is a good thing because this quality results in incomparable nurses.

However, as the text unfolds, one senses a change in Séché's attitude towards the African who previously "amusait par son langage, sa mimique, ses boutades" / amused us with his language, his mimicry and his silliness.[3] Under Séché's gaze the African man is suddenly transformed from a clownish child into a masculine rival: "Gâtés par les infirmières, admirés par la population, ils ont acquis d'eux-mêmes une opinion que leurs mérites ne justifient pas toujours. Ils entendent être traités comme des Européens." / Spoiled by nurses, admired by the population, they have acquired an opinion of themselves that is not always justified by their merits. They believe they should be treated like Europeans.[4] Uncomfortable with the notion of being the equal of an African man, and wishing to establish access to European male culture as based on merit rather than on the accident of birth, Séché ends his text by informing his reader of the action taken by the hospital administrator to resolve this problem: "[il] décida de se priver du concours que les dames de la Croix-Rouge lui prêtèrent tout d'abord." / [he] decided firstly to do without the support that the women of the Red Cross had offered him.[5] Both Séché and the hospital administrator conclude that by removing white women from spaces inhabited by African men and thus creating a homosocial space shared by white men and black men, colonial authorities will better insure that black men will not imagine they could gain access to European masculinity, as if European women provided a gateway to this state of being.

The masculine and racial economy which Séché describes in a hospital in France parallels those portrayed in Francophone colonial novels, narratives which attempt to represent the homosocial space that is colonial society.[6] Known for a preponderance of male protagonists, and a lack of important female characters, colonial literatures also often display a formidable black virility which is always eventually subdued by a superior European masculinity. As such, Francophone colonial novels often function as displays of

---

3 Alphonse Séché, *Les Noirs (d'après des documents officiels)* (Paris: Payot & Cie, 1919), 235.
4 Ibid., 246–247.
5 Ibid., 256.
6 Didier Gondola, *The History of Congo* (Westport, CT: Greenwood Publishing Group, 2002), 66. Gondola notes that "From the colonial perspective, the African city [...] was a male bastion from which women had been excluded."

hypermasculinity within a homosocial framework, presenting examples of manliness which necessarily favor Europeans – be they French or Belgian. However, these expressions of masculinity also hold multiple implications of homoerotic desire. This chapter presents evidence of male homoerotic economies in two colonial Francophone texts, Herman Grégoire's *Makako, singe d'Afrique* (1921) and Pierre Mille and André Demaison's *La Femme et l'Homme nu* (1924). It focuses on the male homoeroticism at play in the voyeuristic activity implicit in writing, not only about colonized and racialized Others, but also about the colonial man, who himself becomes a special type observed through the lens of colonial fiction. Also crucial in these narratives is the presence of white female characters, whose seduction by the black African further allows for a voyeuristic homoeroticism, but who can only be disowned by the Eurocentric narrative once she has given in to the temptations of African sensuality.

Co-written by Frenchmen Pierre Mille and André Demaison, *La Femme et l'Homme nu* recounts the love affair which develops between a Russian aristocrat and a black African. Vania Sélianova, who leaves her husband in Russia to travel to France, remains there in part due to the Soviet Revolution. Living in France during WWI, she becomes a *marraine*, volunteering in a military hospital in Fréjus. There she meets Tiékoro Nouma Sandé, a wounded *tirailleur* from the village of Ifane, in what is now Niger. Though it is Vania who takes the initiative, and who seems to dominate Tiékoro, her decision to follow him to Dakar, Senegal reveals the depth of her emotional attachment. Having arrived in Africa, she is soon disappointed to find their relationship is impossible due to the cultural differences between them and the disapproval she encounters in African colonial society. Tiékoro takes an African mistress and soon decides to leave Dakar and return to his village.

Makako, singe d'Afrique, the second novel of Belgian Herman Grégoire, is so named because the hero's monkey, Makako, functions as both a trickster – *malin comme un singe* – and a mimic with a proclivity for mockery – alluding to the expression "singer quelqu'un". Set at the dawn of a revolt by a group of African subjects of the Congo Free State (the Belgian Congo) it is the story of a Frenchman, Romain Clausel, who is stationed as a colonial administrator in M'Toa, along with his boss, M. Delvèze and Delvèze's young and beautiful wife Hélène, whose acquaintance Romain had made years before. Though he has already had a child with his black African wife and slave, Mwesa Moke, Romain and Hélène fall madly in love and attempt to find a way to be together. While Romain's morals prevent him from acting on his desires, Hélène becomes the mistress of Romain's best friend Landor Carré, and then of her African houseboy, Fataki, after the latter has raped her. Though Romain never learns of

Hélène's affair with Fataki, his knowledge of her tryst with Landor effectively ends his desire to be with her. Imprisoned for a year for having shot several Africans, Romain, after his release, manages to put down the uprising and regains the respect of both the Africans of the region and the colonists who had condemned him the year before.

Though *Makako* and *La Femme et l'Homme nu* clearly center on colonial masculinity, two female characters, Hélène Delvèze in Grégoire's novel and Vania Sélianova in Mille and Demaison's text, expose the social, racial and narrative requirements at play in both works, as they are written into scenes of eroticism with African men. Each novel presents aspects of these women's character which make it possible for the white male authors of these novels to symbolically give them as gifts to African men.

European colonization in Africa has been described through the metaphor of rape: rape of African land and of African women by white men. This tendency is particularly prevalent among African authors such as Léopold Sedar Senghor, David Diop and Laye Camara. Aissata Sidikou notes a tendency among Francophone intellectuals to view "Africa (female), [as] raped by Europe (male), [and as needing] her dignity restored."[7] Ironically, what we might call a counter-discourse to that of Africa as a feminized rape victim also emerged from colonialist France in the form of a paranoia surrounding the bodies of white European women. Though this fear of black men raping white women well precedes the height of the European colonial period in Africa as is evidenced in William Shakespeare's *The Tempest* and Denis Diderot's *Bijoux indiscrets* there is a marked proliferation of this theme in literature and popular culture during the early twentieth century.[8] In some instances this paranoia reveals itself as a desire; a homosocial exchange between the white, European novelists and African men. Such relations within narratives allow for a kind of "prostitution of hospitality"[9] between white women and black men, which is directed by the white authors of colonial narratives. And although the interracial affair in each text ends, and, in the case of *Makako*, Fataki, the

---

7   Aissata Sidikou, *Recreating Words, Reshaping Worlds: The Verbal Art of Women from Niger, Mali, and Senegal* (Trenton: Africa World Press, 2001).

8   See Jan Nederveen Pieterse, *White on Black: Images of Africa and Blacks in Western Popular Culture* (New Haven: Yale University Press, 1992); Martine Van Woerkens, "Guerre, 'Race' et Sexes dans *Le Masque d'or* de Charles Vidor," in *L'Autre et Nous: "Scènes et Types,"* eds Pascal Blanchard, Stéphane Blanchoin, Nicolas Bancel, Gilles Boëtsch, Hubert Gerbeau (Paris: ACHAC and SYROS, 1995), 171–174; Sylvie Chalaye, *Du Noir au nègre : l'image du Noir au théâtre : de Marguerite de Navarre à Jean Genet (1550–1960)* (Paris: L'Harmattan, 1998); and especially Serge Bilé, *La Légende du sexe surdimensionné des Noirs* (Monaco: Éditions du Rocher, 2005).

9   Simone de Beauvoir, *The Second Sex*, trans. and ed. H.M. Parshley (Paris: Gallimard, 1949), 89.

rapist-turned-lover of Hélène is killed, the narratives do describe the affairs as consensual. In effect, these narratives give these women to their African lovers.

Mille and Demaison devote one section of their novel to a detailed description of Vania, who is descended from royalty and born into a wealthy military family:

> A quatorze ans, précocement devenue femme, à peine si elle savait lire et écrire. Mais elle avait conquis la souplesse et la dureté des muscles d'une amazone, ne manquait pas un coq de montagne, à toute volée, avec son petit hammerless calibre 20, et savait prendre en automne, avec un nœud coulant suspendu au bout d'un long roseau, les brochets engourdis dans l'eau glacée des lacs.[10]

> At the age of fourteen, having suddenly become a woman, she could barely read and write. But she had developed the supple and hard muscles of an Amazon. With her twenty-caliber she could hit a mountain rooster from any distance and in autumn could fish out pike from the frozen waters of the lakes using only a knot suspended from a reed.

The narrative stresses not only Vania's savagery by comparing her to an illiterate and an Amazon, but accentuates her "masculine" qualities: her supple muscles, her proclivity for hunting and fishing. Her skill with a gun during an era when the use of firearms was an exclusively male activity symbolizes her phallic power and implies her potential to emasculate the men around her. Though we know she has become a woman, the text suggests that her kind of femininity is the wrong kind. It is one which dismisses and replaces men. It divorces itself from the traditions of her mother and grandmother, in which well-mannered young women were expected to be well-read and educated within the home, not outside of it.

Rather than reinforcing her identity as an aristocrat, Vania's studies at the Pensionnat des Demoiselle Nobles in Saint Petersburg give her more opportunity for rebellion. She finds herself in the company of other, like-minded girls:

> Elles étaient toutes à la Révolution, ou, comme on disait encore, au nihilisme. Celles-là portaient sur la poitrine, comme un scapulaire, le portrait de Véra Sassoulitch, meurtrière et martyre. Elles s'affiliaient à des

---

10   Pierre Mille and André Demaison, *La Femme et l'Homme nu* (Paris: Les Éditions de France, 1924), 9.

groupes révolutionnaires, tenaient dans l'enceinte même du Pensionnat des conciliabules ardents et mystiques.[11]

They had all given themselves to the revolution, or, as was still being said, to nihilism. Those girls wore a picture of the murderer and martyr Vera Zasulich on their breasts like a scapular. They became affiliated with revolutionary groups, and convened, even in the heart of the boarding house, mystical and passionate secret meetings.

As adherents to the Russian nihilist movement of the late nineteenth and early twentieth century, these aristocratic girls discovered Anarcha-feminism, an international, anti-patriarchy and anti-government movement which originated in the work of Russian-born American Emma Goldman in the late 1800's. According to the Anarcha-feminist Manifesto written by the Dark Star Collective in *Quiet Rumors: An Anarcha-Feminist Reader* "a Woman's Revolutionary Movement must not mimic, but destroy, all vestiges of the male-dominated power structure, the State itself ...".[12] Simone de Beauvoir's *The Second Sex* gives an account of Russian feminism in the period in question:

> It is in Soviet Russia that the feminist movement has made the most sweeping advances. It began among female student intellectuals at the end of the nineteenth century, and was even then connected with violent and revolutionary activity.[13]

Despite her early feminist ties, Vania was not a supporter of the Soviet Revolution. However, the text suggests the danger posed by the anarcha-feminism of Vania and her cohorts who took to nihilism and violence as if they were part of a religion – thus the reference to mystic assemblages and the wearing of a scapular with the image of Véra Zasulich, a young woman of aristocratic exrtaction who, in 1878, attempted to assassinate the head of the Russian Police. By evoking this blasphemous and secret religious activity within a group of women, the text hints that, more than pupils, these young women were part of a coven, that their activities were a danger to society-at-large.

11   Pierre Mille and André Demaison, *La Femme et l'Homme nu* (Paris: Les Éditions de France, 1924), 11–12.
12   *Quiet Rumors: An Anarcha-Feminist Reader*, eds Dark Star Collective (San Francisco: AK Press, 2002), 11.
13   Simone de Beauvoir, *The Second Sex*, trans. and ed. H.M. Parshley (Paris: Gallimard, 1949), 126.

When her anarchist activities make her undesirable in Saint Petersburg and
put her at risk of imprisonment, Vania – though married – is sent to Paris with
her mother. Here, she takes various "Occidental" lovers and becomes a "poule
de luxe" / high-class whore.[14] In the various affairs she has with Western men
the clash of cultures is apparent:

> Ils ne pouvaient … surtout les Français et les Anglo-Saxons – s'accoutumer
> à ses imprévoyances, à son inexactitude, à son incapacité radicale d'arriver
> à l'heure, ou seulement avec un retard excusable, à un rendez-vous; à
> ses familiarités avec ses domestiques brusquement interrompues
> d'injures ou d'incompréhensibles antipathies ; à une insouciance ma-
> térielle qui jetait le désordre dans ses affaires, sans qu'elle daignât s'en
> inquiéter.[15]

> They were incapable … especially the Frenchmen and the Anglo Saxons,
> of getting used to her thoughtlessness, her impreciseness, her extreme
> inability to arrive on time or even with an excusable lateness to at date,
> to her informality with her domestics suddenly followed by insults or by
> an incomprehensible disagreeableness; to a material carelessness which
> threw her affairs into disorder, and with which she didn't deign to preoc-
> cupy herself.

Despite Vania's superior standing in Russian society, she possessed none of the
social graces Western men desired and were accustomed to in their women.
The preceding passage is filled with negative prefixes (*in, im, anti*) meant to
underline Vania's un-Western, and particularly un-French-like conduct. Her
protean behavior towards those whom she considers beneath her reveals the
abuse of power of an aristocrat for whom the notion of *noblesse oblige* carries
no meaning. Further, the passage notes Vania's lack of personal organization
in relation to her Western counterparts. Although Brett A. Berliner argues that
"The main characters in this racial drama could not be more different, save
their status as outsiders"[16], Vania's lateness and, by extension, her slowness,
as well as her lack of preoccupation with the future consequences of her actions, place her out of time and within the same realm of the Africans who

---

14   Roger Little, *Between Totem and Taboo: Black Man, White Woman in Francographic
      Literature* (Exeter: University of Exeter Press, 2001), 69.
15   Pierre Mille and André Demaison, *La Femme et l'Homme nu* (Paris: Les Éditions de France,
      1924), 18.
16   Brett A Berliner, *Ambivalent Desire: The Exotic Black Other in Jazz-Age France* (Amherst:
      University of Massachusetts Press, 2002), 57.

appear later in the text. In one instance the text describes both lovers as "savages": "Tiékoro est un vrai primitif, c'est-à-dire l'esclave de puissances sociales, religieuses, magiques, impératives; Vania est peut-être aussi une sauvage, mais déchaînée, tout le contraire." / Tiékoro is truly primitive, that is, he is a slave to social, religious, magical and natural powers ; Vania is perhaps also a savage, but a violent savage, and, as such, completely different from Tiékoro.[17] Though the text differentiates between Tiékoro the slave and Vania the free spirit, she is described with the same vocabulary which the narrative implies is more logically applied to Tiékoro. Like the Lacanian representation of all women, which Anne McClintock describes as "a riddle, unknowable and un-representable … the Dark continent, the Sphinx"[18] *La Femme et l'Homme nu* uses "exoticized and implicitly racist images drawn from an Africanist iconography"[19] to describe the Russian heroine.

Like Berliner, Roger Little has noted that the narrative hinges on the striking contrasts between Vania and Tiékoro.[20] However, the descriptions of Vania which show her as Other vis-à-vis Western women also suggest she has much in common with the African. This passage in the novel stresses what we already know: when the narrative delivers Vania to the bedside of the ailing African, it is not a Frenchwoman that it gives to the black man, but a Slav. This is apparent during a scene at a café in Fréjus, when colonial administrators react to the sight of the lovers:

> – Y a de quoi être dégoûté ! grogna plus loin un adjudant. Dire que les femmes nous préfèrent un moricaud!
> – C'est pas une Française …
> – Je te dis que si …
> – Je te dis que non. Écoute plutôt son accent.[21]

Now that's disgusting! Groaned a warrant officer sitting close by. To think that women prefer this darkie to us!
She's not French …

---

17   Pierre Mille and André Demaison, *La Femme et l'Homme nu* (Paris: Les Éditions de France, 1924), 118.

18   Anne McClintock, *Imperial Leather: Race, Gender, and Sexuality in the Colonial Contest* (New York: Routledge, 1995), 193.

19   Ibid., 193.

20   Roger Little, "Blanche et Noir aux années vingt," in *Regards sur les littératures coloniales, Afrique Francophone: Approfondissements*, ed. Jean-François Durand (Paris: L'Harmattan, 1999), 32.

21   Pierre Mille and André Demaison, *La Femme et l'Homme nu* (Paris: Les Éditions de France, 1924), 161–162.

Sure she is.
I'm telling you she isn't. Just listen to her accent.

Initially, Vania falls under the category of "les femmes," which implies that she is to be considered one of "nos femmes," and which infers ownership by the French men observing her. The politicizing of her sexual choices reflects the fear of the degradation and of the diminution of France's population, which leads to a Foucauldian surveillance of her sexuality.[22] However, their fears of exogamy are allayed and their attention shifts to Tiékoro when they realize that Vania is not one of *their* women. Allowing her to be with the African while she is a guest in their domain performs a curious operation in which the practice of gift-giving resolves a crisis of hospitality, defined by Mireille Rosello as a situation in which "some individuals are expected to be set aside, excluded, banned from the community". These individuals "are not total outsiders, but their mode of belonging makes them eternally fragile guests."[23]

For the men who bristle at Tiékoro's presence at the café it is evident that the *tirailleur* is a guest in their country. As potentially good hosts they would not only welcome him, but also present him with a gift, something of value which they possess.[24] It is particularly crucial that the Frenchmen enact this form of potlatch hospitality as Tiékoro has already presented them with a gift by risking his life in their war with Germany. Providing the companionship of a *marraine* to the convalescent African might qualify as a gift, but Tiékoro has taken permanent possession of a gift meant to be temporary. With this gesture, he becomes an unwelcome guest[25] who, nonetheless, remains within the borders of the community. This crisis of hospitality is resolved when the Frenchmen realize that Vania is *also* a guest. However, her willing participation in breaking the rules of gift-giving makes her, like her lover, present in the community without the full benefits of belonging.[26] Though she does not inspire the same disdain as does Tiékoro, the Frenchmen still consider her a "bad Guest".[27] And because as a bad guest, she is no longer desirable, she becomes the Bad Gift,

22   Michel Foucault, *Discipline and Punish: The Birth of the Prison*, trans. Alan Sheridan (New York: Vintage Books, 1979), 26.

23   Mireille Rosello, *Postcolonial Hospitality: The Immigrant as Guest* (Stanford: Stanford University Press, 2001), 165.

24   Marcel Mauss, *The Gift: Forms and Functions of Exchange in Archaic Societies*, trans. Ian Cunnison (London: Cohen & West, 1966), 37–39.

25   Ibid., 10.

26   Alain Milon, *L'Étranger dans la ville: du rap au graff mural* (Paris: PUF, 1999), 22.

27   Mireille Rosello, *Postcolonial Hospitality: The Immigrant as Guest* (Stanford: Stanford University Press, 2001), 33.

given without any underlying rights of possession, relinquished to Tiékoro in an act of bad faith by men who are relieved she is not one of their own.

A particularly venomous review of the novel, listed under the category "Romans mauvais, dangereux ou inutiles pour la généralité des lecteurs"[28] does express concern over representing "des amours malsains de la grande dame russe et du nègre." / the unhealthy love affair between the great Russian lady and the Negro.[29] Written shortly after the publication of *La Femme et l'Homme nu* the review laments:

> Il y a quelque chose de lamentable à voir déshonorer ainsi un membre de la haute société russe, au lendemain du jour où les Soviets se sont installés à Paris, en l'ambassade de la rue de Grenelle, menaçant de mille maux nouveaux les malheureux proscrits de l'ancienne Russie.[30]

> There is something lamentable in seeing a member of Russian high society be so dishonored so soon after the Soviets established themselves in Paris, in the embassy on Rue Grenelle, threatening with a thousand fresh evils those poor exiles of old Russia.

While showing disdain for Africans, this reviewer does express some empathy for Vania. Nonetheless, the review underlines the heroine's status as a foreigner. The protests within the review reinforce Vania's otherness in French society and reveal Mille and Demaison's reasoning in making their heroine Russian and not French. For, although she is living in France, Vania is no different from the stateless Russian exiles mentioned in the review. This aspect of Vania's otherness, coupled with her penchant for sexual adventure and her feminism make her a prime candidate for a tryst with an African man. Writing and witnessing this love affair through narrative satisfies a voyeuristic need to eroticize both Vania and Tiékoro without compromising the integrity of the nation. This refusal of African penetration into French sexuality is represented by the almost complete absence of Frenchwomen in the narrative. Three Frenchwomen appear in the novel once it moves to Dakar, but these colonial women are peripheral characters for whom sexual contact with an African is precluded by their age, physical beauty, station in life – one of them is a nun – and by their adherence to colonialist doctrine which casts Africans as their

---

28   C.H. Bourdon, "Les Romans," *Revue des lectures*, 13. 1 (Jan. 15, 1925): p. 25.
29   Ibid., 27.
30   Ibid., p. 27.

inferiors. We can read this absence as the archetypal Frenchwoman's refusal – mediated by Mille and Demaison – to give herself to an African.

The woman who gives herself to her African houseboy in *Makako* is, like Vania, a foreigner, for she is French and not Belgian. Pierre Halen observes the tendency in Belgian colonial texts to make characters of questionable morals foreigners rather than Belgians: "tout s'explique et l'honneur est sauf" / all is understood and the [country's] honor is safe.[31] Like Vania, Hélène is the wrong kind of woman. A satirical description provided by Landor, the steamship captain, exposes her inadequacies:

> Madame que voici est instruite; elle a fait des études de droit. Malgré ce que tu pourrais croire, elle est encore très naïve, mais se tait beaucoup, pour ne pas le laisser deviner. Elle traite volontiers les hommes en camarade; elle adore monter à cheval; elle aimera la brousse. Elle a oublié d'emporter des culottes et des guêtres, ce qui prouve qu'elle n'a pas le sens très net de sa vocation.[32]

> Well now, it seems Madame is educated. She has studied Law. In spite of what you might believe, she is still very naïve, but she keeps quiet, so as not to be found out. She gladly treats men like friends. She loves to ride horses. She will love the bush. But she forgot to bring her breeches and her gaiters, which proves that she does not have a very good sense of her vocation.

Landor's acute description of Hélène and the more formal register he uses to convey his disdain for her indicate the uppitiness of her attempt to take on practical, "masculine" traits. However, despite her desire to impress her male companions with her skill in various segments of the masculine domain, she is still a woman. She is ill-equipped, both literally, because she has forgotten her riding gear and figuratively, because she is naïve, forgetful, and transparent despite her duplicity. Rather than presenting her real self, she has sought to manipulate those around her by convincing them of her superiority, that is, of her masculinity.

Makako does seem to paint Hélène as desirous of masculinity, or at least, of the power it would bring her. Upon observing a female monkey who tries unsuccessfully to attract Makako – who himself has seen fit to "rape" both a dog

---

31   Pierre Halen, *Le Petit Belge avait vu grand: Une Littérature coloniale* (Brussels: Éditions Labor, 1993), 81.

32   Herman Grégoire, *Makako, singe d'Afrique* (Paris: La Renaissance du Livre, 1921), 51–52.

and a duck – Hélène contemplates one of the difficulties of being a woman: "la petite femelle frileuse, dédaignée par Makako, ne peut violer ni chien, ni canard et, quelle que soit la fièvre qui la brûle, est condamnée à l'attente inutile et à la résignation." / the skittish little female rejected by Makako can rape neither a dog nor a duck, and no matter how hotly desirous she is, she is condemned to wasting her time waiting, and finally, to resignation.[33] Hélène's dilemma places her between her intellectual education and her sexual instinct. Though she knows that, in keeping with the rules of her society, as a woman she must wait for the sexual advances of men, she wishes, if not to be a man, then at least to possess the sexual agency of men. Hélène suffers from a case of penis envy defined by traditional conceptions of sexual agency. She is incapable of rape as she conceives it because she must always be the insertee and can never be the inserter. That she interprets sexual agency as expressed through rape and that she nonetheless desires this power makes Hélène a highly problematic object for the interest of the white men of the novel.

One of those men, Romain Clausel, first encounters Hélène at a cabaret at the Place Pigalle in Paris, years before they meet again in the Belgian Congo. It turns out that Pigalle, known for its artists, libertines and prostitutes, provides a suitable home for the sexually adventurous Hélène. During a conversation about the nature of love, she wonders: "Pourquoi faut-il que la femme s'adapte à son amant? Pourquoi ne choisirait-elle pas un amant adapté aux circonstances?" / Why must a woman adapt to her lover? Why should she not choose a lover adapted to her circumstances?[34] Hélène then seems to abandon her female agency when she marries the much older Delvèze, who represents the antithesis of colonial masculinity. When encountering her for the first time as Madame Delvèze, Romain wonders why she would marry such a man:

– Je vous croyais partie pour le bon combat, avec héroïsme et indépendance.
– Pensez-vous? Une étudiante pauvre. Ma seule chance de salut était un autre genre de prostitution.
– ... Vive l'antique esclavage!
– ... Où voyez-vous de l'esclavage? ... Avouez qu'il [M. Delvèze] a été privilégié. Et si le don de moi-même lui a paru magnifique, il ne me coûtait rien....
– L'homme est le maître. Il est néfaste d'avoir un maître médiocre.

33 Ibid., 116.
34 Ibid., 44.

– Vielle morale de femmes qui ne savaient pas se garder ... Je suis bien
sûre d'être une femme nouvelle et de n'avoir pas à le regretter.[35]

– I thought you would be fighting the good fight, with heroism and
independence.
– Did you think so? A starving student. My only chance at salvation was
another type of prostitution.
– Long live that old-time slavery.
– Who said anything about slavery? You have to admit that he [Delvèze]
was very lucky to have me. And if my giving myself to him seemed beyond
his wildest dreams, well, it didn't cost me anything.
– The man is the master. It's dangerous to have a mediocre master.
– That's just old feminine morality from women who didn't know how
to protect themselves ... I'm confident in being a new woman, and in not
having to regret it.

Hélène reveals her willingness to compromise the values she held as a young
woman for material gain. By the time she reaches the Belgian Congo, she has
done the exact thing about which she had mused in Paris: she has taken a husband to fit her personal circumstances, and in doing so, has reshaped her ideas
on female existence. She executes her marriage as if it existed somewhere between a business contract and an act of prostitution. She rejects traditional
notions of feminine purity and creates a distinction between the part of herself which she gives to her husband, and a truer identity which lies outside the
role of the passive feminine. Further, her choice of husband, reveals the lack of
value she places on the masculinity of her partner, as if she were prepared to
fill the masculine role in the relationship. This, coupled with her indifference
to traditional notions of women as prizes for deserving men makes her unac-
ceptable as a lover for the ultra-masculine Romain.

Although Hélène and Romain share a mutual attraction, they differ radically in their ideas about ideal femininity. The narrative displays these divergent views on womanhood in order to show that Hélène has lost her way.
Romain's comparison of Hélène to a slave and her description of herself as
a prostitute not only belie her claim of feminine modernity, and show her
as unworthy of the European, but also foreshadow her later submission to
her final sexual partner in the narrative: Fataki, the houseboy, whose name,
aptly, is Swahili for "firecracker" or "rocket". The fact that Hélène's tryst with
Fataki begins in rape further signals a narrative rejection of her as a possible

---

35   Ibid., 53–55.

partner for Romain. Her status as an undesirable partner is solidified in this scene of rape, in which the narrative seems to blame her even more than it does her houseboy:

> Elle avait repoussé le nègre amoureux ... un peu tard! Cette [...] défaillance de sa chair était due [...] à son organisation intérieure. Tout en elle, instincts, sentiments, imagination, avait été subordonné à l'intelligence [...] Les réflexes avaient été supprimés.[36]

> She had rejected the love-struck Negro ... a bit late! This weakness of the flesh was due to her inner makeup. Everything within her, instincts, emotions, imagination, had been subverted by intelligence. Her reflexes had been eliminated.

This description of Hélène's rape links her victimization to her evolution as an intellectual in a tone that exudes an irony similar to that of Landor's description of Hélène as a law student. The text claims that her intelligence, an attribute which is of little use to her, compromises her natural instinct, emotion and imagination. This passage's opposition of the natural and the intellectual in women suggests that for the masculinist project within the narrative, Hélène is far from the ideal woman. In fact, one might argue that Hélène is inferior to Romain's wife and slave Mwesa Moke as the latter is faithful and seeks only to fulfill her husband's desires. White male society's loss of Hélène as a potential partner becomes acceptable in light of her weakness of character. In fact, like the potlatch, she is passed from European to European, and then finally given as a Bad Gift to the black African.

The affairs Hélène and Vania have with black Africans are possible, in part, because of the characterizations of these women as unsuitable for partnership with European males. This rejection facilitates the creation of a European male, homosocial space which excludes certain women and all colonized male subjects. Hélène and Vania, the latter described as thirty-five years old when she meets Tiékoro, also share the status of childless, married women who have thus not completed their feminine functions.[37] And although their affairs

---

36   Ibid., 178–179.

37   See Joshua Cole, *The Power of Large Numbers: Population, Politics and Gender in Nineteenth-Century France* (Ithaca: Cornell University Press, 2000) and Judith Surkis, *Sexing the Citizen: Morality and Masculinity in France, 1870–1920* (Ithaca: Cornell University Press, 2006). Paul Féval sends a clear message regarding reproduction to French women – from France – in the face of the low birthrate and competition from other nations: "Ma fille,

mean they are guilty of adultery, and even more unfit as partners for European men, the lack of offspring guarantees that their contact with black sexuality will not taint the imagined purity of the European gene pool.

The last time Romain and Hélène come face to face, he observes her faded beauty and, reflecting on who may have satisfied her sexual desire, wonders, "Dans quels bras a-t-elle perdu ce tourment qui est notre noblesse?" / In whose arms did she lose that suffering which makes us noble?[38] The suffering to which Romain refers is sexual desire, the control of which is critical for conserving European dignity. By suggesting that Hélène has lost a communal nobility, Romain effectively ejects her from French society as he knows it. And though he cannot guess that her nobility has been lost to an African, he reads in her face that she is no longer the right woman for him.

---

comme celui de mes fils, *ton corps est à moi*. L'impôt du sang dû par la femme, c'est la maternité! ... S'opposer à la conception équivaut à la désertion, et détruire l'enfant conçu équivaut à l'assassinat d'un défenseur." / My child, like the body of my son, *your body is also mine*. The blood tax which the woman must pay comes in the form of motherhood ... Opposition to this belief is equivalent to desertion, and killing the unborn child is equivalent to assassinating a defender of our nation. *Ton Corps est à moi* (Paris: Éditions Radot, 1927), 288.

38   Herman Grégoire, *Makako, singe d'Afrique* (Paris: La Renaissance du Livre, 1921), 243.

"Entre hommes et sous l'équateur": Colonial Masculinity, Race and Desire in *Makako, singe d'Afrique*

Empire was a man's business.

JOHN TOSH, *Manliness and Masculinities in Nineteenth-century Britain*[1]

∴

In *Surréalisme et Sexualité* (1971) Xavière Gauthier comments on the exchanging of female sex partners within the homosocial French Surrealist movement. Anticipating Gayle Rubin's "The Traffic in Women" (1975) and Eve Kosofsky Sedgwick's *Between Men* (1985), Gauthier's work seems to have been informed by that of Lévi-Strauss (1967) on women and exogamy in kinship networks. She contends that "Les rapports de plusieurs hommes qui désirent la même femme sont de nature homosexuelle. La femme, objet de circulation entre hommes, n'est souvent qu'un prétexte." / The relations of men who desire the same women are of a homosexual nature. The woman, an object of circulation between men is often no more than a pretext.[2] Like the Surrealist network, which, especially in the French context, was loath to accept women in any role of power or prestige, colonial power structures were by definition homosocial. Both systems mirror Eve Kosofsky-Sedgwick's description in *Between Men* of homosocial societies. Taking her cue from René Girard's work on mimetic desire (1961), Sedgwick contends that:

> ... in any male-dominated society, there is a special relationship between male homosocial (*including* homosexual) desire and the structures for maintaining and transporting patriarchal power: a relationship founded on an inherent and potentially active structural congruence. For historical reasons, this special relationship may take the form of ideological

---

1 John Tosh, *Manliness and Masculinities in Nineteenth-century Britain* (Harlow: Pearson/ Longman, 2005), 193.

2 Xavière Gauthier, *Surréalisme et Sexualité* (Paris: Gallimard, 1971), 240.

© KONINKLIJKE BRILL NV, LEIDEN, 2018 | DOI 10.1163/9789004365544_004

homophobia, ideological homosexuality, or some highly conflicted but
intensively structured combination of the two.[3]

We find a homosocial, hypermasculine and homoerotic paradigm in Herman
Grégoire's *Makako, singe d'Afrique*, in which the four principal male characters –
the Europeans Romain Clausel, Landor Carré, and Delvèze, and the African
houseboy Fataki – engage in various forms of sexual activity with the sole principal female character, Hélène. Grégoire's novel inhabits an ambivalent space
in which different forms of homosocial and homoerotic desires converge and
in which a conflux of eroticism, romantic love and intellectual love may define
relationships between men, setting different parameters for each homosocial
partnership. For although this erotic sharing of a woman implies a homoerotic fraternity between these four men, there are limits to this brotherhood. In
the same vein as the work of Susan Fraiman, which concludes that "the traffic
in women may involve male status as much as *eros*,"[4] this analysis of *Makako*
maps the effect of the hierarchy presented by the novel's vision of sexual relationships in colonial society. Even though two of the men concerned – Romain
and Landor – share an implicit homoerotic relationship, whose currents verge
toward and then diverge from Hélène as a desired object, the two friends' desire for each other is only possible because each regards the other as a racial
and masculine equal. In *Makako*, constructions of masculinity and hyper-
masculinity are crucial to the creation of homoerotic "in groups" and "out
groups." So too is racial identity. Romain and Landor as well as the narrative
dismiss a homoerotic connection between themselves and both Delvèze and
Fataki as a result of both a racial and masculinist agenda. Thus, the act of sharing a woman in this text involves both amicable and confrontational relations
between men.

We can better understand notions of masculinity in these interpersonal relationships by dividing the men into the categories illustrated by Albert Memmi
in *The Colonizer and the Colonized*. Descriptions of the houseboy Fataki recall
those of what Memmi calls the "mythical portrait of the colonized," a wicked,
wretched figure, not worthy of being trusted.[5] The suggestion, through his
name, that he is a "firecracker" further underlines his unpredictable nature.

---

3 Eve Kosofsky Sedgwick, *Between Men: English Literature and Male Homosocial Desire* (New
   York: Columbia University Press, 1985), 25.
4 Susan Fraiman, "Geometries of Race and Gender: Eve Sedgwick, Spike Lee, Charlayne
   Hunter-Gault," *Feminist Studies*, 20. 1 (Spring, 1994), 82.
5 Albert Memmi, *The Colonizer and the Colonized*, trans. Howard Greenfeld (London: Earthscan
   Publications, 2003) (1957), 126.

As for Delvèze, a local tax collector too frightened of Africans to demand payment from them, he possesses the "humanitarian romanticism" of the "colonizer who refuses":[6] a colonizer but not a colonialist. But in refusing to be a colonialist, Delvèze may also be guilty of bad faith, because he is no revolutionary working for the benefit of Africans. Despite his refusal to acquiesce to the sadistic component of colonization, he does nothing to end the practice, but rather continues to benefit from the exploitation of Africans. Romain and Landor, who can be qualified as colonizers who accept the role of colonialists, proudly embrace sadism as a necessary aspect of imperialism. Proponents of a "colonial racism" which establishes an unbridgeable gulf between themselves and the colonized, these men find their superiority in descriptions of themselves as men of action who, rather than depending on the intellectualization of racism, "draw [their] lessons from experience."[7]

In his description of the colonizer who accepts, Memmi mentions the role of colonial fiction in producing the myth of colonial man: "The model is very ordinary and his portrait flows readily from the top of a pen. The man is generally young, prudent, and polished. His backbone is tough, his teeth long. No matter what happens he justifies everything – the system and the officials in it."[8] To be sure, myths of colonial masculinity, largely disseminated by colonial adventure novels such as *Makako*, describe a strong, independent European whose emotional satisfaction centered on reveling in a male physicality far removed from the feminizing romantic desire left behind in the European metropolis. Robert Aldrich forwards that:

> colonial masculinity and its actions – conquest, pacification, the building of new countries, settlement, promotion of traditional virtues – was seen as compensation for a deficit of manliness in France, as evidenced by military defeat in 1870–71, a falling birth rate and depopulation, fears of degeneration, and contestatory social and cultural currents.[9]

Certainly, by presenting themselves as men of action, who rejected passivity, colonial men represented a new Europe. They were, as Richard Laurent Omgba notes, "tout différents des aristocrates oisifs de Paris et des bourgeois repus des campagnes françaises. Ils constituent 'un peuple neuf', qui s'est forgé

---

6   Ibid., p. 65.
7   Ibid., 114–115.
8   Ibid., 90.
9   Robert Aldrich, "Colonial Man" in *French Masculinities: History, Culture and Politics*, eds Christopher E. Forth and Bertrand Taithe (New York: Macmillan, 2007), 125.

à l'épreuve et s'est endurci devant l'adversité." / completely different from the do-nothing aristocrats of Paris and the overstuffed bourgeois of the French countryside. They embodied a new people, forged in hardship and hardened by adversity.[10] Ironically, as William B. Cohen notes, the vast majority of recruits to the École Coloniale issued from the middle class.[11] Cohen associated the lure of the colonies in some men with their bourgeois origins:

> In republican France, the feudal order had long disappeared, but the colonies represented a world in which the sons of the bourgeoisie could exercise an authority which not even their forefathers had possessed, to become part of the ruling caste.[12]

The colony, then, became a pivotal space for personal reinvention through class. While these men may have quit Europe as members of the bourgeoisie, Africa allowed them to recreate themselves, to form a new kind of masculinist aristocracy reminiscent of the crusaders of France's distant past.

The hypermasculine sexuality constructed by this new class of man provided a dual extension of the hardiness and endurance which he sought to embody. This sensuality was nonetheless epitomized by genital restraint:

> ... wild sexual impulses have been tamed, and the genitals do not monopolize passion. The complete colonial man, unlike the stereotype of the African, Asian, or Oceania is one who, in Greco-Roman and Judeo-Christian style, can master his base urges and subsume lust to the superior goals of civilization: a 'higher' masculinity reserved for the white man.[13]

Thus, erotic power from the idealized colonial man comes not from displaying his ability to have sex, but rather from his choice to abstain from genital contact. However, considerations of genital restraint in the colony extended

---

10   Richard Laurent Omgba, "Mythes et Fantasmes de la Littérature Coloniale," in *Regards sur les Littératures Coloniales, Afrique Francophone: Approfondissements*, Tome II, ed. Jean-François Durand (Paris: L'Harmattan, 1999), 131.

11   William B. Cohen, "The Lure of Empire: Why Frenchmen Entered the Colonial Service," *Journal of Contemporary History*, 4.1 (Jan. 1969): 106.

12   Ibid.: 111.

13   Robert Aldrich, "Colonial Man" in *French Masculinities: History, Culture and Politics*, eds Christopher E. Forth and Bertrand Taithe (New York: Macmillan, 2007), 135.

beyond heterosexual desire. Jonathan Rutherford, writing on the English colonial context, contends that:

> Like war, the imperial mission offered men the opportunity to displace their homosexual desire. The empire provided an ideal screen for its projection onto black and brown young men. [...] One of the central imperatives of colonialist culture was the white man's fear of the sexuality of the voracious native. While women were constructed as the primary victims of this black and brown peril, its impetus lay in the projective fantasies of the white man who was enmeshed in anxieties of homosexual rape.[14]

Makako resides squarely within a category of colonial fiction which forwards the model of colonial masculinity described above, applying the world views of Romain and Landor to the construction of a truly masculine colonial hero, and allowing each of them to perform masculinity for the benefit of the other. As Michael Kimmel writes, "Masculinity is a *homosocial* enactment. We test ourselves, perform heroic feats, take enormous risks, all because we want other men to grant us our manhood."[15] The need to display masculine discipline may inspire these two men to resist the attractive Hélène Delvèze. But their heterosexual genital restraint results from the romantic friendship between them. Thus, hypermasculine conversations about pursuing or denying a woman represent only displaced homosocial desires, as does the physical domination of colonial subjects. The homoerotic tensions which underpin the relations of these two colonials thus complicate any notion of genital restraint. The amalgam of French and Belgian masculinity in *Makako*, creates a space for homoeroticism in the colonial project through both its positioning and eventual exclusion of women and its celebration of male physicality.

The hypermasculinity of Romain, the novel's colonialist hero manifests in his physical traits, his relationship with indigenous populations, and his attitude towards desire. The narrative presents him as a perfect balance of physical hardiness and intelligence:

> Il est de taille petite, mais on le sent vigoureux, entraîné aux sports les plus rudes. Sa démarche est très affirmative. Mais son visage, trop intelligent,

---

14   Jonathan Rutherford, *Forever England: Reflections on Race, Masculinity and Empire* (London: Lawrence & Wishart, 1997), 29–30.

15   Michael Kimmel, *Manhood in America* (New York: Free Press, 1996), 7.

l'est moins. Il donne l'impression de penser et, par là, dans le troupeau des humains, demeure inquiétant.[16]

He is small, but one can sense that he is vigorous, trained in the roughest sports. His gait is very assertive. But his aspect, too intelligent, is less so. He gives the impression of one who thinks and thus, within the herd of humans, remains a cause for concern.

As his name suggests, Romain illustrates the Greco-Roman notion of an ideal man, achieving a balance in the development of the body, mind, and spirit through stoical interactions with the world. In his confidence Romain impresses himself upon others. His intelligence, though vital, subordinates neither his physical strength nor his spirit as a natural leader. The heterosexual fulfillment of his need for physical pleasure seems the result of a logical conclusion rather than a capitulation to passion.

The narrative emphasizes Romain's physical connection with Africa and its colonized subjects who provide an outlet for his masculine energies. We witness this in a description of Romain, who, sick with fever, travels through the territory to collect taxes:

... il écoutait les plaintes individuelles, faisait donner le fouet s'il y avait lieu. Ici, nouvelle souffrance. La fièvre ne manquait pas d'exciter en lui cette pointe de sadisme que contient la flagellation et, pour ne pas continuer à frapper quand le sang coulait, il lui fallait faire un pénible effort qui augmentait sa nervosité.[17]

He listened to individual plaintiffs, ordered whippings if it was necessary. Here there was a new hardship. The fever had not failed to excite in him that edge of sadism which flagellation incited and it became necessary for him to go to great lengths in order not to continue whipping when blood began to flow.

The whip as Romain's phallic extension provides a means of contact between him and the people in his charge, within the mainly-homosocial public sphere of the colony. Though he treats beating African men as only one of many aspects of his job as a colonial administrator and bravely bears the suffering he must endure in administering this form of torture, the text moves

---

16   Herman Grégoire, *Makako, singe d'Afrique* (Paris: La Renaissance du Livre, 1921), 21.
17   Ibid., 122–123.

from Romain delegating the use of the whip to the sexual pleasure he experiences while using the whip himself. And while the narrative provides the context of a "fever" to explain the passion with which Romain seeks to violate the bodily integrity of colonized subjects, this fever is both erotic and viral.

His sadism towards African men has not, however precluded his taking of an African mistress. Mwesa Moke, described as little more than a tool: "lui sert d'esclave et d'épouse" / serves him as both slave and wife.[18] He feels a contentment with her that is undisturbed by feelings of romantic love: "cette perfection était sans désir" / this perfection involved no desire.[19] Hélène's arrival and the desperate longing he feels for this white woman disturbs this utopia. Here too, his conception of masculinity – and of interactions with women – condition his notions of how to deal with his debilitating desire:

> Et pourtant, se dit-il, elle est faite comme toute autre femme. Un sexe et peu de cervelle. Si la raison a pris le dessus, c'est que l'instinct a été étouffé. Il suffira de la violer pour lui rendre son authenticité.[20]

> And yet, he told himself, she's just like any other woman. A vagina and no brain. If her reason has taken over it is because her instinct has been stifled. One only needs to rape her in order to help her reclaim her authenticity.

Romain's concern over returning Hélène to some originary state falls in line with his desire to retain and renew his own masculinity. Afraid the romantic desire he feels for Hélène has feminized him, Romain uses a fantasy of rape to imagine what sexual violation might do for *him*, how raping Hélène might make him her master, while transforming her into a real woman, something more like his African concubine. His wish to separate her intellectual pretensions from her physicality takes the form of an imagined cutting-up of her body into its two primary parts: her genitalia and her small brain.

We find the same regard for emotional attachments in Clausel's friend, Landor Carré, operator of the steamship *Le Communard* and contraband smuggler, whose first name recalls the French term *lendor* and connotes a withdrawn, apathetic attitude, and whose family name suggests a man defined by frankness and a disdain for fussiness: "La commodité de son existence vagabonde le poussait aux mêmes conclusions que Romain, son érotisme

---

18   Ibid., 65.
19   Ibid., 67.
20   Ibid., 96.

intellectuel: partager les joies amoureuses, écarter les troubles sentimentaux."
/ The convenience of his vagabond existence led him to the same conclusions
that Romain had reached through his intellectual eroticism: share sexual pleasures but avoid sentimental disorder.[21] If Landor feels at home on the river
it is due to his disdain for fixity and emotional attachments. Though he and
Romain belong to different social classes, the former of working-class roots
and subject to the life of a vagabond, the latter guided by a certain middle-
class intellectual curiosity, each understands the other in part because of a
complicit refusal of sentimentality. This stoical vein which runs through their
friendship creates an intimacy between them, the likes of which they explicitly
refuse to share with women.

Landor, even more so than Romain, defines himself by his hypermasculine
traits with which he justifies his own brand of sadism:

> Que demande le peuple? interrogeait-il avec conviction, en distribuant
> des coups de fouet à ses porteurs. Et il avait une façon de dire 'le peuple'
> qui signifiait: tout ce qu'on peut cingler de canaille avec des bras comme
> les miens. Pour cette puissance toute physique, mais rayonnante, Landor
> l'aimait.[22]

> "What more could the people ask for?" he would demand with conviction
> while distributing lashes to his porters. And he had a way of saying 'the
> people' which meant: everything in sight that was savage and with arms
> like mine. It was for this totally physical but radiant power that Landor
> loved him.

As if foreshadowing the characters later found in Jean Genet's *Querelle de
Brest* (1953), Landor's persona presents lower-class machismo and inspires
male homoeroticism. Within this passage, there are two forms of erotic *jouissance*, that of Landor as torturer and that of Romain as spectator. Just as the
whip acts as an extension of Landor's phallic power, Landor himself becomes
an extension of Romain's erotic desires vis-à-vis African men. By brutalizing
African men, they share an affirmation of their possession of hegemonic
masculinity.[23] And though the genital restraint of colonial masculinity does

---

21   Ibid., 71.
22   Ibid., p. 47.
23   For more on hegemonic masculinity, see John Beynon, *Masculinities and Culture*
      (Philadelphia: Open University Press, 2001). See also Raewyn Connell, *Masculinities*

not permit heterosexual romantic desire, it does, in this case allow for a homoerotic, romantic friendship.

Despite their valuing of hyper-masculinity, and despite their mutual rejection of heterosexual romantic desire, there is a tenderness to the relationship
between Romain and Landor. This becomes most apparent during a scene in
which Landor has taken the gravely-ill Romain on board his steamer:

> Landor le contemplait. Il avait une sympathie fraternelle et un peu at-
> tendrie pour ce jeune homme de taille petite, mais si vigoureux et ner-
> veux que son adresse pouvait rivaliser avec sa force brutale à lui, Landor.
> Maintenant il est très faible et Landor peut le porter dans ses bras, comme
> un enfant.[24]

> Landor gazed at him. He held for this young man an affection that was
> both fraternal and somewhat tender. Romain was small but yet so vigor-
> ous and so nervous that his agility might even rival Landor's brute force.
> Right now, he's very weak and Landor can carry him in his arms like a
> child.

Despite the narrative's careful description of Landor's brotherly love for
Romain, there are also signs of a romantic attachment. Landor, thoroughly
aware and admiring of his own hypermasculinity, surveys his friend's small
body, which, though weak with fever, still evokes a masculine strength.
Additionally, Landor's vision of an ailing Romain allows the former to take
the sick and thus inactive man into his arms. The tenderness of his gaze upon
Romain's body and vision of Romain as an infant blurs the line between his
romantic and filial ties to the latter and echoes the Baudelairian concept of
the lover as both child and sibling.[25] Further, as an infant, or one who does not
speak, Romain remains passive while the scene of homoerotic desire unfolds,
but retains his status as a hypermasculine heterosexual.

It is in part this hypermasculinity of both Romain and Landor that allows
for the implicit homoerotic desire between the two friends. Their homoerotic
bonding expresses itself most forcefully when it takes place at the expense
of Africans, who are often the butt of Landor's jokes and the objects of his

---

(Cambridge: Polity Press, 1995) and Máirtín Mac an Ghaill, *The Making of Men:
Masculinities, Sexualities and Schooling* (Buckingham: Open University Press, 1994).

24   Herman Grégoire, *Makako, singe d'Afrique* (Paris: La Renaissance du Livre, 1921), 130.

25   Charles Baudelaire, "L'Invitation au voyage" in *Fleurs du mal* (Paris: Librairie Générale
Française, 1972, 1857), 73–75.

physical violence. For the two, both racist humor and violence constitute aspects of being between men and below the equator. Romain and Landor occupy a zone that is geographic, racialized, and gendered, and in which actions, normally unthinkable in the metropolis occur unquestioned. It is a space that they share based on their espousal of a hegemonic colonial masculinity which feeds upon the subordination of African men.

Being below the equator also echoes the centuries-old discourse which located sexual licentiousness in Africa. While this myth implies an invitation to participate in acts forbidden in Europe, Romain and Landor never engage in direct sexual contact with each other. Of course, this would be impossible in such a novel – whose author was at the time celebrated for his service to the cause of colonial literature.[26] The novel's supposedly authentic presentation of colonial man also bars displaying the reality of European homosexuality in colonial spaces even though homoerotic relationships were fairly common in the colonies as is noted by Christopher Lane (1995); Anne-Laura Stoler (1995) and Joseph Boone (1989, 1995). However, in Grégoire's text, despite the attraction that each colonial man feels to the other's displays of masculinity, their romantic friendship precludes any sexual relationship between the two, for this brotherhood allows sexual intercourse only where there is physical desire but no love. So, while Romain has no misgivings about bedding his African concubine, the sentimentality of his feelings for Hélène conflict with the principles of colonial masculinity. Landor holds no reservations about engaging in emotionless sex with women, all the while privileging, as does Plato's Phaedrus, a chaste, same-sex love between friends who are honest and loyal.[27] Like those of Zeno's Stoics their erotic desires are ambivalent, but display a valuing of "love that involved more than desire."[28] As such, Landor and Romain embrace a chaste homoeroticism, somewhere between *eros*, or physical desire, and *philia*, or romantic love.

Being *entre hommes* also signals the forms of sharing which define their relationship. They share women, not just Hélène, but also Romain's wife, Mwesa

---

26   Joseph-Marie Jadot, "La Littérature coloniale de Belgique, Conférence faite, le mai 1922, aux Mardis des Lettres Belges," *La Revue Sincère*, No. 2 (Nov. 15, 1922), 78, accessed May 26, 2016, http://gallica.bnf.fr/ark:/12148/bpt6k5741863c.image.hl.r=Grégoire.f14 langEN.pagination.

27   Graeme Nicholson, *Plato's Phaedrus: The Philosophy of Love* (West Lafayette, IN: Purdue University Press, 1999), 212.

28   Louis Crompton. *Homosexuality and Civilization.* (Cambridge: Harvard University Press, 2003), 67, accessed September 26, 2017, https://books.google.com/books?id=TfBYd9xVa XcC&lpg=PA66&dq=homosexuality%20stoics&pg=PA67#v=onepage&q=homosexuali ty%20stoics&f=false.

Moke, who Landor suggests should become his once Romain has taken Hélène from her husband, Delvèze. Secondly, though Romain and Landor also share a mutual admiration in their disdain for romantic love, they experience an erotic, physical melding while gazing at and falling for Hélène, during an evening spent on Landor's boat:

> [...] rien n'empêchait qu'Hélène fût là, sous leurs yeux, et que la vision de sa robe légère ne libérât leur cœur d'une étreinte volontaire: pour Landor, celle du bon sens; pour Romain, celle de son intelligence.[29]

> Nothing was stopping Hélène from being there, under their gaze, and nothing was stopping the sight of her summer dress from freeing their hearts from a voluntary grip: for Landor one of common sense; for Romain, one of intelligence.

Though the phrase alludes to two pairs of eyes gazing at Hélène, it also evokes an image in which Romain and Landor share eyes, vision, heart and erotic desire. And though they share these things in their admiration of Hélène's beauty, it is the corporal and spiritual proximity to each other that provides at least an aspect of the erotic tension of the passage. The two friends sublimate their homoerotic attraction for each other and express this attraction through Hélène but without actually losing the bond formed by male friendship and homoeroticism. In fact, the narration implies a preference for the homoerotic tension of the passage over the folly of heterosexual desire as the latter demands that one forfeit both intelligence and common sense.

When, later in the narrative, Romain suspects an affair between Landor and Hélène, their friendship loses none of its tenderness:

> – Mon cher Landor, dites-moi la vérité. Que s'est-il passé entre Hélène et vous?
> Ayant posé sa question, Clausel regardait au large. Les deux amis s'étaient adossés au bastingage du *Communard*. Dans le soir très doux, il éprouvait de la gêne à discuter. La rêverie leur paraissait préférable. Pour Romain surtout qui prévoyait un déchirement.[30]

> – My dear Landor, tell me the truth. What happened between you and Hélène?

29   Herman Grégoire, *Makako, singe d'Afrique* (Paris: La Renaissance du Livre, 1921), 72.
30   Ibid., 151.

Having asked the question Clausel gazed off into the distance. The two friends leaned against the railing of the *Communard*. Romain felt uncomfortable about arguing on such a beautiful evening. Dreaming seemed preferable to them. Especially for Romain, who perceived a looming separation.

The moment of silence which follows Romain's question reminds us again of the knowledge of the homoerotic implications of sharing a woman and the discomfort this acknowledgement causes. The difficulty they have speaking about Landor's relationship with Hélène and their inability to look each other in the eyes does not, however, take away from the romantic atmosphere of the evening. Once again they are on Landor's boat, which has served as their *stoa*, a safe, protected sphere. But once again Hélène comes between them. However, the role of desire in this scene differs from that of the former scene, in which Hélène is physically present. Her physical absence implies the privileging of male romantic friendship over heterosexual carnal desire and lust. Romain does not fear a separation in the form of an unconsummated tryst with Hélène, but rather a breakup with Landor.

In contrast, Romain's feelings for Hélène change radically after he discovers that Landor and Hélène have been lovers. He chooses his friendship with the former over a love affair with the latter: "Vous m'excuserez, ma chère, lui avait-il confié en partant, mais je ne peux consentir à créer une telle gêne entre mon ami et moi." / You will excuse me, darling, he said to her as he was leaving, but I cannot allow the creation of such bad feelings between me and my friend.[31] Romain leaves Hélène because he discovers she has been unfaithful to him, but he also leaves her because she threatens his relationship with Landor. She represents the "gêne," the interloper, which Romain cannot allow to come between them. In effect, Romain leaves his *amie*, or mistress for his *ami*, the latter a term which, in the context of the narrative, implies something between friend and lover.

The homoerotic relationship which connects Romain and Landor, and which first uses Hélène as a conduit before discarding her as an obstacle, remains nonetheless off limits to the two other men with whom Romain and Landor share her: her husband Delvèze, and her houseboy Fataki. Even though ostensibly, the four men are connected by homoerotic bonding, the narrative excludes Delvèze and Fataki from any possible implied sharing of a lover with the other principal male characters by placing them at the bottom of a racial and masculine hierarchy.

---

31   Ibid., 155.

Not a man of action like Romain, Delvèze might be called a "négrophile en chambre" /a salon negrophile, who prefers to keep his distance from his colonized subjects.[32] Despite his position as the administrator of the territory and as Romain's supervisor, he fears the very people he is meant to govern, all the while failing to challenge the status quo of colonial domination. He seems also to fear his own sexuality, and sexuality in general, declaring to Romain that Remy de Gourmont's *Physique de l'amour* "était un traité de cochonner-ies antinaturelles et son auteur [...] un dégoûtant salaud." / was a treatise full of unnatural filth and its author a disgusting bastard.[33] The work in question, a study of natural science, also ventures into the study of human sexual-ity. In comparing human sexuality with that of the animal world, Gourmont proposed an abolition of notions of the un-natural and of debauchery.[34] Delvèze's preference to intellectualize the natural physical world illustrated by Gourmont reveals his fears and inadequacies vis-à-vis sexuality, and casts him as un-masculine. This fear carries over into interactions with his wife: "l'administrateur [Delvèze] n'éprouvait aucun plaisir à piloter sa femme. Il ne jouissait de sa présence que lorsque Romain, entre eux, animait la conversation." / The administrator took no pleasure in controlling his wife. He only enjoyed her presence when Romain, occupying a place between them, made the con-versation livelier.[35] The sexualized nature of the passage suggests Delvèze's fear of sexuality in general not only extends to a dread of female sexuality but also implies a hypo-masculine nature which finds no joy in domination and control. His only *jouissance* takes place with the presence of Romain. The effects of placing Romain between himself and his wife signal Delvèze's am-bivalent sexuality, for it remains unclear whether his joy comes from the pro-tection Romain offers him from his own wife, from the voyeuristic pleasure he feels in seeing another man dominate her or perhaps even from his physical proximity to Romain. Delvèze's failure to command his wife, like his failure to command the Africans who are nominally under his authority, points again to his lack of colonial masculinity. Like the collection of taxes in the region, a task which, uncompleted by Delvèze falls to Romain, the job of commanding Hélène also falls to the latter. In fact, Delvèze often leaves Hélène in the hands of both Romain and Landor, believing that she is frigid, and thus secure in her

---

32   Maurice Delafosse, *Broussard ou les états d'âme d'un colonial suivi de ses propos et ses opin-ions* (Paris: Comité de L'Afrique Française, 1923), 53.

33   Herman Grégoire, *Makako, singe d'Afrique* (Paris: La Renaissance du Livre, 1921), 112.

34   Remy de Gourmont, *Physique de l'amour : essai sur l'instinct sexuel.* (Paris: Société du Mercure de France, 1903).

35   Herman Grégoire, *Makako, singe d'Afrique* (Paris: La Renaissance du Livre, 1921), 68.

constancy. And although he does visit Romain's home one night to "réclamer sa femme" / reclaim his wife,[36] he fails to display the sexual agency and masculinity with which a "real" colonial man would mark his property.

Delvèze's deficiency in masculinity renders him unfit for the homosocial and homoerotic community formed by his fellow Europeans Landor and Romain. Despite his race and his status as a colonial administrator he cannot claim colonial masculinity. The unmanly picture painted of Delvèze notwithstanding, we can assume some sexual activity between him and Hélène – at least in the consummation of their marriage. And though Romain's attitude towards Delvèze suggests a challenge of the sexual prowess of the latter, Romain himself never actually beds Hélène. Though he has ample opportunity to make her his mistress, both in Paris and in the Belgian Congo, and though the two share a few kisses, his sexual activity relies almost purely on fantasy and points either to a failure in sexual agency or to the triumph of sexual restraint. He writes her letters, but never sends them. He fantasizes of raping her but stifles his violent desires. In fact, of the four men in the narrative romantically involved with Hélène, Romain is the only one who we can be sure never beds her. This reality challenges his role as a man of action but also provides an example of colonial masculinity as, if not misogyny, then at least a rejection of romantic heterosexuality. Romain can thus play the hero of this narrative because he has resisted desire, and exhibited a masculine will as solid as his physicality. In contrast, if Delvèze shows no interest in his wife's sexuality, he does so out of fear, not because of an authentic colonialist masculinity.

In truth, Landor and Fataki exercise the greatest sexual agency vis-à-vis Hélène, and actually do what Romain can only imagine. The exclusion of Fataki from a homoerotic complicity is made possible, not by a lack of masculinity in the African but by the perceived inferiority of his race. The text introduces Fataki as "le plus beau nègre de la tribu" / The most handsome Negro of his tribe[37] and as a master hunter. The narrative also describes the brute force he uses to subdue Hélène. This masculinist discrimination is thus tightly bound to race, and indicative of the views held of Africans by Romain. For example, after being brought to trial for shooting three African men during an excursion, Romain defends himself by denouncing the Africans who testified against him:

> Je regrette infiniment, croyez-le, que mon éducation coloniale n'ait rien retenu des excellents principes qui justifient votre estime du nègre et

---

36   Ibid., 147.
37   Ibid., 9.

qu'un séjour de trois ans dans la brousse m'ait enseigné à garder ma dignité de telles compromissions.[38]

I am infinitely sorry, please believe me, that my colonial education has retained none of those excellent principals that justify your esteem of the Negro, and that three years in the bush have taught me to keep my dignity free of such compromises.

True to his display of colonial hegemonic masculinity, Romain's ironic self-defense emphasizes his practical experience over the defective intellects of his accusers, who themselves, have given up their self-respect by valuing the lives of Africans. By Romain's standards, Hélène's love affair with Fataki would equal the ultimate self-debasement, not only for her, but also for himself, as such an affair would symbolically put him within the proximity of the sexuality of an African.

This disdain for African men emerges later in the narrative, when Romain puts down a native revolt, a plot device which Pierre-Philippe Fraiture observes as paralleling challenges to black African masculinity and sexuality.[39] After killing its leader, a "nègre arabisé," / an Arabicized Negro,[40] who represents the trope of the "bad Negro" in Belgian colonialist narrative[41] he tells the Africans who surround him, now subdued and ready to follow his orders: "Celui-ci est la moitié d'un homme; je suis un homme; je suis un homme tout entier!" / This one here is only half a man. I *am* a man. I am one hundred percent man![42] In order to realize his masculinity as a colonizer, Romain must fully evacuate that of any African who seeks a status similar to his. The description of the rebel leader as "arabisé" points to Romain's belief that black Africans blindly welcome contamination by revolutionary currents. He opposes this Arab influence with a European ideology that seeks to keep African men subservient. But in his repetition of "je suis un homme" lies a speech act whose pleasurable conjuring of virility also endeavors to make African masculinity disappear.

---

38   Ibid., 165.

39   Pierre-Philippe Fraiture. "De l'influence du Goncourt sur le corpus colonial: le cas de *Batouala*," in *Prix Goncourt*, 1903–2003: essais critiques, ed. Katherine Ashley (Bern: Peter Lang, 2003), 99.

40   Herman Grégoire, *Makako, singe d'Afrique* (Paris: La Renaissance du Livre, 1921), 234.

41   Pierre Halen, "Les Fictions amoureuse et l'idéologie coloniale au Congo belge," in *L'Exotisme* eds Alain Buisine and Norbert Dodille (Saint-Denis, Île de la Réunion: Cahiers C.R.L.H, 1988), 247.

42   Herman Grégoire, *Makako, singe d'Afrique* (Paris: La Renaissance du Livre, 1921), 234.

Similarly, even though Fataki appears in scenes in which Hélène becomes an object of admiration for both Landor and Romain, and though Fataki's admiration for Hélène is clear the first time he sees her, he remains essentially invisible when in the presence of the two Europeans:

> Fataki entra portant une soupière fumante [...] Mais, à la vue de *la madame*, – la première blanche qu'il voit, – Fataki se trouble. Le vase tremble dans ses mains, Hélène, amusée, un peu flattée aussi, déclare qu'elle entend battre son cœur. Et comme, à cette expression naïve, Romain a eu un regard narquois, elle rougit et se tait.[43]

> Fataki entered carrying a steaming-hot soup tureen [...] But in seeing the lady – the first white woman he has ever seen – Fataki becomes agitated. The liquid trembles in his hand; Hélène amused, as well as a bit flattered, declares she can hear his heart beating. And when, in reaction to this naïve chatter, Romain looked at her snidely, she blushed and fell silent.

Romain's disgust is not directed toward Fataki, who, despite being the subject of Hélène's teasing, remains invisible to the European man. Rather, he regards the Frenchwoman disdainfully as if she had reacted in a vulgar manner to something whose presence would otherwise not be noted. For aside from being forced by Hélène's behavior to notice Fataki's attraction to her, Romain barely acknowledges the houseboy's existence. In fact, even in other portions of the narrative in which they are both present – when Romain is still smitten with Hélène and Fataki has not yet become her lover – there are no exchanges between the two characters. The novel compartmentalizes Hélène's various affairs, so that Fataki's rape of and subsequent affair with her only take place once Landor has rejected her and Romain has left M'Toa to work at another outpost. Whereas Landor has sex with Hélène while Romain simply contemplates doing the same, these events take place in the first half of the novel, whereas Fataki's conquest of Hélène happens in the latter part of the narrative. And though Fataki rapes her while taking her to see, and ostensibly to make love to Romain, they never reach their destination and Hélène does not see her European admirer again until a few years later, when he has lost all desire for her.

This narrative allows for homoerotic entanglements which uphold the banner of colonial masculinity, but avoids those which undermine the prestige of the novel's hero and which taint racialized colonial ideologies. Herman

43   Ibid., 34.

Grégoire accomplishes this through the disappearance of some of *Makako*'s male characters. For example, Landor disappears from the narrative after confessing his affair with Hélène to Romain. And though Romain's fear of a fissure between them foreshadows Landor's removal from the story, the latter's absence also allays the discomfort of having shared Hélène as well as any distress resulting from implications of homoeroticism.

Delvèze too disappears. Even though we know that he is still present, as he is mentioned in the description of a party given by Hélène and referred to in the last pages of the text, we never see him again. Rather, we note that Hélène has taken on his role as master of the house. For when Romain enters the "salon de Mme. Delvèze" he sees that "elle préside" / she is presiding.[44] Hélène, acquiring the gravitas suited to her station as an administrator's wife, replaces the ineffective masculinity of her husband.

As for Fataki, he disappears through death, what the narrative calls an act in which "l'on reconnaît le doigt de Dieu" / One could see the hand of God.[45] Having been seen slapping his European mistress and pressing himself against her, Fataki is shot by Isidore LeFranc, a friend of Hélène's. Killing Fataki accomplishes what Abdul JanMohamed, in referring to colonial or "kidnapped romance" calls the justification of "the social function of the dominant class [...] to idealize its acts of protection and responsibility" by ridding itself of the threatening Other.[46] JanMohamed attempts to read the function of colonialist fiction written by authors hailing from colonizing as well as colonized societies in relation to what he calls the "dominant" and "hegemonic phases of colonialism". For JanMohamed, whereas the "dominant phase of colonialism" is that "which spans the period from the earliest European conquest to the moment at which a colony is granted 'independence'"[47] the "hegemonic phase (or neocolonialism)" is that in which "the natives accept a version of the colonizers' entire system of values, attitude, morality, institutions, and, more important, mode of production."[48] The production of colonialist fiction during the dominant phase reflects the production of goods through the exploitation of the colony and its peoples:

---

44   Ibid., 240, 241.
45   Ibid., 121.
46   Abdul R JanMohamed, "The Economy of Manichean Allegory: The Function of Racial Difference in Colonialist Literature," *Critical Inquiry* 12. 1 (Autumn 1985): 59–87. See also Northrop Frye, *The Secular Scripture: A Study of the Structure of Romance*, Charles Eliot Norton Lectures, 1974–1975 (Cambridge, Harvard University Press, 1976), 57.
47   Ibid., 61.
48   Ibid., 62.

Just as imperialists 'administer' the resources of the conquered country, so colonialist discourse 'commodifies' the native subject into a ste-
reotyped object and uses him as a 'resource' for colonialist fiction. The
European writer commodifies the native by negating his individuality, his
subjectivity, so that he is now perceived as a generic being that can be
exchanged for any other native (they all look alike, act alike and so on).[49]

JanMohamed posits that the kidnapped romance "is not only suited to but is an
integral and necessary part of the dominant phase of colonialism".[50] Reading
the account of Fataki's death through the theories of JanMohamed we can conclude that it is not by chance that Hélène's champion is named Isidor LeFranc,
for this man, whose Greek first name signifies "a gift from god" and who, like
a *deus ex machina* arrives near the end of the narrative, represents the totality of Franco-European masculinity in its possession of *translatio imperii* and
its domination of colonial spaces. He engages in a "chivalric fallacy" in which
Hélène symbolizes "the intact national body, which must be shielded from
penetration by dark alien forces."[51] He saves the day by defending French womanhood and, by extension, Franco-European masculinity, from the African
male. And although LeFranc murders Fataki in the Belgian Congo, the African's
death ensures the protection of Belgium itself.[52] Additionally, relating Fataki's
death to an act of god forwards a world view in which French European colonizers maintain exclusive domain over both might and right. Killing the houseboy crystallizes the principal message of *Makako*, a novel which espouses the
superior masculinity of the European male.

Only after Fataki dies does the narrative allow Romain – freed from prison, and recalled to Europe – to come face to face with Hélène once again. By
killing Fataki, the narrative creates an erotic buffer zone, a space for Romain
to exist without exposing him, or the reader, to a disturbing and competing
African masculine sexuality. The strategy of the narrative makes contact between Romain and Fataki impossible because the African's sexual agency
threatens that of the Frenchman. This protection is necessary not only because
Fataki has done what Romain has fantasized but failed to do, in taking Hélène
by force and then becoming her lover, but also because Fataki's sexuality

---

49   Ibid., 64.
50   Ibid., 72.
51   Susan Fraiman, "Geometries of Race and Gender: Eve Sedgwick, Spike Lee, Charlayne
     Hunter-Gault," *Feminist Studies*, 20. 1 (Spring, 1994): 71.
52   On rape and territoriality see Tanya Horeck, *Public Rape: Representing Violation in Fiction
     and Film* (New York: Routledge, 2004), 47–50; 74–76.

creates a homoerotic panic in Romain, as the houseboy's rape and seduction of the European female suggests a sexual violence which might also target the European male.

Fataki's disappearance from the narrative also indicates another textual strategy which seeks to replace his sexual agency (literally destroyed) with that of Romain, and which intimates Romain's mimetic desire vis-à-vis black men. A passage early in the text in which Romain is gravely ill also exposes his fantasized relationship with Africa and African men: "il est bien le chef du pays; c'est dans ces fonctions qu'il veut mourir; c'est comme un sultan nègre qu'il veut être inhumé." / He is very much the chief of this land; it is in performing these functions that he wishes to die; it is as a Negro sultan that he wishes to be buried.[53] Romain does not envision himself as a sultan who rules Negros but rather as a Negro sultan, who in his imagination represents the zenith of masculine authority. Despite his racist attitudes towards blacks, and despite his continual displays of a European hegemonic masculinity, the thoughts evoked on what he considers his death bed naturally turn to what he desires most, a racial transformation which is not literal but psychological, and which will – in his mind – make him an ideal man. The homoerotic tension evoked in Romain's fantasy of racial transformation belies his espousal of white superiority and illustrates his desire for communion with black men. Jonathan Rutherford notes a similar homoerotic tension in British imperial adventure stories and describes Englishmen who "donned a disguise to pass themselves off as a native."[54] When this Belgian text presents such a fantasy as the ramblings of an ailing colonial, who, once healed, resumes his display of disdain for African men, the narrative strategy in *Makako* attempts to protect both Romain and an imagined Francophone European male reader from too closely approaching the realities of homosocial colonial society. Channeling desire away from the sensual and into conquest thus seeks to disguise the entanglement of the lust for colonial conquest with homoerotics, not only for black African men but also for any sufficiently masculine force encountered in the colonial project.

---

53   Herman Grégoire, *Makako, singe d'Afrique* (Paris: La Renaissance du Livre, 1921), 123.

54   Jonathan Rutherford, *Forever England: Reflections on Race, Masculinity and Empire* (London: Lawrence & Wishart, 1997), 30.

Nothing but a Thing: The African Male as Fetishist and Fetish in *La Femme et l'Homme nu*

Il était pareil à un fétiche de bois dur, poli par les caresses des croyants.
PAUL MORAND, *Magie noire*.[1]

∵

As a critique of the representation of interracial love in colonial fiction Roger Little's *Blanche et Noir aux années vingt* (1999) offers a comparative reading of Pierre Mille and André Demaison's *La Femme et l'Homme nu*, Lucie Cousturier's *Des Inconnus chez moi* (1920) and Louise Faure-Favier's *Blanche et Noir* (1928) theorizing that in each text the treatment of interracial eroticism was influenced by the gender of the authors. Little credits the female writers with carrying out a "révolution douce" / soft revolution,[2] particularly in their non-exploitive development of African male characters, and notes a tendency in *La Femme et l'Homme nu* to treat Tiékoro, the African protagonist as more of an anthropological specimen than as a man. One of the few presentations of Mille and Demaison's novel to venture beyond a cursory glimpse at the narrative, Little's analysis of *La Femme et l'Homme nu* marvels at the ubiquitous display of African sexuality. Comparing Mille and Demaison's work to that of the two female writers, Little notes: "C'est chez Mille et Demaison, non chez Cousturier ni chez Faure-Favier que l'on retrouve le mythe déformant du 'gros phallus braqué sur le cercle magique de l'innocence blanche." / It's in the work of Mille and Demaison and not in those of Cousturier or Faure-Favier that one finds the distorting myth of the 'huge phallus trained on the magical circle of white innocence.[3] Though Mille and Demaison create in the novel's white

---

1 Paul Morand, *Magie noire* (Paris: Bernard Grasset, 1928), p. 172.

2 Roger Little, "Blanche et Noir aux années vingt," in *Regards sur les littératures coloniales, Afrique Francophone: Approfondissements*, ed. Jean-François Durand (Paris: L'Harmattan, 1999), 47.

3 Ibid., 41. See also Pius Ngandu Nkashama, "The Golden Years of the Novel," in *European-language Writing in sub-Saharan Africa* Vol. 1, ed. Albert Gérard (Budapest: UNESCO, 1986), 107.

Russian heroine, Vania, an explicitly sensual persona, the text focuses keenly on the sexuality of the African.

At its most basic narrative level, *La Femme et l'Homme nu* embraces the pleasures of voyeurism firstly because it begins and ends with a nude Tiékoro. He is nude before we meet him, in the title of the novel, and even though, once he leaves his village, he dons clothing in the pages which follow, he is seen running on a European battlefield "sans armes et à moitié nu" / without a weapon and half naked.[4] Also, the narrative culminates with the African returning to his village after leaving Vania in Dakar, Senegal, retreating to a society in which nudity is the norm. Further, as Little notes, Tiékoro's many sexual escapades punctuate different stages of the narrative, from the young women in his village to a prostitute in St. Raphaël, France, to Vania, and finally, to a Mandingo woman in Dakar.[5] Little does not, however, relate Mille and Demaison's insistence on exposing Tiékoro's sexuality to the larger homoerotic implications of the authors' project. His heteronormative astonishment that it is male and not female authors who sexualize an African male character, stops short of examining the source of the irony within his interesting observation of race, gender, and sexuality in colonial fiction. To be sure, one should hesitate to conclude that either Mille or Demaison was homosexual, though Little's analysis seems to imply this without fully exploring such a possibility. Though limited in this respect, Little's reading of the text, based on a gender binary with implied heteronormative expectations, is productive as it invites further investigation of the sexualities underpinning colonial fiction. In a narrative in which one of the central tropes is the fetishistic practices of an African, the authors participate in a form of homoerotic fetishism in which the pleasures of the text are sometimes derived from reducing the African to a "penis symbol."[6]

This interpretation of *La Femme et l'Homme nu* illuminates the function of sexual fetishism in the novel by exposing how it informs the actions of its heroine, Vania, of her lover Tiékoro, and of the French colonial men who oppose their relationship. And though the central problematic of the narrative is the doomed love story of Vania and Tiékoro, this analysis examines how their

---

4 Pierre Mille and André Demaison, *La Femme et l'Homme nu* (Paris: Les Éditions de France, 1924), 114–115.

5 Roger Little, "Blanche et Noir aux années vingt," in *Regards sur les littératures coloniales, Afrique Francophone: Approfondissements*, ed. Jean-François Durand (Paris: L'Harmattan, 1999), 41.

6 Frantz Fanon, *Black Skin, White Masks*, trans. Richard Philcox (New York: Grove Press, 2008), 137.

romance is predicated upon each partner's fetishistic use of the other and considers the role of the novel itself in fetishizing the African.

A fetish, broadly defined as an element of magical or religious practice, has also come to be viewed as "an object or bodily part whose real or fantasized presence is psychologically necessary for sexual gratification and is an object of fixation to the extent that it may interfere with complete sexual expression.[7] We can thus conceive of the fetish as having an alternately religious and sexual function while standing in for a desired object or state of being. The attention paid in this colonial text to fetishism reflects a general interest among Europeans in animism and in both religious and sexual fetishism at the turn of the century and an association of fetishism with perversion. This is evidenced in psychological studies of the era by Jean-Martin Charcot and Valentin Magnan (1882), and by Richard von Krafft-Ebing (1894) and in the anthropological work of Edward Taylor (1873), Andrew Lang (1900), and Lucien Lévy-Bruhl (1922). Alfred Binet's *Études de psychologie expérimentale* (1888) treats both religious and sexual fetishism. This interest in the sexual fetish was not limited to academic circles, but revealed itself in what Emily Apter describes as a "clinical realism" in literature, that is "a genre anchored in the art of describing the morbid symptoms of the body."[8]

Lucien Lévy-Bruhl proposes an abandonment of the notion that "primitive" peoples were incapable of deep thought in order to embrace, "sans idée préconçue [...] l'étude objective de la mentalité primitive" / without any preconceived notions [...] the objective study of primitive mentality[9] and presents a plethora of information on religious practices in West and Central Africa, including those specific to fetishists. In the field of psychology, Jean-Martin Charcot and Valentin Magnan laid the foundation for pre-Freudian theories of sexual fetishism. Though they do not specifically mention the term fetishism in their much consulted "Inversion du sens génital et autres perversions sexuelles," / "Genital Inversion and other Sexual Perversions" their recounting of the sexual excitement related to inanimate objects will later be labeled sexual fetishism. Charcot and Magnan's work would prove critical in defining fetishism as a male illness, and aligning it with homosexuality, so that the psychoanalytical discourse often labeled the fetishist a closeted male homosexual.

---

7   "Fetish," Merriam-Webster, accessed April 4, 2010, http://www.merriam-webster.com/dictionary/fetish.

8   Emily Apter, *Feminizing the Fetish: Psychoanalysis and Narrative Obsession in Turn-of-the-Century France* (Ithaca: Cornell University Press, 1991), xii.

9   Lucien Lévy-Bruhl, *La Mentalité primitive* (Paris: Presses Universitaires de France, 1960), 15.

Alfred Binet, who also laid much of the groundwork for Freud's work on fetishism,[10] viewed sexual fetishism as widespread within human interactions, and as playing a critical role in sexual attraction. Binet compared extreme cases of sexual fetishism cited by Charcot and Magnan, to the religious practices of some non-European societies:

> L'adoration de ces malades pour des objets inertes comme des bonnets de nuit ou des clous de bottines ressemble de tous points à l'adoration du sauvage ou du nègre pour des arêtes de poisons ou pour des cailloux brillants, sauf cette différence fondamentale que, dans le culte des dégénérés, l'adoration religieuse est remplacée par un appétit sexuel.[11]

> The adoration these sick individuals hold for inert objects such as night bonnets or boot studs resembles in all aspects the adoration that savages or that the Negro holds for fish bones or for shimmering stones, with the difference being that in the worship performed by degenerates, religious adoration is replaced by a sexual appetite.

Anne McClintock (1995) notes the importance of Binet's definition of modes of fetishism in the transformation of the way we regard objects of desire:

> With Binet, a critical transition occurred as fetishism became a switchboard term, mediating between race and sexuality, colony and metropolis. Following Freud's adoption of the term as crucial for an analysis of the 'perversions,' one witnesses, at the same time, a disciplinary shift as the discourse on fetishism moved from anthropology and the study of religion – out of the inverted realm of imperial nature, that is – into psychoanalysis and the realm of metropolitan culture.[12]

---

10   See Sigmund Freud, "Fetishism," in *The Standard Edition of the Complete Works of Sigmund Freud*. Vol. 22, trans. James Strachey et al. (London: Hogarth Press and the Institute of Psychoanalysis, 1957), 152–157.

11   Binet, Alfred, *Etudes de psychologie expérimentales*. (Paris: Octave Doin, 1888), 3. Jean-Martin Charcot and Valentin Magnan, "Inversion du sens génital," in *Archives de neurologie : revue des maladies nerveuse et mentales*, Tome 4, n. 10–12 (1882), 296–322, accessed April 4, 2010, http://jubilotheque.upmc.fr/ead.html?id=CN_000032_004.

12   Anne McClintock, *Imperial Leather: Race, Gender, and Sexuality in the Colonial Contest* (New York: Routledge, 1995), 189.

Indeed, although Binet attempts a distinction of religious and sexual fetishists, his initial comparison invites his reader to consider points of contact between several modes of being and desiring. Establishing a correlation between mental illness and sexual degeneracy, he also creates a trinal construction composed of unhealthy Westerners, savages and Negroes. Binet thus intimates that only mental defect within a European would create in him/her an eroticism resembling that of the savage in general and of the African specifically. Finally, Binet suggests that European psychological and erotic deviancy and "African" religion share a framework based on fetishism. Comparing European sexual fetishists to Africans allows Binet to underscore the alien nature of sexual maladies all the while creating a heightened tension by introducing the possibility of an African-like sexual psychology in the metropole.

With a narrative that shifts between Africa and Europe *La Femme et l'Homme nu* follows a path similar to that which McClintock describes. Beyond the geographic trajectories of the story, the novel also oscillates not only between heterosexual and homoerotic desire, but also between fetishist practices both religious and sexual. Instances of junction and overlap and the resultant challenges to strict divisions of colony and metropolis parallel aspects of a European cultural angst of the late nineteenth century.

The European reader of *La Femme et l'Homme nu* experiences a narrative peppered with foreign terms and emphasizing the strangeness of both the African and his fetishistic practices. The reader learns of the *tanna*, meaning totem; *igwar*, the divinity that protects a village; *oungher*, meaning fetish; and *faleg* or man. The text suggests that the sacredness of a "faleg" equals that of the *tanna* and the *igwar* implying the importance of virility for Tiékoro. Later, in his interactions with Vania and his confrontations with European males, Tiékoro transposes his belief system onto European culture and looks to both his divinities and to those of the Europeans for guidance. By way of this deciphering of fetishes he concludes that Vania's statue of the Virgin Mary is her *oungher* or fetish and that the war in which he is fighting opposes the Rooster *tanna* (France) and the Eagle *tanna* (Germany). The question of understanding and possessing *tannas* remains crucial to Tiékoro, who, before going off to fight in WWI, is secure in his virility as a young man living in the forest of Ifane. With his limited knowledge of white men, he learns to both fear and desire their power:

> il y a, de par l'univers, des êtres dont la peau est comme celle d'un homme écorché ; ils ont l'apparence des humains, mais ils sont blancs comme des Génies ; ils ont des *tannas* puissants et ne craignent pas la mort ; on ne les

aperçoit presque jamais et ils commandent partout ... La crainte de les voir se mêla en lui au désir de les approcher.[13]

There are, throughout the universe, beings whose skin is like that of a flayed man; They look human, but they are as white as genies; they have powerful spirit animals and do not fear death; one almost never sees them and yet they rule everywhere ... The fear of seeing them mingled with the desire within him to encounter them.

The folklore of Tiékoro's people transforms white men into something between human and god, invisible entities who, like *djinn*, are made of smoke, and cannot be captured, or subdued. This equation of whites and the dead both disturbs and rouses Tiékoro. Attracted to their omnipotence he hopes in getting closer to them, to increase his own power and masculinity. This fetishizing of the European by an African counters the stereotypical vision of the colonizer desiring to possess and subdue the African. By changing the direction of the desiring gaze, *La Femme et l'Homme nu* asks us to consider the complex forms of desire and domination which colonization implies.

It is this desire to be closer to the European male and the power he possesses which first leads Tiékoro to fight alongside French forces in the first world war. Having risked his life on European battlefields, he feels he has gained some of this power, especially because his acts of bravery are so lauded by white men. But more than his role as a soldier fighting for France, it is his relationship with Vania, whom he perceives as a gift from white men, that allows him the possibility of equaling their supremacy:

Il crut même certain que les *tannas* des Hommes-aux-oreilles-rouges lui étaient favorables dès qu'ils lui accordaient la récompense d'une de leurs filles choisies. Il ne douta pas d'être en possession d'un moyen rapide et supérieur de parvenir à capter avec l'aide de cette femme les secrets des Puissances qui étaient encore pour lui un mystère.[14]

He was even sure that the spirit animals of the Men-with-the-red-ears approved of him as soon as they had granted him the reward of one of their most prized girls. He was confident that he had gained a rapid and

---

13   Pierre Mille and André Demaison, *La Femme et l'Homme nu* (Paris: Les Éditions de France, 1924), 55–56.

14   Ibid., 155.

superior method of attaining, with the aid of this woman, the secrets of
the Powers which remained a mystery to him.

Tiékoro can only conceive of Vania as a form of exogamic currency and in relation to the men who, in his view, possess her. Though it is Vania who initi-
ates a sexual relationship, Tiékoro sees her as lacking the agency with which
she might give or withhold her sexuality. Rather, this sexuality is a gift from
white men refashioned by Tiékoro into a fetish. Vania exists only as a talisman,
a helper opening the gates to white men's power. Her value as an object of exchange is purely reflective of the regard white men must have for him. In their
coitus he imagines himself as completing the equivalent of a Promethean trial,
stealing power from white men. He is not, then, motivated by sexualized and
racialized revenge.[15] Nor is he captivated by a desire to become white.[16] Rather
he is lured to power, be it sexualized or otherwise. He does not judge Vania as
superior to African women. Rather, her significance lies in her role as fetish,
in her function as a conduit; a means to an end. And although Tiékoro makes
love to her entire physical body, this experience is an instance of synecdochic
fetishism in which the female body represents a relatively insignificant part
of the totality with which he seeks spiritual and sexual communion. Despite
Vania's gender, for Tiékoro she is representative of white masculine power.
Through her he experiences a syncretism of religious and sexual fetishism
which open up new possibilities for communion with white men.

However, inherent in this presumed communion is the African's misunderstanding of Vania's position vis-à-vis the French men whom he believes are
her keepers. Because Tiékoro cannot distinguish Russians from the French he
fails to grasp the fact that Vania, also a foreigner in France, belongs neither to
French men nor to French culture. Nonetheless, the possibility of communing
with white men allows Tiékoro to feel more confident in his masculinity. This
confidence further develops when Vania has him fitted for a khaki uniform
that transforms him into something resembling the African American officers
stationed in France:

> Il ne douta plus d'avoir franchi en hâte plusieurs des barrières qui sépa-
> raient encore des hommes porteurs des Pouvoirs. L'aisance de son corps
> dans un uniforme qui ne gênait plus ses mouvements élargit sa superbe.

---

15   See Frantz Fanon, *Black Skin, White Masks*, trans. Richard Philcox (New York: Grove Press,
      2008), 51.
16   Ibid., 45.

Il pouvait maintenant regarder quiconque dans les yeux, jouissant des prérogatives des gens élevés.[17]

He was now sure he had swiftly crossed several barriers which had separated him from those holders of Power. The ease of his body in a uniform which no longer constricted his movements increased his haughtiness. He could now look anyone in the eyes, enjoying the prerogatives of the upper class.

In *Paris Noir* Tyler Stovall notes that positive stereotypes of African American soldiers in wartime France distinguished them from the black African, who, while known for his bravery on the battlefield, remained nonetheless a savage in the thoughts of many of the French.[18] It is no accident then that Tiékoro's new khaki suit becomes a fetish which transforms him from a colonized subject into a non-colonized, African American soldier and bestows upon him a concomitant societal capital. In "becoming" African American and imitating these "whites with black skin"[19] he retains his blackness but also almost attains whiteness, which is understood by him not as skin color but as the possession of power. Not only does Tiékoro begin to see himself as an equal to the white officers around him, he also begins to feel superior to them. While previously he trembled under the fear of and desire to encounter white men, having the full knowledge of the invisibility which their magic allowed them, he now feels confident that he can not only see them, he can also return their gaze. But beyond employing the uniform-fetish as a transformative tool for the purposes of personal satisfaction, Tiékoro, in an expression of the "original erotic component, the desire for recognition"[20] uses his new clothes to attract the gaze of the white soldiers to whom he once felt inferior. In doing so he transforms himself into a fetish in the form of an African dandy.

---

17   Pierre Mille and André Demaison, *La Femme et l'Homme nu* (Paris: Les Éditions de France, 1924), 160–161.

18   Tyler Stovall, *Paris Noir: African American in the City of Light* (Boston: Houghton Mifflin, 1996), 16–20.

19   Ch. Didier Gondola, "The Search for Elegance among Congolese Youth," *African Studies Review*, 42.1 (April 1999): 27.

20   Jessica Benjamin, "Master and Slave: The Fantasy of Erotic Domination," in *Powers of Desire: The Politics of Sexuality*, eds Ann Snitow, Christine Stansell and Sharon Thompson (New York: Monthly Press Review, 1983), 281.

Tiékoro's experience of his new clothes, resembles an "inapprehensible be-ing-for-others in the form of *possession*."[21] He is "possessed by the Other"[22] and henceforth can only exist in conjunction with the gaze of the white men he tries to impress. His own "hungry gaze"[23] seeks out these white men in order to impress himself upon them as an object of admiration. Clothed in what amounts to a costume, he invites the desire of European men by becoming an object which seeks power in the intimacy it achieves with those who acknowl-edge it.[24] But he not only desires to be seen, he also seeks to return the white men's gaze. This returned gaze is "a gesture that presupposes a sense of self," "an action that performs and is a process of subjectification that incorporates, rather than denies desire."[25]

In this vision of himself face to face with the white men whose commerce he has so long desired, Tiékoro keeps Vania by his side. However, he sets his sights not on her, but on the white men to whom she belongs. As his fetish, she has served her purpose in protecting him and allowing him access to these men. But his primary goal is both the fulfillment of this desire and the creation of a new desire in his white counterparts. This can truly be read as a case of male homoerotic desire, that is, the desire of one man to attract another.

If Vania has unknowingly become Tiékoro's religious and sexual fetish, she is nonetheless explicit in her appropriation of Tiékoro as an erotic fetish. Their encounters allow the narrator and the reader a voyeuristic exploration of the taboos of interracial sex. Though Vania's initial attraction springs from her role as a *marraine de guerre*, a friend to an ailing soldier, she soon begins to objec-tify the African: "Tiékoro l'a d'abord amusée comme un jouet, comme des serfs [sic], géant ou nain, que ses aïeux nourrissaient dans leurs vastes maisons." / Initially, Tiékoro amused her as if he were a toy, as if he were one of those serfs [sic], either giant or miniature, that her ancestors kept as pets in their vast mansions.[26] Though it would be difficult to draw any concrete conclusions in noting the use of *serf* here when surely the authors meant for its homo-phone *cerf* or "deer" to appear, either term would establish Vania's initial view

21   Jean-Paul Sartre, *Being and Nothingness: An Essay on Phenomenological Ontology*, trans. Hazel E. Barnes (New York: Citadel Press, 1966), 364, original emphasis.
22   Ibid. 364.
23   Miles Ogborn, "Locating the Macaroni: Luxury, Sexuality, and Vision in Vauxhall Gardens," *Textual Practice* 11.3 (1997): 453.
24   Achille Mbembe, *On the Postcolony* (Los Angeles: University of California Press, 2001), 111.
25   Monica L. Miller, *Slaves to Fashion: Black Dandyism and the Styling of Black Diasporic Identity* (Durham: Duke University Press, 2009), 69.
26   Pierre Mille and André Demaison, *La Femme et l'Homme nu* (Paris: Les Éditions de France, 1924), 117.

of Tiékoro as having a status beneath her own.[27] However, she goes further than that, animalizing him, all the while fantasizing that by creating a relationship of dependence between them, she could easily tame him. Although Vania possesses great wealth, relative to the poverty of her new African friend, in her fantasies, Tiékoro as a fetish transports her to an even greater moment of wealth and prestige epitomized in her family's past.

Vania's admiration of Tiékoro further develops when during her attempt to seduce him, the African proposes to kill the Soviets who have taken over her country. Her reaction to this offer of masculine domination reveals Vania's masochistic desires: "Il parut si grand à Vania qu'elle eut peur de lui – peur et désir. Elle l'enlaça par la taille. Ces grands muscles étaient capables de briser les Soviets ... et elle aussi sans doute." / He seemed so tall to Vania that she became afraid of him – afraid and desirous. She put her arms around his waist. Those large muscles were capable of breaking those Soviets, and, without a doubt, of breaking her as well.[28] Vania's fetishistic relation to the black body before her lies somewhere between negrophilia and negrophobia. As with Frantz Fanon's problematic conviction that "a negrophobic woman is in reality merely a presumed sexual partner,"[29] Vania's conception of Tiékoro is not as a real person, but as an archetypal African man whose functions are uniquely based in sex and violence.

Erotic violence frames their lovemaking as Vania manages to seduce Tiékoro by inciting him to attack her. After putting a metal collar around her neck, she picks up the horsewhip she once used for riding in Russia:

> D'un bond elle sauta sur la cravache, et avant que Tiékoro pût prévenir le geste, elle le frappa deux fois en aller-et-retour ... Le Noir saisit le premier objet qui lui vint sous la main, et le lança à toute volée à la tête de Vania.[30]

> Leaping suddenly, she pounced on the riding crop and before Tiékoro could anticipate her intentions, she slapped him back and forth across

---

27   This seems to be one of several editorial errors. In another instance, the blond Vania is described as "rousse" or 'read-headed" instead of "russe" or "Russian".

28   Pierre Mille and André Demaison, *La Femme et l'Homme nu* (Paris: Les Éditions de France, 1924), 139–141.

29   Frantz Fanon, *Black Skin, white Masks*, trans. Richard Philcox (New York: Grove Press, 2008), 135.

30   Pierre Mille and André Demaison, *La Femme et l'Homme nu* (Paris: Les Éditions de France, 1924), 143.

the face ... The black man seized the first thing at hand and hurled it at
Vania's head.

Vania's use of both the whip and collar suggest a desire to both dominate and
be dominated. After Tiékoro breaks a statue of the Virgin Mary in a fit of rage –
arguably a metaphor for the breakdown of the Russian's relative sexual "purity"
in the arms of the African – he believes he is condemned for having destroyed
Vania's personal fetish. Seeing his distress,

> Vania se rapprocha, et, timidement, lui posa les mains sur les épaules.
> Comme il ne réagissait pas, elle le poussa doucement pour qu'il s'étendît.
> Docile, il se laissait faire [...] Dans le silence, le choc des boutons d'uni-
> forme sur le parquet accompagna le bruit mou des habits [...]
> – Sauvage! cria Vania, tendrement ...[31]

> Vania went to him, and, timidly, put her hands on his shoulders. When he
> didn't react, she lowered him gently so that he would lay down. Docile,
> he let himself go [...] In the silence, the clatter of uniform buttons on the
> floor accompanied the soft sound of clothing [...]
> – Savage! Vania cried out tenderly ...

Vania's indulgence in eroticized violence allows her to conceive of Tiékoro as
her slave, as if, through the phallic gesture of whipping she were living out
a colonial fantasy. The narrative suggests Vania's latent masculinity, making
her a more cogent representative of white male colonial aggression. The whip
here can also be characterized as what Frank Graziano calls the *picana* or
picota, an object which is imbued with fetishistic powers. Graziano theorizes
that "Whoever has the phallus, whoever wields the *picana* (the 'magical object' of the myth), whoever controls the *picota* exercises the sovereign power it
affords."[32] Vania's actions towards Tiékoro exemplify the critique Roger Little
makes of Demaison and Mille's treatment of the African:

> Demaison ne méprise pas ouvertement Tiékoro; au contraire, il prend
> très au sérieux les croyances et le milieu social qui pèsent sur lui d'une

---

31   Ibid., 143–144.
32   Frank Graziano, *Divine Violence: Spectacle, Psychosexuality & Radical Christianity in the
      Argentine "Dirty War,"* (San Francisco: Westview Press, 1992), 161.

manière si positiviste. Le traiter toutefois en spécimen n'équivaut pas à le traiter en homme.[33]

Demaison does not show overt disdain for Tiékoro; rather, the author is quite serious about portraying his adhesion to personal beliefs and to his social milieu, both of which influence him in an extremely positivist manner. However, treating Tiékoro like a specimen does not equate to treating him like a man.

Little's observation can be read as implying the fetishistic use of Tiékoro for the purposes of ethnographic exposition, an attempt to show the African as the sum of his cultural norms, which fails to present him as an individual. More than this, however, is the continual portrayal of Tiékoro, both by Vania and in the descriptive aspects of the larger narrative, as a sexual object. To be sure, Tiékoro acts as a fetish in Vania's scene of sadomasochism. Vania becomes the sexual torturer who derives pleasure from the power she holds over him as both her victim and her fetish. Mastery of the African is made more significant by the violence he expresses towards her, confirming both the stereotype of the African as a savage and her conviction that she has the power to subdue him.

While Tiékoro enjoys making love to Vania, and although Vania seems to have tamed him, the African becomes more interested in her as a fetish than as a mate. The joy he experiences in her presence comes, not so much from the pleasure she gives him, as it does from the prestige which possessing her affords him. And though this arrangement causes barely a stir among the ordinary residents of Fréjus in southern France, where African soldiers have been stationed for three years, the sight of an African escorting his white mistress is simply too much for those Frenchmen in the southern city who, having lived in Africa, have played the role of colonialists. Mille and Demaison describe the grounds for these men's' objections:

Les promenades en voiture, les manières hautaines de Tiékoro, l'uniforme de fantaisie, les regards de Vania qui ne dissimulait plus leur ardeur,

---

33   Roger Little, "Blanche et Noir aux années vingt," in *Regards sur les littératures coloniales, Afrique Francophone: Approfondissements*, ed. Jean-François Durand, Paris: L'Harmattan, 1999), 48.

même en public, tout cela mit le comble à l'exaspération des hommes qui, moins favorisés, n'obtenaient plus du sort de pareilles faveurs.[34]

The car rides, Tiékoro's haughty manner, the novelty uniform, Vania's gaze which no longer sought to hide their ardor, even in public, with all of this, men who were less lucky in love and who no longer received such favor were pushed over the edge.

Tiékoro transforms from what Ada Martinkus-Zemp terms the "Noir-heureux," who admires the white man and is submissive to him, to the "Noir-prétentieux," who feels the white man is his equal.[35] This Janus-faced distinction of the two types of black men reflects a stereotype disseminated in colonial discourse. In *Les Noirs* (1919), Alphonse Séché suggested a need for a "re-senegalization" of Africans living in France; a re-acculturation which would train blacks who had been exposed to whiteness to again accept their inferior status vis-à-vis Frenchmen. As mentioned previously, Séché complains of *tirailleurs* who had taken to western culture and of the dandyism of these African soldiers, who had been softened by the special care received from white nurses:

> Beaucoup de Sénégalais que l'on a eu le tort de laisser traîner dans les hôpitaux de l'intérieur ont une mentalité complètement déformée. Ils arrivent à Menton remplis de prétentions et d'arrogance. Le contact des blancs leur a été néfaste [...] ils regardent les autres noirs avec pitié sinon avec mépris; ils laissent croître leurs cheveux, font la raie sur le côté et se refusent à manger la cuisine indigène. A tout propos, ils auront des plaintes et des réclamations à faire entendre. Si on ne leur accorde point satisfaction, ils n'hésiteront pas à menacer d'en appeler aux autorités supérieures. Un sergent alla jusqu'à se procurer l'adresse de M. Poincaré, à seule fin de lui écrire ![36]

Many Senegalese men whom we have mistakenly allowed to remain in hospitals in the interior of our country have a completely distorted mentality. They arrive in Menton full of pretension and arrogance. Contact with the white man has been damaging to them [...] They view other

---

34   Pierre Mille and André Demaison, *La Femme et l'Homme nu* (Paris: Les Éditions de France, 1924), 161.

35   Ada Martinkus-Zemp, *Le Blanc et le Noir* (Paris: A.G. Nizet, 1975), 172.

36   Alphonse Séché, *Les Noirs (d'après des documents officiels)* (Paris: Payot & Cie, 1919) 246–247.

blacks with pity if not with scorn. They let their hair grow long, parting it on the side and refuse to eat their native foods. At every opportunity they have complaints and reclamations. If they are not satisfied with our response they do not hesitate to threaten to contact our superiors. A Sargent went as far as to get the address of Prime Minister Poincaré in order to write to him!

Séché's objections to the comportment of black men recall the motifs in *La Femme et l'Homme nu*. Common examples of problematic behavior include the penetration of the French interior, manipulation of physical appearance, and challenges to white male authority. As in Mille and Demaison's novel, time spent in hospital wards represents for Séché the initiation of the African's delusions of grandeur. The implication here is that changes in behavior among Africans arise from contact with female nurses and *marraines* so that the ultimate challenge to white male authority is brought about by the actions of white women.

Similarly, in *La Femme et l'Homme nu* it is Vania's behavior which encourages her dandified African lover. It is she who provides his new clothes, arousing the jealousy of colonial officers who witness the offensive spectacle. Tiékoro's uniform becomes all the more significant as a fetish in light of the title of the novel. Initially identifying him as *l'homme nu*, the text transforms its hero into a fetish whose nudity leads to the manner of objectification described by John Berger:

> To be naked is to be oneself. To be nude is to be seen naked by others and yet not recognized for oneself. A naked body has to be seen as an object in order to become a nude. (The sight of it as an object stimulates the use of it as an object.) Nakedness reveals itself. Nudity is placed on display.[37]

Though the narrative attempts to give some insight into the workings of Tiékoro's mind, the authors' use of his body as an object of display and study far overshadows any development of a character capable of self-reflexivity. He is never really naked and recognized for himself in the novel because his body's nudity as fetish always signifies something outside of itself. Tiékoro's nudity is code for the savagery and sexual wantonness of Africa, in short, for its un-European-ness. His nudity in the novel's title underscores the inutility of the novelty uniform, the ersatz clothing simulating civility and worn by a man who can never be fully clothed.

---

37   John Berger, *Ways of Seeing* (New York: Viking Penguin, 1972), 54.

In the early chapters of the novel, before Tiékoro retains his prized uniform the hero behaves like a primitive who wishes to become an *évolué*, often appearing in stages of undress, and in a quest to clothe himself. When we first see him and the people of Ifane, the narrative carefully notes their nudity:

> Et tout ce petit monde, remuant, agité, criant ou chantant, allait tout nu ... Car pourrait-on, en vérité tenir pour vêtement la bande de cuire de chèvre, large d'un pouce, qui distingue les femmes des jeunes filles ; ou bien cet *ipog*, doigt de gant en fibres de palmiers tressées qui protège la virilité des hommes contre la fureur des mouches, l'offense des épines et des broussailles ?[38]

> And all these people, mingling, agitated, screaming or singing, went around completely naked ... Since, in truth, could we really qualify as clothing the band of goat skin, no larger than a thumb which distinguishes girls from women; or even that *ipog*, that protective sleeve made of the braided fiber of palm trees and which protects the virility of men against the furor of flies and the affront of thorns and bushes?

Through the narrative's narrow conception of clothing, the reader is encouraged to think of Ifane as a natural world, in which the activities are basic and unsophisticated. But because the text uses this declared nudity as a sign of something other than itself, as an indication of non-European simplicity – the people of Ifane can never really be naked, that is, they can never, in the context of the novel, be themselves.

After going on a quest to procure new sources of power for his people, Tiékoro and his best friend Inabougi arrive in a colonial settlement, where other Africans laugh at their nudity. In a narrative turn which resembles the biblical creation myth, their contact with a greater source of civilization and knowledge, leaves them ashamed. After buying their first pairs of pants, the two friends, proud to have attained a higher level of civilization, remove their penis cases. Because they have abandoned their traditional dress out of feelings of shame brought about by the gaze of others, the young men continue to be nude even in their newly-purchased clothing. And even though others in the settlement as well as the reader are invited to gaze upon the clothed bodies of these men, their attempts to re-define themselves as clothed will always depend on a primary misapprehension and misrepresentation of their nakedness, that is, of their true identities and of the form of dress specific to and

---

38   Pierre Mille and André Demaison, *La Femme et l'Homme nu* (Paris: Les Éditions de France, 1924), 26.

legitimate in their culture. If Tiékoro continues to be a fetish throughout the narrative for both Vania, the narrator, and the reader, it is in great part because of his unrelenting nudity, because he has been created as a signifier of undress.

When as a *tirailleur* Tiékoro first wears his awkward and uncomfortable uniform – clothing which Vania regards as "lourd, sale et disgracieux" / heavy, dirty and disgraceful[39] he becomes the victim of a failed mimesis. His inability to effectively wear the clothing assigned to him by his colonial masters points to the same lack of civilization as does nudity. But when Vania re-dresses Tiékoro, the two employ his new novelty clothing as articles of fetish, as "the adoption of alternative aesthetic codes" in "a symbolic gesture aimed at reclaiming power."[40] The fetishistic power embodied by Tiékoro's new uniform frustrates attempts by French colonial soldiers to fetishize the African by dressing him in the manner in which they conceive the African soldier. Despite the title of the novel, because the African is dressed in a suit made specifically for him, and because the suite becomes *his* fetish, he escapes being defined by his nudity.

Tiékoro's newly found confidence resulting of the possession of both Vania-as-fetish and clothing-as-fetish allows him to assert himself when, at a café in Fréjus, he and Vania are berated by the white male clientele: "Tiékoro sentait sa tête s'échauffer. Ses mâchoires se serrèrent : il se leva pour aller voir le patron. En passant à travers les tables, il bouscula celle de l'adjudant, renversa les verres sur la belle culotte de drap du sous-officier." / Tiékoro felt his head getting hotter. He clenched his jaw: he rose to find the owner of the establishment. Passing between the tables, he overturned that of the warrant office and spilled the drinks on the NCO's beautiful pants.[41] Tiékoro can only express his indignation because he has decided he is equal to white men. Soiling the official's clothing is not only a direct challenge to the latter's station but also a tainting of the fetishistic power of the colonial officer's uniform.

As if by coincidence, not long after Tiékoro's confrontation with the white colonial officers, he is repatriated, effectively cast out of the space in which he has disrupted the *status quo* of colonial power. But repatriation also holds challenges for a newly westernized Tiékoro, especially because Vania has followed him to Senegal. In Dakar, they encounter an even more intense opposition to their relationship. The objections of the mostly male colonialist population of Dakar stem in part from their value of beautiful white women, who, according to the narrative, are rare in the colony. Finding Vania impervious to their

---

39   Ibid., 160.

40   Dominic Thomas, *Black France: Colonialism, Immigration and Transnationalism* (Bloomington: Indiana University Press, 2007), 161.

41   Pierre Mille and André Demaison, *La Femme et l'Homme nu* (Paris: Les Éditions de France, 1924), 162.

charms these men turn their gaze upon the African she has taken as her lover: "Il arriva, passa timidement entre les tables, voulut repartir, intimidé par tous ces 'Hommes-aux-oreilles-rouges' qui inspectaient son casque, ses habits coupés à l'européenne." / He arrived, passed timidly between the tables, decided to leave, intimidated by all those "Men-with-red-ears" who scrutinized his helmet, his clothing cut in the European style.[42] Despite Tiékoro's timidity, the spectacle of his European clothes reflects the fetishistic power they hold to magically duplicate European masculinity. Though the French colonials understand he is an African – thus their astonishment at his access to European clothes – their gaze comes to rest not on Tiékoro himself, but on what he is wearing. Indeed, he disappears inside his suit and helmet which come to represent the Europeanized African.

As they did in France, these clothes possess what Michael Taussig refers to as a "mimetic faculty," that is "the faculty to copy, imitate, make models, explore difference, yield into and become the other."[43] Like Taussig's model, Tiékoro's mastery of European clothing appears in stages, between the moment he abandons his *ipog* in order to copy a new form of dress, to his donning of a novelty uniform which allows him to almost become the object on which he has modeled himself. However, a novelty uniform represents a contradiction in terms, as the fantasy of the clothing implies that which has no basis or model in reality even though it attempts, as a uniform, to become one with those it seeks to imitate. The novelty uniform is an aspect of un-reality which attempts to become real through mimicry but which, lacking authenticity, misses the mark.[44] Compromised by the visual barrier of race, Tiékoro's novelty uniform cannot wholly transform him into a European. Although his new clothes allow him to "draw on the character and power of the original" and to "assume that character and that power"[45] the imitation rings false. The fantasy of the uniform and Tiékoro's misunderstanding of its authenticity replicate his misapprehension of the Russian Vania as a gift from his French masters and solidifies the authors' portrayal of Tiékoro as unable to correctly identify and use the "tools" of Western society.

Nonetheless, for a short while, before the difficulties of an interracial relationship force him to leave Dakar, Tiékoro is able to quench his desire for contact with white men, communing with them through Vania, and offering

42   Ibid. 184.
43   Michael Taussig, *Mimesis and Alterity: A Particular History of the Senses* (New York: Routledge, 1993), xii.
44   Ibid., xii.
45   Ibid., xiii.

himself to them as a visual object of desire. However, Tiékoro, finds that despite his success in acquiring some of the power of white men through his possession of Vania as a fetish and through his transformation into an African dandy, his life has in fact been made more difficult:

> S'il s'était réjoui dès l'abord de pénétrer dans l'intimité des hommes possesseurs d'Influences secrètes par l'intermédiaire d'une de leurs femmes, il se trouvait maintenant comme ces pauvres hères qu'une fortune subite pousse au premier rang et qui s'en épouvantent.[46]

> Even though he had rejoiced after having entered into the private sphere of these men who possessed secret Influences, using one of their women as an intermediary, he now found himself in a miserable position having been pushed by fortune to the heights of success, only to suffer from vertigo.

The invocation of Tiékoro as desirous of penetrating white men's private lives demonstrates the spiritual and sexual syncretic fetishism of the novel. While the act of penetration is easily linked to sexuality, *intimité* indicates religious, spiritual, sensual, or sexual practices, or even genitalia.[47] The narrative allows Tiékoro limited access to the domain of power and sexuality ruled by white men, and acts as a documentation of a homoerotic desire expressed thorough mimesis and through the conduit of a white female. However, it is also careful to display the consequences of Tiékoro's aspirations, as if it were a warning against the impossibility of both interracial heterosexual and homoerotic desire. Like Prometheus, punished for eternity for having stolen fire from Zeus, Tiékoro must suffer mistreatment from the colonial men who believe the African has stolen a white woman: "Chacun voyait en lui l'usurpateur d'une femme isolée qui, par le droit des Tropiques, pouvait appartenir à tous." / Each of them saw in him the usurper of a single woman who, by the law of the Tropics could have belonged to each one of them.[48] Happy to circulate her among themselves, in a white male homoerotic exchange of sexual goods, Vania's colonialist admirers nonetheless refuse to share her with an African.

---

46   Pierre Mille and André Demaison, *La Femme et l'Homme nu* (Paris: Les Éditions de France, 1924), 187.

47   "Intimité" definitions I.A. ; IIA- 1. ; IIA- 2a ; IIA- 2b, Trésor de la langue française, accessed April 14, 2010. http://atilf.atilf.fr/dendien/scripts/tlfiv5/advanced.exe?35;s=2172564045;.

48   Pierre Mille and André Demaison, *La Femme et l'Homme nu* (Paris: Les Éditions de France, 1924), 199.

Loving the Alien: Rape of the African Immigré in Ousmane Sembene's *Le Docker noir* and Saïdou Bokoum's *Chaîne*

> – Ah, ça non! protestai-je. Il n'y a pas de cela dans mon pays. Là-bas, un homme est fait pour vivre avec une femme. Un homme est fait pour se marier et pour avoir des enfants. – Tu ne nous connaîtras jamais assez, toi! dit-elle. Nous avons des vices, ici! Vous êtes purs, vous, les Africains. Vous ignorez les artifices et les perversions.
>
> LAYE CAMARA, *Dramouss*[1]

∴

As part of a long tradition of Francophone-African postcolonial narratives which depict the experiences of the male African immigrant during his travels in France, Ousmane Sembene's *Le Docker noir* (1956) and Saïdou Bokoum's *Chaîne* (1974) deal with the implications and consequences of crossing physical, cultural and racial boundaries. *Le Docker noir* and *Chaîne* both present what can be considered a reverse colonization: contested immigration into metropolitan France as both an imperialist country – in Sembene's work – and a post-imperial state – in Bokoum's text. In both narratives, the entrance of a black African immigrant protagonist into restricted spaces results in the crystallization of racialized masculine identities. Immigration into France acts as a catalyst for some of the white Frenchmen of these narratives to fortify their group identity and play the role of the protectors of France. However, the black African men of these texts also maintain or take on certain archetypal qualities in order to distinguish themselves from white Frenchmen. Despite the many commonalities between the novels, each author deals differently with the intellectual underpinnings of immigration. Sembene presents an African who, though desirous to penetrate French space and culture, vigilantly rejects the influences of the metropole. Bokoum's hero, on the other hand, wishes for complete assimilation within France and her population, only to be rebuffed

---

1 Laye Camara, *Dramouss* (Paris: Librairie Plon, 1966), 82.

by Frenchmen who act as sentinels for Frenchness, whiteness and masculinity. Though these texts differ in their immigrant hero's relationship with France, both ask us to consider the sexualized nature of this reverse colonization. Both texts employ expressions of homoeroticism and homophobia in the dissemination of a racialized masculinity which opposes a decadent European sexuality to a heteronormative, authentic African sexuality. This chapter examines how in both narratives African immigration to France leads to the creation of racialized, hypermasculine group identities and how these hypermasculine agendas of racial segregation also view homoeroticism as either a corrupting force or as a tool of domination. Finally, the chapter considers how novels which might be characterized as acts of anti-racist definitional activism, that is as the creation of modes for responding to prejudice,[2] are also expressions of homophobia.[3]

In *Le Docker noir* Senegalese writer and filmmaker Ousmane Sembene tells the story of Diaw Falla, a young Senegalese man who, while working on the docks of Marseille, hopes to publish the novel he has written: *Le Dernier voyage du négrier Sirius*. Unable to publish his book without paying exorbitant fees, he accepts the aid of a white Parisian woman, Ginette Tontisane, who has connections in the literary world. When Diaw finds that Ginette has published the novel under her name, and that she has won a literary prize with his work, he travels to Paris to confront her. The Frenchwoman dies during their heated argument and Diaw is tried not only for murder, but also for an attempted rape of which there is no physical evidence. His claim of having written the novel attributed to Tontisane is rejected, and he is convicted and left to die in prison.

In *Chaîne*, the sole novel of Guinean writer and political activist Saïdou Nour Bokoum, protagonist Kanaan Niane is a Guinean law student in Paris whose *ennui* and obsession with fulfilling the Hamitic Hypothesis, which justifies the enslavement of black African peoples, leads him to drop out of school. His fixation on bedding white women and his involvement in homoerotic encounters and auto-erotic mutilation serve as symbolism for the African immigrant's degradation. These misadventures culminate in Kanaan's rape by a gang of hooded white teenagers in the woods of Fontainebleau. In this highly didactic work, it is only Kanaan's departure from heterosexual contact with white women and homoerotic activities with white Frenchmen – solidified by

---

2   Elisabeth Young-Bruehl, *Anatomy of Prejudice* (Cambridge: Harvard University Press, 1996), 198.

3   See Martin Summers, "'This Immoral Practice' The Prehistory of Homophobia in Black Nationalist Thought," in *Gender Nonconformity, Race, and Sexuality: Charting the Connections*, ed. Toni Lester (Madison: University of Wisconsin Press, 2002) 21–43.

his relationship with a black woman – which allow his ascent from the state of a victim of homoerotic domination to that of a possessor of "legitimate" (heterosexual) phallic power. He re-integrates himself into the African Diaspora of Paris, and eventually becomes involved in an organized-labor strike during which some of his fellow Africans are murdered. The end of the narrative reveals that the narrator, Saïdou – Kanaan's real name and the name of the author – has just awoken from a dream. He prepares to leave his home for a protest, as an evolved and politically engaged African.

The reverse colonization represented in these narratives disturbs and threatens to overturn power structures established under colonialism. Dominic Thomas writes that though *Le Docker noir* is set during the colonial period, it "already constituted what are today commonly categorized as immigrant narratives."[4] Thus, like Bokoum's novel, the location of Sembene's narrative in France creates a setting for African immigrants to challenge racial hierarchies. As David Murphy has noted: "le plus grand crime commis par Diaw Falla ... est celui d'avoir trahi la confiance et l'amour paternalistes de la France pour ses enfants coloniaux." / the gravest crime committed by Diaw Falla ... is that of having betrayed the trust of the paternalist love of France for its colonial children.[5] One might argue that for the French, African masculinity and its implied rejection of the persona of the "grand enfant" lies at the heart of this betrayal. Additionally, for the white Frenchmen in each text, these contestations of imperial power are predicated upon the threat posed by the physical proximity of the masculine alien. The spatial aspects of *Le Docker noir* are key to the narrative, which depicts the world of the *vieux quartier* inhabited by African immigrants living and working in Marseille. Many critical readings of Sembene's novel have stressed the importance of Marseille in the narrative. Lydie Moudileno has noted the destabilizing effect of placing the bulk of the narrative in Marseille rather than in Paris where so many other immigration narratives are set.[6] Christopher Miller likens the racially diverse community of Marseille to that of the "Négrier Sirius" the slave ship in Diaw Falla's

4   Dominic Thomas, *Black France: Colonialism, Immigration and Transnationalism* (Bloomington: Indiana University Press, 2007), 115.
5   David Murphy, "La Danse et la parole: l'exil et l'identité chez les Noirs de Marseille dans *Banjo* de Claude McKay et *Le Docker noir* d'Ousmane Sembene," *Canadian Review of Comparative Literature* (September 2000): 476.
6   Lydie Moudileno, *Parades postcoloniales: la fabrication des identités dans le roman congolais* (Paris: Éditions Karthala, 2006), 89.

novel,[7] while Willfried Feuser suggests that the spatial segregation in Marseille is akin to "an expression of psychological distance."[8] Dominic Thomas argues for Marseille's significance as the location of a global black community and as a symbol of France's historical connection with Africa.[9]

The narrator of Sembene's novel refers to this *vieux* Marseille as "cette Afrique méridionale de la France" / that southern-African region of France.[10] This neologism can be read as a reference to Africa's relatively close proximity to Marseille and to the historic cultural and commercial traffic between the two locations. As David Murphy observes: "la ville phocéenne est connue comme la porte de l'Afrique."[11] / The Phocean city is known as the port to Africa. However, Sembene's renaming of Marseille could also be taken as a form of reverse colonization in which established geographical spaces are both settled and re-named by outsiders – in this case, the protagonist and many of his fellow dock workers.

After Diaw's arrest, some of the non-African residents of *vieux* Marseille express their intolerance of this penetration. According to an account given in a newspaper article: "L'opinion des commerçants est ébranlée; ils ont fait passer une pétition dans le quartier, protestant auprès des conseillers municipaux et demandant l'expulsion des Noirs et des Arabes qui ne vivent que de rapines." / The merchants are in shock ; they have circulated a petition in the neighborhood, protesting to municipal councilmen and demanding the expulsion of the blacks and Arabs who live only on what they steal.[12] The attempt by the business people of Diaw's neighborhood to take back the command of their space through a forced exodus of racialized Others and through the functioning of their local government mirrors the independence movements of many African nations which sought the expulsion of their European colonizers. Both the petition and the newspaper article which publicizes it could symbolize

7   Christopher L Miller, *The French Atlantic Triangle: Literature and Culture of the Slave Trade* (Durham: Duke University Press, 2008), 367–368.

8   W.F. Feuser, "Richard Wright's *Native Son* and Sembène Ousmane's *Le Docker noir*," in *Essays in Comparative African Literature*, eds Willfried F. Feuser and I.N.C. Aniebo (Lagos: Center for Black and African Arts and Civilization, 2001), 261.

9   Dominic Thomas, *Black France: Colonialism, Immigration and Transnationalism* (Bloomington: Indiana University Press, 2007), 96.

10   Ousmane Sembene, *Le Docker noir* (Paris: Présence Africaine, 1973), 78.

11   David Murphy, "La Danse et la parole : l'exil et l'identité chez les Noirs de Marseille dans *Banjo* de Claude McKay et *Le Docker noir* d'Ousmane Sembene," *Canadian Review of Comparative Literature* (September 2000): 462.

12   Ousmane Sembene, *Le Docker noir* (Paris: Présence Africaine, 1973), 28.

attempts to *reprendre la parole*, that is, to fully take control of the discourse and thus of their threatened community identity.

The notion of violating space in the text is not only specific to Marseille, but implicates France in general. Much of the intrigue of *Le Docker noir* centers on the perception of Diaw as an African immigrant, an outsider who has penetrated the geographic, economic, intellectual, and, perhaps, even the sexual boundaries of France. It is the protagonist's penetration of the sacred spaces of the State and his challenge to State discourse which lead to his demise. This perception is noteworthy because if colonization and the breaching of borders it entails are akin to rape, we must consider the implications of the immigration from the postcolony to the imperial state which forms the basis for Sembene's narrative. Thomas makes this observation when he notes that in *Le Docker noir* "rape functions metaphorically as a violation of the domestic space that is by association inextricably linked to the broader territorial space of the Hexagon itself."[13]

Diaw's *prise de la parole*, which represents another crossing of boundaries, permits him to write a novel in French. This accomplishment marks his entrance into the closed space of Francophone literary production; an area long reserved for those of European descent. In addition to eventually being tried for murder and accused of rape, Diaw is also accused of attempting to plagiarize Ginette Tontisane. This is why the prosecutor in Diaw's trial finds it so natural to talk of the attempted rape of Ginette and then, in the very next breath, express disgust over the African's claims of authorship: "Cette insulte à nos lettres est aussi un délit." / This insult to our literary traditions is also a crime.[14] These juxtaposed reactions echo the French expression "violer la langue," which creates an analogy between a raped woman and a feminized and disrespected French language.

Ginette thus symbolizes the French language and France itself, both violated and destroyed by a "savage" African immigrant. Her death conjures notions of an attack on both French womanhood and French language and literature. The journalistic accounts of Ginette's death, describe her not only as a woman, but also as "la célèbre romancière" / the famous female novelist.[15] One newspaper account tells the public that "La victime était aimée de tout son quartier. Avant d'être lauréate du grand prix, elle avait déjà écrit deux livres, l'un sur la vie des paysans, l'autre sur la Résistance." / The victim was loved by

---

13   Dominic Thomas, *Black France: Colonialism, Immigration and Transnationalism* (Bloomington: Indiana University Press, 2007), 100.

14   Ousmane Sembene, *Le Docker noir* (Paris: Présence Africaine, 1973), 69.

15   Ibid., 26.

her entire neighborhood. Before being awarded the Grand Prix, she had written two books, one on the life of the peasantry, the other on the Resistance.[16]
Here Ginette is the perfect woman, highly educated but retaining links to the
every-day citizen. She follows the late-nineteenth-century French tradition of
glorifying the peasant – subjects of her earlier novel – and aligns herself, postwar, with the now popular Resistance. This last affiliation also implies Ginette's
resistance of Diaw's attempt to penetrate the borders of French womanhood,
as if she were a Joan of Arc, fighting to keep foreigners at bay. Claiming justice
for Ginette through Diaw's trial and incarceration thus becomes a manner of
drawing parallels between "the immediate/biological and the future/political,
between woman's body and the future state ... of the nation."[17]

    Another aspect of Diaw as an intruder in French society is his work on the
docks of Marseille, where he earns less than his white, French counterparts,
some of whom feel threatened by the presence of what they perceive are un-
qualified Africans stealing their jobs. That both groups are traditionally oppressed makes no difference. For although Guy Rozat and Roger Bartra observe
in drawing a parallel between the freed slave, the colonized subject in colonial
contexts and the proletarian worker that: "Emancipating the slave was tanta-
mount to turning him into a proletariat in order to make him work harder and
produce more and bind him more firmly into the production system based
on the class structure,"[18] belonging to the same theoretically assigned class of
workers guarantees neither cohesion nor solidarity. Nor does it preclude mar-
ginalizing behaviors by relatively dominant class members. Once again, a passage from a local newspaper describes "ces êtres incapables de réagir devant
le progrès, qui se disent navigateurs et ignorent jusqu'au fonctionnement des
machines modernes." / these beings, incapable of keeping up with progress,
call themselves navigators and don't know the first thing about how modern
machines work.[19] The goal of this unofficial State discourse is to place the
African outside of humanity and modernity, thus the invocation of *être* rather
than *homme*, the ironic tone of *se disent*, and the juxtaposition of *incapables*
and *progrès*, of *ignorent* and *modernes*. The danger Diaw poses emerges from

---

16   Ibid., 29.
17   Barbara Bair, "Remapping the Black/White Body: Sexuality, Nationalism and Biracial
     Antimiscegenation Activism in 1920s Virginia," in *Sex, Love, Race: Crossing Boundaries in
     North American History* ed. Martha Hodes (New York: New York University Press, 1999),
     408.
18   Guy Rozat and Roger Bartra, "Racism and Capitalism," *Sociological theories: Race and
     Colonialism* (Paris: Unesco, 1980): 298.
19   Ousmane Sembene, *Le Docker noir* (Paris: Présence Africaine, 1973), 28.

his abilities as an educated individual who sees himself as an equal to white Frenchmen capable of occupying the same social and physical space. Much to the chagrin of Diaw's French bosses and even to that of some fellow Africans, his education as a colonized subject and his natural abilities as a leader allow him to protest the treatment of African dock workers. In one instance, the sight of Diaw challenging the authority of his boss draws comments from a woman boarding a ship to the colonies: "– Si ce n'est pas malheureux, ils viennent ici mendier de quoi vivre et encore ils veulent nous commander. Ces communistes, on devrait tous les pendre!" / How sad this is. They come here begging for work and still want to order us around. These Communists, we should hang them all.[20] The irony of this passage is of course the theme of penetrating foreign spaces, the African dock worker's entry into France and the Frenchwoman's journey to the colonies where France commands the lives of millions of non-French people. The use of the term *mendier* which implies a sometimes pitiful, sometimes aggressive request for goods creates an imagined scenario which replicates the French imperial project. Sembene thus uses the irony of the scene to indirectly contest French colonial exploitation.

What proves even more ironic in *Le Docker noir* is that these agents of a reverse colonization remain wary of assimilating into French society, which the novel portrays as the source of a decadent non-normative sexuality. Though *Le Docker noir* does not explicitly assert that homoeroticism is the norm for all Frenchmen, the narrative hints at this, opposing a strict African heterosexuality to homosexuality, which can only be white and French. In a deceptively unremarkable scene, the carnivalesque atmosphere of a *kermesse*, or street fair, unfolds beneath the narrator's gaze. Food vendors advertise their wares, as do the "madeleines," or prostitutes of the neighborhood. Pickpockets abound within a noisy, undulating crowd. Close by "Les homosexuels déchaînés, guettaient leurs proies." / Rabid homosexuals stalked their prey.[21] Placing these criminals inside the *kermesse* signals the decadence of this very European tradition. For although the term describes a street fair, *kermesse* also connotes "des fêtes orgiaques qui comptent de nombreux participants" / orgiastic feasts with numerous participants.[22] The sexualized criminal activity of the *kermesse* involves not only the explicit activities of homosexual desire and prostitution, but also the implicit crime of non-productive eroticism. While the prostitute

---

20 Ibid., 147.
21 Ibid., 119.
22 "Kermesse," *Dictionnaire Sexuelle: Lexique / Glossaire des Expressions Sexuelles*, accessed March 1, 2010, http://www.dictionnaire-sexuel.com/definition-k.html.

represents a misuse of sexuality, the homosexual betrays the possibility of sexual pleasure as coupled with procreation.

As if protecting themselves from this taboo sexuality, the Africans place themselves at the exterior of this scene: "les Noirs palabraient, ne jetant que de temps à autre un regard indifférent sur ce qui se passait devant eux." / the blacks conversed, only occasionally turning an indifferent gaze upon what was unfolding before them.[23] The construction of this scene distinguishes blacks from non-blacks as well as immigrants from natives. According to the narrator, homosexual desire holds no interest for black men: "Tout ce qu'ils se disaient se rapportait au pays, à la femme, aux parents [...] aux promises, aux bêtes qu'on avait achetées pour célébrer une union [...] leur village et leur lopin de terre." / Everything they discussed was related to back home, to their women, to their families, to their fiancées, to animals they had bought to celebrate a marriage [...] to their village and their plot of land. The African's topics of conversation are all suggestive of heterosexual structures: his mother and father; a wife or a fiancée; a marital union, the cultivation of land, which itself symbolizes the planting of a man's seed in the (female) earth. Even though the pickpockets, prostitutes and homosexuals are directly in front of them, the black men in this scene refuse to admit them into their collective consciousness. So, although they cannot deny the spatial proximity of their expatriate community to homosexuals, they can at least remain emotionally and intellectually rooted in Africa.

The scene at the *kermesse* presents one of two brief-but-explicit portrayals of homosexuality within Sembene's novel. In the final section of the narrative a letter from an imprisoned Diaw written to his uncle specifically mentions *pédérastie* as one of the ills plaguing Africa and links it to corrupt institutions and high unemployment.[24] We deduce from both the letter and the description of the *kermesse* that homosexuals are white and French, that they are hunters, or perhaps even animals of prey. The narrative also suggests a socio-economic and political causality between French imperialism and homosexuality in Africa and implicitly rebuts accusations by white characters in earlier sections of the text that animalize and sexualize Africans. Even in implying that all homosexuals are European and that male homoerotic desires inform France's imperial project, Sembene does not suggest the inverse, that all Europeans are driven by homoeroticism. The homosexuals in the street scene represent only one aspect of French society. Associating them with prostitutes and pickpockets through physical proximity implies that homosexuals do not represent

---

23   Ousmane Sembene, *Le Docker noir* (Paris: Présence Africaine, 1973), 119.
24   Ibid., 216.

whiteness or "frenchness" *per se*, but rather the decadence and criminality found in imperial French society.

Like Diaw Falla's entry into imperial France, in *Chaîne*, Kanaan's crossing of borders and the reverse-colonization it implies is portrayed as a threat to white French masculinity. The homoerotic violation which counters this threat represents an expression of an "El Cid ideology": manifested in tactics employed by white European males to keep out racialized male Others through hypermasculine behaviors. In *Chaîne* the contestation of the African's presence in France represents a traumatic turning-point in the narrative in the form of rape. This challenge to Kanaan's crossing of boundaries comes relatively late in the narrative, after he has already lived in France for over four years,[25] a fact which underlines the protagonist's lack of awareness in relation to the implications of his presence in the *métropole* and specifically, in Paris. His rape by a gang of white teenagers wearing black ski mask is precipitated by his visit to an arcade in Paris, where he meets them for the first time. Kanaan's entry into the arcade underlines a contrast between the heroes presented by Bokoum and Sembene. Whereas Diaw and the men of his African expatriate community choose to keep a certain distance between themselves and the French, Kanaan seeks out this intimate contact with white society and finds it in an almost exclusively homosocial space. Before the young men sodomize Kanaan, they remove him from the highly symbolic space of the arcade and take him to the woods of Fontainebleau, allowing him to remain in France, but depositing him outside of their Parisian territory.

Similar to the African men in *Le Docker noir*, the white teenagers of *Chaîne* come together to create a hypermasculine, racialized in-group. However, the young men's use of homoerotic rape puts them in sharp contrasts with Sembene's African men. Whereas the former view homoeroticism as a crime and as a potential destroyer of their society, the white teenagers of *Chaîne* treat it as a punishment for attempts at racial mixing, and as a display of masculine power which edifies their white masculine identities and nullifies Kanaan's black masculine power. Despite the divergences in the use of homoeroticism, both Sembene and Bokoum are hinting at the same thing: white men are inherently prone to homoerotic behavior while real black men reject it. Even in black homosocial spaces, the notions of women and heterosexual reproduction are always present. What's more, the authors' portrayal of white men suggests those men lack an understanding of the purpose of the phallus, and of the use of sex in general. Sembene's Africans show a kind of elegant reserve in their conversations which imply heterosexual encounters, but which never

---

25   Saïdou Bokoum, *Chaîne* (Paris: Éditions Denoël, 1974), 23.

describe them explicitly. In contrast, Bokoum's white teenagers participate in a gang rape, a collective, violent, vulgar and non-productive form of sexuality. And so, two texts which seem predicated upon a definitional activism which writes against the anti-black racist tropes common in French society also reveal their own racist agendas.

Kanaan's violators make a point of denying that they are racists: "C'est pas qu'on est raciste, mais on ne veut plus vous voir dans la zone." / It's not that we're racist, we just don't want to see you in our hood.[26] Kanaan's physical presence in the haunts of these young white males allows him to see them and – perhaps unknowingly – to dominate them through his gaze. This declaration seems to go against the acknowledged power of the white male gaze within colonial contexts.[27] In the colonized space the phallic power behind the gaze of the *indigène* might also pose a threat to white males. But since the crossing of borders which is so important in colonization already implies the violation and domination of the African male, the gaze of white colonizers might function to keep in check what white men have already conquered. In *Chaîne* we see the African immigrant penetrating post-imperial borders. If we couple this geographical penetration with the ever-present myth of African virility, we can then conclude that despite his relatively low social status and his generally-limited ability to grasp symbolic capital within European spaces, the African wields a great deal more power than he did in colonial contexts. Try as they might, these boys cannot be blind to Kanaan's power. As such their narrative function is to display the sexual aspects of seeing, being seen and avoiding the gaze of the African.

While raping Kanaan, their wish not to see him reveals a desire not to be seen by him. Immediately before raping him, the teenagers take several steps so that Kanaan will no longer see them. They ride late at night to a dark wooded area. They turn off their motorcycle lights to insure their victim will be disoriented. They order him to disrobe but choose *themselves* to wear black facemasks. The young men order Kanaan down on all fours and make him turn away from them. However, the use of facemasks and the avoidance of light is ironic, since Kanaan's attackers have already spent hours face-to-face with their future victim. The function of the mask here seems more emotional and psychological than practical in that it allows its wearer to enter highly symbolic states.

There are several possibilities for reading the use of masks by Kanaan's attackers. Masking in this scene is linked to hiding, transforming, revealing the

---

26   Ibid., 75.

27   See, for example, Christopher L. Miller, *Blank Darkness: Africanist Discourse in French* (Chicago: University of Chicago Press, 1985).

true self, and ultimately to a construction of white masculinity with the goal of ejecting the African from their territory. Freud used the concept of the mask to speak about the latent content of dreams – the elements we hide behind the mask of the subconscious which are judged as too "perverse" for the dreamer to reveal to himself/herself. Freud likened these urges to "masked criminals."[28] We can also compare these un-acknowledgeable desires to aspects of Jung's shadow-self and to the notion of the Jungian archetype, the *persona* – or mask – which consists of the roles played by our public selves "behind which we hide our private selves."[29] Jung believed that the fulfilling of these roles was a "projection of the collective unconscious" and that it often satisfied specific societal expectations in which the individual is reduced to rigid, "universal and impersonal archetypal images."[30] He states that one resultant of highly guarded personas is the "irritability" of the subject who must work tirelessly to fit into narrow preconceived roles and to retain the mask of what we might call self (non)representation. Applied to this scene of rape, these theories of hiding and shame suggest a denial of homoerotic urges, the facemasks allowing Kanaan's rapist to hide their homoerotic desires even while they sodomize him. Ironically, they never actually attempt to verbally deny that they are driven by homoerotic desire after raping Kanaan. It is as if the masks they are wearing allow them to dissociate from the sexual implications of their violence.

For Frantz Fanon, masking represents not only an alienation from the true self, but also a desire to become an Other. Fanon's *Black Skin, White Masks* is, in part, informed by Alfred Adler's general theories on comparison and appearance.[31] Like Fanon, Adler conceives of masking as a means towards *fictional goals* or "subjective guiding ideals that represent mastery of [the subject's] sense of inferiority," a compensation for failure in one area by claiming to succeed in another.[32] So, although *Black Skin, White Masks* treats the black individual who desires to be white, the issues of comparing the self to another and masking the self also prove useful in an analysis of white teenagers

---

28   Christopher F. Monte and Robert N. Sollod, *Beneath the Mask: An Introduction to Theories of Personality* (Hoboken, NJ: John Wiley & Sons, 2003), 132.

29   Ibid., 139.

30   Ibid., 139.

31   Frantz Fanon, *Black Skin, White Masks*, trans. Richard Philcox (New York: Grove Press, 2008), 170–175. Fanon dedicates half of the chapter "The Black Man and Recognition" to a discussion of how his theories depend on and diverge from Adler's theories of comparison.

32   Christopher F. Monte and Robert N. Sollod, *Beneath the Mask: An Introduction to Theories of Personality* (Hoboken, NJ: John Wiley & Sons, 2003), 170.

wearing black masks. One must wonder if the transformative power of these masks allows their wearers the experience of being black males, of wielding the phallic power with which their wearers endow black African men. One would still be correct in associating the wearing of these masks with the creation of archetypal subjects. But the myth at play here is that of the virile, sexually aggressive African male. In this case, rather than ejecting this manifestation of blackness in the manner that they seek to banish Kanaan, these youths might be driven to emulate black phallic power. The black masks would then reveal attempts at compensation for the impotence of these self-identified white youth and call into question notions of white male hegemonic domination. And while Fanon concedes that "... there is but one destiny for the black man. And it is white,"[33] *Chaîne* seems to imply that for white men in need of affirmations of their sexual hegemony, there is but one destiny, and it is black.

Finally, it is possible that the black masks worn by Kanaan's attackers reveal the young men's true selves; what they fear they really are: black men. In the teenagers' confrontation with Kanaan the gaze of the African immigrant becomes a reflection. The donning of black masks allows them peer out from behind their metaphorical black skins. Read through the theories of personal constructs espoused by George Kelly in which the mask holds the possibility of revealing the identity of the subject and of acting as a metaphor for social roles taken on by an individual, but which may eventually become enduring aspects of that person's identity,[34] the white teenagers' black masks signal their identification with the African immigrant. After all, Kanaan describes these boys as "des voyous de banlieue" / thugs from the ghetto and "[des] marginaux" / dropouts,[35] terms often used in a variety of Western contexts to describe black men. Their marginality and ghettoization also indicate that both spatially and socially, these young white men reside on the outskirts of French society. Perhaps they identify with the African male because even as nominally-white males, they, like the African immigrant, remain subject to domination by those who more securely possess white male power. Although they declare ownership and protection of their own zone, they are in fact on the fringes of white society. The arcade in which they encounter Kanaan might be their own physical space, but any notion of ownership of the city of Paris results from a collective delusion. Their enactment of the El Cid ideology gives

---

33   Frantz Fanon, *Black Skin, White Masks*, trans. Richard Philcox (New York: Grove Press, 2008), xiv.

34   Christopher F. Monte and Robert N. Sollod, *Beneath the Mask: An Introduction to Theories of Personality* (Hoboken, NJ: John Wiley & Sons, 2003), 541.

35   Saïdou Bokoum, *Chaîne* (Paris: Éditions Denoël, 1974), 70, 76.

purpose to their roles as sentinels opposing the invading African. But perhaps on some level they know that they two are trespassing. Keeping company with Kanaan opens up what Julia Kristeva calls "la possibilité ou non *d'être un autre*" / the possibility and impossibility *of being an other*,[36] not necessarily as a result of empathy with the African, but as the consequence of seeing his racial condition as closely resembling their own.

In this reading of *Chaîne* the black mask reveals shades of whiteness; the elusiveness of a purely white identity. The inability to confidently claim essential whiteness binds the teenagers together in a state of "fraternalistic deprivation," defined by Walter Runciman as feelings of lack within one's identity group as related to another group,[37] and which expresses itself in their ejection of Kanaan from their *zone*. This ejection results from the implication that sharing the same space confirms that the African and his attackers are all equally un-white. Homoerotic rape re-establishes an imagined hierarchy, literally allowing them to be on top, if only momentarily.

---

36   Julia Kristeva, *Étrangers à nous-même* (Paris: Fayard, 1988), 25. Original emphasis.

37   Walter Garrison Runciman, *Relative Deprivation and Social Justice: A Study of Attitudes to Social Inequality in Twentieth-Century England* (University of California Press, 1966), 33–34.

CHAPTER 5

Is Looking Merely the Opposite of Doing? Rape and Representation in *Le Docker noir*

> ... the pornographic body shows itself, it does not give itself, there is no generosity in it ...
>
> ROLAND BARTHES, *Camera Lucida, Reflections on Photography*[1]

∴

In his discussion of sexual violence Mark Seltzer, author of *Serial Killers*, asks: "Is looking merely the opposite of doing?"[2] For Seltzer:

> There is something magical in the understanding of the imagined or symbolic simply as the opposite of 'real' sex. (As if there were not always a symbolic and fantastic component in 'real' sex.) And there is something incoherent in the simple antinomy of 'merely looking' at images and robotic or automatic acts of sexual violence.[3]

Seltzer's argument against a stark distinction of the visual and the physical, intimates that we have, at least where rape is concerned, been duped by the Cartesian tradition which separates the body from the mind and thus looking as an intellectual act from doing. Accepting this distinction makes fantasy rape, if not innocent, then at least harmless. Though it might prove a challenge to argue that fantasy rape and physical violation are indivisible, as does the work of feminist activist Catharine MacKinnon[4], Tanya Horeck contends that representations of rape are part of the same process, separate but concurrent

---

1   Roland Barthes, *Camera Lucida: Reflections on Photography*, trans. Richard Howard (New York: Hill and Wang, 1980), 59.
2   Mark Seltzer, *Serial Killers: Death and Life in America's Wound Culture* (New York: Routledge, 1998), 188.
3   Ibid., 188.
4   Catharine MacKinnon, *Only Words* (London: Harper Collins, 1993).

events found along the same trajectory of rape.[5] In *Public Rape*, Horeck moves from an initial discussion of representations of rape to assert that representation *is* a part of psychic rape particularly in instances of pornography in which the represented subject is unaware of or un-consenting to representation. It is surely pertinent in *Le Docker noir* in which the protagonist loses all power of self-representation and control over the capturing and wide dissemination of his physical image in French newspapers, and in which representations of his person as violent and sexually obsessed can be likened to pornography. The valence of this comparison of photographic representation and pornography stems from the gratuitously performative nature of the imagery (both verbal and pictorial) and its power to create and reinforce inequality. For as Catharine MacKinnon notes: 'Social inequality is substantially created and enforced ... through words and images.'[6] Additionally, photographic documentation of the African's image in *Le Docker noir* can also be compared to rape because of the fantasy infused with fear and desire which it incites within the viewer.

Following the example of critics such as Dominic Thomas, who, as mentioned above, likens rape in the text to a violation of space, and Patrick Day, who also invokes the notion of space and territory by proposing that Diaw's transgression was not the murder of Ginette Tontisane, but rather his personal relationship with her,[7] I explore the concept of rape in the context of homosocial French spaces. This chapter thus examines the fact and fantasy of rape in *Le Docker noir* by underlining the deployment of specifically male-generated discourses designed to penetrate the physicality and sexuality of the protagonist by imagining the immigrant as a rapist of a white woman. Going beyond setting the imagined rape of Ginette Tontisane within an unquestioned heterosexual context, in what follows, I attempt to deepen the critical understanding of rape in *Le Docker noir* by examining how the narrative uses an accusation of heterosexual rape to illustrate the homoerotic tensions within a male-dominated public sphere, and to suggest that the truly significant rape in the narrative is a homoerotic violation of the African immigrant.

Public representation as sexual violation informs Tanya Horeck's chapter in *Public Rape* on what has come to be called "New Bedford's 'Big Dan's' Gang Rape". The event, which took place in a Portuguese-American community in Massachusetts in 1983, involved the rape of a 21-year old, Portuguese-American

---

5   Tanya Horeck, *Public Rape: Representing violation in fiction and film* (New York: Routledge, 2004), 80.

6   Catharine MacKinnon, *Only Words* (London: Harper Collins, 1993), 13.

7   Patrick Day, "A Comparative Study of Crime and Punishment in Ousmane Sembène's *Le Docker noir* and Albert Camus's *L'Étranger*," *Africa Today*, 52. 3 (Spring 2006): 87.

woman by fellow customers at Big Dan's Tavern; other customers in the bar wit-
nessed the rape but did not intervene. What particularly disturbed many was
the image of those who may not have touched the victim, but who participated
in the rape as spectators. Horeck reports that in the months following the incident, "The Portuguese-Americans of New Bedford were constructed as 'Other'
to white Anglo American"[8] as its men were regarded as displaying the same
sexual licentiousness with which black men have been branded. According to
sociologist Lynn Chancer "the Portuguese community began to feel that it, not
the woman, had been raped, and as if the woman, not the Portuguese [men
were] the rapist."[9]

Horeck also points to the significance of the media coverage of the case, the
first nationally televised trial on CNN:

> The act of viewing a spectacle of violence was revealed as participation
> in that violence, muddying a distinction between those who raped and
> those who watched. Having the rape trial aired on national television
> raised a troubling question about the complicity between the television
> audience and the spectators at Big Dan's.[10]

Ousmane Sembene's fictional work elicits a similar disquietude. Like the efforts
of CNN and of the American justice system, the attempts by the French media
and by the French judiciary in the narrative of Le Docker noir to procure justice
for the imagined victim of what is – at least in this case – an unsubstantiated
sexual violation leads to the metaphoric public rape of both the alleged victim
and the accused, a kind of second rape "stemming from the dissemination of
testimony and evidence."[11] Fantasy rape in Le Docker noir feeds three desires:
the first, to see the African victimize a white Frenchwoman and to share in
this imagined experience; the second, to dominate the African by abstractly
controlling his body; the third, to experience the fear and thrill of imagining
that the African could potentially rape the viewer. This fantasy of rape which

---

8   Tanya Horeck, *Public Rape: Representing Violation in Fiction and Film* (New York:
     Routledge, 2004), 74.
9   Lynn S Chancer, "New Bedford, Massachusetts, March 6, 1983-March 22, 1984: The 'Before
     and After' of a Group Rape," *Gender & Society*, 1.3 (1987): 248–249. Cited in Tanya Horeck,
     Public Rape: Representing Violation in Fiction and Film (New York: Routledge, 2004), 75.
10   Tanya Horeck, *Public Rape: Representing Violation in Fiction and Film* (New York:
     Routledge, 2004), 87.
11   Laura Hengehold, "An Immodest Proposal: Foucault, Hysterization, and the 'Second
     Rape'," *Hypatia*, 9.3 (Summer 1994): 100.

reifies and manipulates the body of Sembene's hero in order to *make him* a rapist is an attempt to seize control of that body, of its drives and its actions. In seeking to validate the stereotype of the black man as a sexual violator of white women, the disseminators of public discourse in the narrative repeat the tropes of sexual possession which were part and parcel of chattel slavery. In the enslavement of Africans, the sometimes-forced couplings and some-times-forced reproduction represented not only a means of replenishing and "breeding" workers[12], but also of commandeering the sexuality of an Other. The narrative presents this latter motivation as a driving force in the discourse created around Diaw Falla as a rapist. Those who devote their energies to mak-ing him a rapist undertake an operation which will allow them to metaphori-cally crawl under his skin, to dictate his desires and to take pleasure in fulfilling those desires themselves. They participate in a mimesis fed by contact with the Other, or with his image.[13] Through this process of mimesis, they grant them-selves the pleasure of the out-of-body experience, but only so that they might take possession of the African's sexuality or, at least, the wanton sexuality he is believed to possess. This imagined sexual prowess is contradicted by a narra-tive which carefully notes that Diaw Falla has only one sexual partner, his girl-friend Catherine. However, the voyeuristic desire of Diaw's spectators, "linked to the scopophilic instinct," is an eroticism fed by witnessing others engaged in coitus, and specifically, in this case, in an imagined act of rape.[14]

Rape then, is never a physical event in *Le Docker noir*. Rather, in the text, rape is representation, the corollary of "cultural fantasies of power and domination, gender and sexuality, and class and ethnicity."[15] Rape is firstly an imagined act in the case of Diaw Falla as Ginette Tontisane's attacker. But Ginette's rape does not in fact occur until after she has died, when speculation within the pub-lic sphere over her as a rape victim becomes what Jacquelyn Dowd Hall calls

---

12   For an illuminating discussion of the practice of breeding African slaves and the long-term cultural repercussions within see Angela Y. Davis, *Women, Race, & Class* (New York: Random House, 1981).

13   Michael Taussig, *Mimesis and Alterity: A Particular History of the Senses* (New York: Routledge, 1993) explores the magical process of mimesis and its connection to and de-pendence upon physical and symbolic contact between subject and object.

14   Ann E Kaplan, "Is the Gaze Male?" in *Powers of Desire: The Politics of Sexuality*, eds Ann Snitow, Christine Stansell and Sharon Thompson (New York: Monthly Press Review, 1983), 310–311.

15   Tanya Horeck, *Public Rape: Representing Violation in Fiction and Film* (New York: Routledge, 2004), 3.

"public fantasy."[16] Tanya Horeck notes that "Although the rape is obviously told, rather than shown, during the course of a rape trial, several theorists argue that the re-telling of a rape in the courtroom always conjures up a visual image of that rape."[17] Further, considering the stakes for female rape victims testifying at trial Carol Smart argues: "The judge, the lawyers, and the public can gaze on her body and re-enact her violation in their imaginations."[18] Although the description of the possible violation of a now-deceased Ginette Tontisane creates a "rape in absentia," wherein she does not actually suffer through the public scrutiny of her trauma, it is still worth noting how the consequences to her person bear similarities to those of actual rape victims who witness the creation of stories meant to represent the unrepresentable by wresting the experience of trauma from the victim so it can be shared and re-shared with new witnesses.

This witnessing of rape becomes, in turn, the rape of Diaw Falla. Though Diaw's trial is not televised, it is highly publicized and open to public spectators, and thus provides an opportunity to speak about Diaw as a victim of a "rape by society."[19] This, in turn, expresses Diaw's vulnerability as an immigrant in imperial France. Like the tradition of lynching following the abolition of slavery in the u.s., this public rape provides violent and tangible proof of the African man's otherness. As David Halperin observes in *One Hundred Years of Homosexuality*, citizenship also implies the impossibility, at least among males, of being sexually violated.[20] Some feminist critiques have offered a similar theory of the vulnerability of women as victims of rape, though in this logic it is social power and not the technicalities of citizenship which these theories have deemed instrumental.[21] By these lines of thinking, immigrant males who become victims of rape, whether this rape entails explicit, physical contact or public fantasy, are at once sexually and civically powerless.

16   Jacquelyn Dowd Hall, "'The Mind that Burns in Each Body': Women, Rape and Racial Violence" in *Powers of Desire: The Politics of Sexuality*, eds Ann Snitow, Christine Stansell and Sharon Thompson (New York: Monthly Press Review, 1983), 335.

17   Tanya Horeck, *Public Rape: Representing Violation in Fiction and Film* (New York: Routledge, 2004), 88.

18   Carol Smart, *Feminism and the Power of Law* (London: Routledge, 1992), 39.

19   Noreen Abdullah-Khan, *Male Rape: The Emergence of a Social and Legal Issue* (New York: Palgrave Macmillan, 2008), 76.

20   David Halperin, *One Hundred Years of Homosexuality: And other Essays on Greek Love* (New York: Manchester University Press, 1990), 96.

21   Noreen Abdullah-Khan, *Male Rape: The Emergence of a Social and Legal Issue* (New York: Palgrave Macmillan, 2008), 64–65. Abdullah-Khan notes this treatment of rape in Deena Metzger, "It is always the woman who is raped," *American Journal of Psychiatry* 133 (1976): 405–408.

Though textual evidence supports the argument of a sexualized discourse surrounding the persecution of Diaw Falla, the notion that French society's collective sexual desire of Diaw and its wish to dominate him are linked specifically to male homoerotic desire via patriarchal power is less obvious. After all, half of French society consists of women. And women too might participate in the sexualization of and in fantasies of control over Diaw's body. However, acknowledging hetero-erotic desire and domination – that is, imagining that Diaw's prosecution permits some women of the French society presented in the narrative to sublimate their yearning to dominate and/or be dominated by an African male – does not disqualify the existence of male homoerotic fantasies in women. Nor does it preclude asserting that some of the novel's Frenchmen might be driven by the very same desires. As Adrienne Rich notes in her discussion of patriarchy:

> Patriarchy is the power of the fathers: a familial-social, ideological, political system in which men – by force, direct pressure or through ritual, tradition, law, and language, customs, etiquette, education, and the division of labour, determine what part women shall or shall not play, and in which the female is everywhere subsumed under the male. It does not necessarily imply that no woman has power, or that all women in a given culture may not have certain powers.[22]

Rich's assertions about the role of women in patriarchal systems are directly in line with this reading of Sembene's text, in which power goes beyond gender roles and becomes a question of race and citizenship. So, although the white Frenchwomen of the text may hold considerably less power than do their male counterparts, both their race and citizenship permit them some powers of desire, however unspoken, over the African immigrant. While acknowledging the role feminine desire might play in the public rape of Diaw Falla, we can recognize the massified, phallogocentric presence in the machines of discourse and law which drive the persecution of the African immigrant and in which specific interest groups control the opinions and prejudices of individuals.[23]

---

22   Adrienne Rich, *Of Woman Born: Motherhood as Experience and Institution* (London: Virago, 1977), 61.

23   See Karl Mannheim, "The Problems of Generations," in *Essays on the Sociology of Knowledge*, ed. Paul Kecskemeti (New York: Oxford University Press, 1952), 276–320; C. Wright Mills, *The Power Elite* (London: Oxford University Press, 1956); David Riesman, Nathan Glazer, and Reuel Denney, *The Lonely Crowd: A Study of the Changing American Character* (New York: Doubleday, 1955).

The policemen who arrest Diaw are male, as are the officers of the court which tries him, as well as the photographers whose cameras fix him in their gaze and shoot him with the intensity of machine-guns. The members of the jury which finds him guilty of murder and the judge who sentences him to a life of forced labor are all men.[24] Although heterosexual rape represents the central narrative problematic, acknowledging this over-arching masculine presence in the narrative allows us to go beyond imagining erotic power structures in *Le Docker noir* as solely heterosexual and permits us to grasp the link between patriarchy, the control of public discourse and the deployment of homoerotic desire.

And still, the novel makes clear that not all of its white characters partake in the public rape of Diaw Falla. Sembene is careful to introduce characters such as "Maman," the kind laundry woman and second mother to the Africans of the neighborhood,[25] and Pierre and Janine, proprietors of the bar which the Wolofs frequent. Though one could argue that Pierre's friendliness with "ses Sénégalais," denotes more than a soupçon of paternalism, his attempt at building fraternity makes his role noteworthy. He calls Diaw his "frère," and when the latter rejects this term of endearment – "Je ne suis pas ton frère et je n'aime pas que ta moitié me donne des pseudonymes." / I'm not your brother and I don't like it when your kind gives me nicknames – Pierre retorts: "Tu es mon frère. Je suis né le jour et toi la nuit." / You are my brother. I was born in the daytime and you were born at night.[26] We see other examples of this fraternity in Diaw's defense lawyer, M. Riou, who recognizes that Diaw is the victim of racism and of French imperialist culture rather than the criminal portrayed by the French media, and in Edmond Lazare, father of the *bourgeoise* who died after a botched abortion, and with whom Diaw shares a tender moment of mourning.

Diaw is also not the only character in the narrative to be sentenced to prison. Two white, secondary characters share a similar fate – Madame Lazare and the doctor accused of taking her daughter's life. Though Dorothy S. Blair has

---

24   French women gained the right to serve on juries in 1944. However, the jury in *Le Docker noir* is referred to as "Messieurs les jurés," suggesting that there are no women on this particular jury. Ousmane Sembene, *Le Docker noir* (Paris: Présence Africaine, 1973), 71.

25   In Yaël Simpson Fletcher, "Catholics, Communists and Colonial Subjects: Working-Class Militancy and Racial Difference in Postwar Marseille," in *The Color of Liberty: Histories of Race in France*, eds Sue Peabody and Tyler Edward Stovall (Durham: Duke University Press, 2003), 338–350, the author writes that Maman is "an African woman" and the owner of a laundry (345). In addition to the highly improbable instance of an African woman owning her own business in 1950s Marseille, there is nothing in the narrative to suggest that Maman is anything but a white, French woman and a native of Marseille.

26   Ousmane Sembene, *Le Docker noir* (Paris: Présence Africaine, 1973), 100.

questioned the usefulness of this secondary plot to the narrative as a whole, calling it the "most unsatisfactory aspect of the novel [...] adding nothing to the presentation of Diaw Falla's predicament,"[27] the inclusion of this plot line reminds us to avoid falling into the trap of racial stereotypes on both sides of the black/white racial divide and also demonstrates the possibility of tragedy to which all classes of society might be subject. It is thus not Diaw's condemnation that is remarkable especially since the narrative does not deny that he at least accidentally caused Ginette's death. But the sexualized discourse which surrounds and justifies his trial and its production within a patriarchal, imperial society begs for a closer inspection. The effectiveness of Le Docker noir lies partially in distinguishing between citizens who participate in the state's attack on foreign bodies and those for whom loving the alien is actually possible. When the narrative does point to those Frenchmen who perceive the African immigrant as an invader, a body which they desire to dominate, Sembene implicitly criminalizes them by emphasizing the act of one group of men preying upon another.

The visual scrutiny and verbal debasement of Diaw Falla performed by these agents of the state rob him of physical and intellectual power over his person. These two elements of the discourse of the public sphere are employed, even before Diaw's trial, in the French press which becomes the site of a kind of "folk pornography."[28] Journalistic representation in Le Docker noir is a form of erotic anthropology. The newspaper images of Diaw create a racialized dichotomy in which the African immigrant can be seen but cannot himself see: "Le magnésium l'aveuglait, il ferma les yeux. Il était mitraillé sous tous les angles, les photographes le harcelaient." / The magnesium flash blinded him. He closed his eyes. He was fired at from all angles, photographers harassed him.[29] The violence of capturing Diaw's image in a photograph originates in his position of non-participation in the profilmic event, from his metamorphosis into an object, into the Spectrum, to use Roland Barthes' terminology, which is no longer the subject of the photograph, but a sort of residue, a ghost.[30] With each exposure, Diaw loses part of himself, stripped away by the camera's Opérateur,

27   Dorothy S. Blair, African Literature in French: A History of Creative Writing in French From West and Equatorial Africa (New York: Cambridge University Press, 1976), 231.

28   Jacquelyn Dowd Hall, "'The Mind that Burns in Each Body': Women, Rape and Racial Violence" in Powers of Desire: The Politics of Sexuality eds Ann Snitow, Christine Stansell and Sharon Thompson (New York: Monthly Press Review, 1983), 335.

29   Ousmane Sembene, Le Docker noir (Paris: Présence Africaine, 1973), 44.

30   Roland Barthes, Camera Lucida: Reflections on Photography, trans. Richard Howard (New York: Hill and Wang, 1980), 9.

who now commands Diaw's representation and insures that for Diaw there will be no self-representation, because there will be no self. Journalistic photographs of Diaw are in fact evidence of an attack. After the initial production of identity by the camera comes the reproduction of the seen-unseeing object within the panopticon of the press. And because, as Walter Benjamin tells us, photographic reproductions peel away the "aura" and diminish the historical testimony of an object, the mass publication and distribution of Diaw's image further prevents his self-representation.[31]

Control, or not, over one's image can distinguish photography conceived of as art or photography that aims to inform from photography whose agent, without or against the wishes of the subject seeks to excite the viewer. Such photography is prostitution of another and defines itself through the intent of both the cameraman and the viewer. In their Introduction to *Sex and Violence: Issues in Representation and Experience* Penelope Harvey and Peter Gow, expanding on theories of Susanne Kappler's *Pornography of Representation* (1986) state that,

> Our unease about the actions which result from our images of the other reaches its fullest form in the suspicion that the truth of our relationship to the other is purely that of the domination of the image of the other. This is the suspicion that all representations of the other are pornographic.[32]

Though perhaps the question of intent in the photographer, the viewer and the subject might make room for representation of the Other that is *not* pornographic, this would require an accord between all three participants. One would have to feel, even in the static space of a photograph, that the subject was looking back at them. However, in *Le Docker noir* the gratuitous nature of the photographs taken of Diaw satisfies the criteria of pornography as he can never look back. Rather, his body bears the mark of the cameraman's and eventually the public's violent gaze. In describing the capturing and presentation of Diaw's image, the narrative challenges Michel Foucault's claim of the

---

31   Walter Benjamin, *Illuminations*. ed. Hannah Arendt, trans. Harry Zohn (New York: Schocken Books, 1969), 189.

32   Penelope Harvey and Peter Gow, "Introduction," in *Sex and Violence: Issues in Representation and Experience*, eds Penelope Harvey and Peter Gow (New York: Routledge, 1994), 5. Harvey and Gow cite Susanne Kappler, *The Pornography of Representation* (Oxford: Polity Press, 1986).

"disappearance of torture as a public spectacle."[33] For this violent pornography blurs the line between simply looking at a body and acting upon that body. More precisely it exposes violent representation as an integral part of physical violence, so that the trajectory of Diaw's body from the police station to the newspaper, to the courtroom, to the prison, belongs within a seamless process of violence. As such, "fantasy or intention" is not so much "the *cause* of an act" as it is "*part of* an act."[34]

The press' photographing of Diaw enacts Kobena Mercer's notion of the fulfillment of the "phallocentric fantasy in which the omnipotent male gaze sees but is never itself seen."[35] In his analysis of Robert Mapplethorpe's portrait series *Black Males* (1980), which displays the nude bodies of black men, Mercer notes that the images:

> ... reveal more about the absent and invisible white male subject who is the agent of representation than they do about the black men whose beautiful bodies we see depicted. Insofar as the nude studies facilitate the projection of certain sexual and racial fantasies about the 'difference' that black masculinity is assumed to embody, they reveal the tracing of desire on the part of the I/eye placed at the center of the camera's monocular perspective. On this view, the position to which the spectator is invited to identify can be described as a white male subject-position, not so much because Robert Mapplethorpe is himself white and male, but because of the fantasy of mastery inscribed in the 'look' which implies a hierarchical ordering of racial identity historically congruent with the power and privilege of hegemonic white masculinity.[36]

We can assume that men and women of diverse ethnicities within Francophone society will consume the journalistic photographs of Diaw. The international dissemination of these photographs which will serve as a warning to those immigrants who might follow in his footsteps, reaches even his mother in Senegal – who, unable to read, must learn the story of her son's trial through images. Regardless of whom we imagine will see these photographs, all those who gaze

33   Michel Foucault, *Discipline and Punish: The Birth of the Prison*, trans. Alan Sheridan (New York: Vintage Books, 1979), 7.
34   Mark Seltzer, *Serial Killers: Death and Life in America's Wound Culture* (New York: Routledge, 1998), 187.
35   Kobena Mercer, "Looking for Trouble" in *The Lesbian and Gay Studies Reader*, eds Henry Abelove, Michèle Aina Barale, David M. Halperin (New York: Routledge, 1993), 351.
36   Ibid., 352.

upon these images understand – consciously or unconsciously – the physical and economic white patriarchal power behind the camera. To make this presence clear to his reader Sembene has crafted the narrative to create a kind of *mise en abyme* which takes a snapshot of white photographers photographing a black protagonist.

Even when the narrative does not explicitly describe photographers, we sense their presence and their motivations. In one journal, we see: "une photo de Diaw, menottes aux poignets, encadré de deux inspecteurs, couvr[ant] les trois-quarts de la page." / a photo of Diaw, handcuffed, flanked by two inspectors, a photo which covers three quarters of the page.[37] Diaw falls victim to an isolation effect, whereby only one black man "occupies the field of vision at any one time (thus enabling the fantasy of mastery by denying the representations of a collective and contextualized black male identity)."[38] The mythology expressed here indicates a black beast in the form of the African immigrant whose power to harm the French public is kept in check by the white heroes who enforce French law. The size of the image incites fear by implying the immediacy of the threat posed by the African, all the while creating an erotic tension through the masculine domination of Diaw's body implicit in the act of photography and through the confidence of mastery experienced by the viewer. Further, the photograph itself represents control through the reproduction and stereotyping of this body so singular and unwavering is its function.[39] As a way of reiterating the mythology of control and domination suggested in the photograph, the accompanying news story tells the public of twenty-four hours of interrogation by the police.

Newspaper articles on the arrest and trial of Diaw Falla act in tandem with the discourse of the actual court trial to portray Diaw as a sexual object. We see this in the attention given by the media and by the prosecution at Diaw's trial to vivid, fantastical descriptions of the protagonist's body and in the insistence in both arenas on imagining a scene of rape whose occurrence is not supported by any physical evidence. One newspaper reports that Diaw is "De taille moyenne, le cou épais, les cheveux lui couvrent presque tout le front, ce qui lui donne l'air assez obtus; ses bras sont anormalement pendants." / Of medium height, thick necked, with hair covering almost his entire forehead,

---

37   Ousmane Sembene, *Le Docker noir* (Paris: Présence Africaine, 1973), 29.

38   Kobena Mercer, "Looking for Trouble" in *The Lesbian and Gay Studies Reader*, eds Henry Abelove, Michèle Aina Barale, David M. Halperin (New York: Routledge, 1993), 354.

39   See Mireille Rosello, *Declining the Stereotype: Ethnicity and Representation in French Cultures* (Hanover: University Press of New England, 1998).

which gives him a decidedly obtuse appearance; his arms hang abnormally.[40]
The trope of the African-as-ape is easily recognizable here. But if a description of body hair tends to animalize a subject, it also indicates sexual power
and appetite, for as John Berger suggests in *Ways of Seeing*: "in the European
tradition ... Hair is associated with sexual power, with passion."[41] This passion
is further articulated when the journalist declares that "Lorsque l'on considère
sa démarche, semblable à celle d'un fauve traqué, on peut facilement supposer
comment le nègre, sous l'emprise d'une passion sexuelle, a saisi la pauvre
Ginette Tontisane pour la violer." / When one considers his gait, similar to that
of a hunted beast, one can easily imagine how the Negro, under the power of
sexual passion, seized poor Ginette Tontisane to rape her.[42] This discourse allows readers to imagine themselves as participating in a state-sanctioned hunt
of the African. The ease with which the journalist can presuppose the effects of
sexual passion upon Diaw's person suggests that *supposer* in this passage indicates not only imagination, but also fantasy. The sexual passion expressed here
can be more surely attributed to the journalist who has produced the article
and fantasized the rape; who has imagined himself raping while inhabiting
the African's body, tapping into a violent sexuality which he feels he can only
access by becoming black.

Because imagining is literally creating an image, and as such, choosing the
content of that image, the narrative presents a French society which may permit itself to view and sexualize the body of the African immigrant while escap-
ing accusations of the impropriety of erotic desire. Creating and controlling a
violent image of the Other involves a pornography of representation and the
projection of one's own undesirable impulses.[43] Seeing these modes of representation for what they are allows us to link collective imagining of the sexuality of the Other to violence and pleasure.[44]

During the trial André Vellin, a professor of medicine and a so-called expert in African sexuality establishes a pseudo-scientific discourse which characterizes the African male as an "obsédé sexuel". This doctor affirms that for

40   Ousmane Sembene, *Le Docker Noir* (Paris: Présence Africaine, 1973), 27.
41   John Berger, *Ways of Seeing* (New York: Viking Penguin, 1972), 55.
42   Ousmane Sembene, *Le Docker noir* (Paris: Présence Africaine, 1973), 27.
43   See Max Horkheimer and Theodore Adorno, *The Dialectic of Enlightenment* (New York: Seabury Press, 1972).
44   See Penelope Harvey and Peter Gow, "Introduction," in *Sex and Violence: Issues in Representation and Experience*, eds Penelope Harvey and Peter Gow (New York: Routledge, 1994), 2. See also Susanne Kappler, *The Pornography of Representation* (Oxford: Polity Press, 1986).

black men sexual obsession is "une chose naturelle, surtout quand il s'agit d'une femme blanche" / a natural thing, especially where white women are concerned.[45] The further insertion of a white woman in this discussion allows for a seemingly innocent scrutiny of the sexuality of the African male. Deeming their uncontrollable sexuality "natural" reiterates the theme of African men as close to nature, that is, as uncivilized.

The prosecution's expert also declares Diaw capable of killing a white woman who refuses his advances: "– Alors, si Ginette Tontisane avait refusé de céder, il pouvait aller jusqu'au meurtre? – Oui, affirma le professeur." / Thus if Ginette Tontisane had refused his advances, he might have gone as far as killing her? – Yes, affirmed the Professor.[46] This question posed by the prosecuting attorney safeguards Ginette's reputation by suggesting she did, in fact, refuse Diaw's advances. Though this notion does nothing to help Ginette, it does protect the men who claim her as one of their own from the fear that she and Diaw might have been consensual lovers. This protection of white male virility through the abasement of African sexuality reappears in the contention of the witnesses that "La science a déterminé que les hommes de couleur ont des psychoses devant une femme blanche." / Science has determined that men of color are stricken by psychosis when in the presence of white women.[47] This statement seeks to establish the inferiority of black men who are unable to control their sexuality when placed before an object of desire ostensibly already conquered and owned by white men.

More than an object to be possessed, Ginette acts as a stand-in for these men, a reflection of their own sexual panic which arises from an encounter with an imagined African sexual prowess. Generally guaranteed a sexual impenetrability due to their status as white males and as French citizens, these men witness the threatening of their bodily integrity as triggered by the presence of the African immigrant. Their fantasies of Diaw raping Ginette might then reveal not a desire to keep her to themselves, but rather an alternative to homoerotic fantasy, to the fearful desire of contact with black male bodies replicated in a scene of heterosexual rape. Telling the story of Ginette's rejection of Diaw's sexual advances and of the African's eventual domination of the woman is thus a way of both desiring and refusing to desire roles as objects of homoerotic domination.

45   Ousmane Sembene, *Le Docker Noir* (Paris: Présence Africaine, 1973), 54.
46   Ibid., 54.
47   Ibid., 55.

Whatever the motive for Vellin's "scientific" testimony, this discourse reads less as *scientia sexualis* as veers toward an *ars erotica*[48] which reveals the pleasure of seeing that informs a witness's testimony. The erotic aspect of the expert's testimony lays in his co-opting of the African's foreign sexuality, which allows him an unconscious projection of his own fantasies of sexual violence in which Diaw becomes his potential rapist. Like the ethnographer who exposes his own neuroses within declarations about other cultures, the doctor reveals his desire for a masculine power capable of phallic display through his assertions about black male sexuality. The doctor's erotically inspired testimony allows for the establishment of a link between a terrifying African male sexuality and violence while masking traces of ecstatic terror – a fear-driven pleasure – under a layer of scientific discourse. The prosecutor, the judge and the jury can therefore, through the proxy of French womanhood express the collective anxiety of homoerotic pleasure which places them as receptors of the African's sexual power by creating a heterosexual scientific discourse in order to neuter the African and thus neutralize the homoerotic threat he represents. The result of a fear of rape, the persecution of Sembene's hero seems inspired by a fear of a symbolic transfer of power from one group to another.

The narrative provides the opportunity to work within the Francophone literary tradition, firstly to disrupt traditional notions about African immigrants, and secondly to expose the erotic violence to which black African immigrant males are subject. But the novel's implication that French men are motivated by homoerotic domination is hardly objective, and is perhaps one of the elements of the narrative which lead Mineke Schipper-De Leeuw to describe its presentation of Western racism as unconvincing.[49] In illustrating the persecution of Africans the novel risks becoming a participant in the violent system of fantasy and representation it hopes to contest.

---

48   Michel Foucault, *The History of Sexuality Volume 1: An Introduction*, trans. Robert Hurley (New York: Vintage Books, 1990), 71.

49   Mineke Schipper-De Leeuw, *Le Blanc vu d'Afrique: le blanc et l'occident au miroir du roman négro-africain de langue française, des origines au Festival de Dakar, 1920–1966* (Yaoundé: Éditions CLE, 1973), 173.

"L'homme de couleur et le blanc": Interracial Desire and the Fear of the Queer in *Chaîne*

> Arracheur de son propre masque, qu'il avait choisi – qu'on avait plutôt choisi pour lui –, il se découvrait noir à l'extérieur et blanc à l'intérieur ...
>
> GASTON-PAUL EFFA, *Tout ce bleu*[1]

∵

Frantz Fanon dedicates two chapters of *Black Skin, White Masks* to the question of interracial desire between black women and white men and black men and white women, respectively. Through the analysis of Mayotte Capécia's *Je suis martiniquaise* (1948), Abdoulaye Sadji's *Nini, mulâtresse du Sénégal* (1954) and René Maran's *Un homme pareil aux autres* (1947) Fanon theorizes that it is the black's acceptance of the racial division imposed by the European which makes possible the existence of a hierarchy which blacks then feel the need to climb by participating in interracial erotic relations.[2] In the chapter "The Man of Color and the White Woman"[3] Fanon describes the yearnings of black men, newly arrived in metropolitan France to fulfill longtime fantasies of caressing "these white breasts,"[4] components of the white female anatomy which act as avatars for "white civilization and worthiness."[5] Quoting Maran, Fanon posits that the obsession with the sexual conquest of white women that might consume some black men stems in part from "the satisfaction of dominating the European woman [...] made more so by a certain taste for prideful vengeance."[6] *Black Skin, White Masks* also cites the thrill of daring to engage in sexual relations which historically carry a penalty of castration for black men

---

1   Gaston-Paul Effa, *Tout ce bleu* (Paris: Bernard Grasset, 1996), 26.
2   Frantz Fanon, *Black Skin, White Masks*, trans. Richard Philcox (New York: Grove Press, 2008), 63.
3   Ibid., 45.
4   Ibid., 45.
5   Ibid., 45.
6   Ibid., 51.

© KONINKLIJKE BRILL NV, LEIDEN, 2018 | DOI 10.1163/9789004365544_008

as a punishment for the pursuit of white female flesh.[7] Fanon's coupling of interracial desire and revenge suggests firstly that black men wish to challenge the masculinity of European males through the victimization of European women. And although Fanon generally rejects the application of Freudian Oedipal theories to the psychological study of the black man, the second imagined impetus for this desire seems a manifestation of the Freudian death drive, a masochistic return to primordial scenes of domination in which white men may threaten the sexuality of their black counterparts but yet fail to fully dominate them.[8] Rather than rely on Freud in his analysis of the motivations of black men who desire to bed white women, Fanon refers to Germaine Guex's theories of abandonment neurosis (*névrose d'abandon*) described as originating in the pre-genital phase of childhood as the consequence of a traumatic separation from the mother and resulting in an *abandonnique* who is obsessed with re-enacting the past episodes of separation in which he/she is rejected and abandoned.[9] The aspects of the *névrose d'abandon* which Fanon borrows from Guex are "ce trépied de *l'angoisse* ... de *l'agressivité* qu'il fait naître et de la *non-valorisation* de soi-même qui en découle." / the tripod of the *anxiety* aroused by any abandonment, the *aggressivity* to which it gives rise, and the resultant *devaluation of self.*[10]

In instances of black men desiring a white woman Fanon illustrates what we can now call a Girardian mimetic desire in which the woman acts as the desired object, the black man as desiring subject and the white male as mediator. In this triangular desire, the erotic actions of black men result from attempts to imitate a perceived white-male power. Thus, the notion of the white mask in Fanon's work which stems from the black man's desire to transform the self, to become white and to access the prestige which whiteness promises, is related, in part, to sexual conquest. Fanon suggests that black men going beyond this paradigm of racially informed self-hatred and desire of the other, would require a "restructuring the world."[11]

7   Ibid., 137. Fanon wonders: "Isn't lynching the black man a sexual revenge?"

8   See Sigmund Freud, "The Economic Problem of Masochism," in *The Standard Edition of the Complete Psychological Works of Sigmund Freud*, trans. James Strachey Vol. 19 (1923–1925) (London: Hogarth Press and the Institute of Psychoanalysis, 1953–74), 159–170.

9   Germaine Guex, *La Névrose d'abandon* (Paris: Presses Universitaires de France, 1950).

10   Germaine Guex, *La Névrose d'abandon* (Paris: Presses Universitaires de France, 1950), 13; Frantz Fanon, *Black Skin, White Masks,* trans. Richard Philcox (New York: Grove Press, 2008), 54.

11   Frantz Fanon, *Black Skin, White Masks*, trans. Richard Philcox (New York: Grove Press, 2008), 63.

While the implications of Fanon's envisioned world restructuring are revo-lutionary, his theories are limited in that they only consider racial hierarchies within heteronormative contexts, and thus attempt to establish racial equality while leaving sexual hierarchies intact. For even though Fanon briefly discusses homosexuality in *Black Skin, White Masks*, same-sex attraction does not figure into his principal representation of interracial desire. Fanon mentions homo-sexuality by comparing white male Negrophobes to repressed homosexuals and in citing white passive homosexuals "who insist on black partners."[12] In both cases, the homosexual, in Fanon's conception, is always male and always white. He claims that homosexuality does not exist in Martinique and argues this is due to the fact that the Oedipus complex does not occur in the Antilles. Although Fanon does admit the presence of transvestites in Martinique, he denies the possibility of black homoeroticism, assuring his readers that these male transvestites "lead a normal sexual life."[13] In "Saint Fanon and 'Homosexual Territory'" Terry Goldie observes that Fanon's "rejecting the pos-sibility of homosexual Martinicans allows [him] to see homosexuality not as desire which might disrupt homosocial mastery from within, but as an aspect of oppression from without."[14] And as Diana Fuss points out, Fanon's problem-atic conflation of white male racism and homosexuality, where racism might more properly be linked to homophobia, "offers little to anyone committed to both an anti-imperialist and an antihomophobic politics."[15]

Homoeroticism as a white male condition provides a major trope in Saïdou Bokoum's *Chaîne*, which traces the psychological journey of Kanaan, a black African student living in post-imperial France. Kanaan is obsessed with the sexual conquest of white women and lives a life of decadence while turning a blind eye to the struggles of his community. The prescriptions delivered by the narrative bear some resemblance to the heteronormative theories on inter-racial desire posited by Fanon in *Black Skin, White Masks*. Like Fanon's work, *Chaîne* stresses that black male homoeroticism is passive and the result of exposure to European society. *Chaîne* also resembles *Black Skin, White Masks* firstly in that it warns against the dangers of alienation faced by black men whose drive to bed white women issues from a desire to imitate white men and secondly in that it portrays white men as desirous of homoerotic contact with

---

12   Ibid., 155.

13   Ibid., 158, note.

14   Terry Goldie, "Saint Fanon and 'Homosexual Territory'," in *Frantz Fanon: Critical Perspectives*, ed. Anthony C. Alessandrini (New York: Routledge, 1999), 79.

15   Diana Fuss, "Interior Colonies: Frantz Fanon and the Politics of Identification," *Diacritics*, 24. 2/3, *Critical Crossings* (Summer-Autumn, 1994): 32.

black men. However, Bokoum's narrative diverges from the theories of racialized sexuality presented in *Black Skin, White Masks*. Rather than limiting itself
to Fanon's construction of a black male desire of the white male based solely on
social alienation,[16] *Chaîne* fully considers the manner in which the black man's
desire for sexual revenge upon the white man – through sexual contact with
white women – and the black man's embracing of the decadence of the global
north create a path towards homoerotic desire. As such, *Chaîne* more closely
resembles the rhetoric of black American activists such as Eldridge Cleaver[17]
and Marcus Garvey.[18] While Bokoum seems to view Fanonian theories of desire through a queer lens, like *Black Skin, White Masks, Chaîne* does not valorize
homoeroticism. Rather, in a homophobia more radical than Fanon's, *Chaîne*
envisions black, male homoeroticism and black, male rejection of the African
community as one in the same. In *Chaîne*, the black male who betrays his race
is as alien to his people as is homoeroticism. Additionally, both homoeroticism
and alienation from blackness are punishable by sexual violence.

Rarely the object of close critical analysis, *Chaîne* has most effectively been
treated by Chris Dunton and Chantal Zabus, whose readings of the text provide keen insight into the multi-layered narrative.[19] Dunton first explored the
thematic intersections of *Chaîne* and Jean-Paul Sartre's "Orphée Noir" (1948).
Zabus has contributed a keen analysis of the intertextuality between *Chaîne*
and both "Orphée noir" and *La Nausée* (1938), further illustrating the hero's
existential crisis, and situating this immigration novel within a larger literary context. Following Zabus' and Dunton's lead, I examine how homoeroticism manifests within Kanaan, the protagonist, as the result of his presence in
the *métropole* and following his abandonment of a normative black identity.
Finally, I consider how his re-integration into black-African society "frees" him

---

16   Françoise Vergès, "Creole Skin, black Masks: Fanon and Disavowal," *Critical Inquiry* 23
      (Spring 1997): 589.

17   See Kobena Mercer, "Decolonisation and Disappointment: Reading Fanon's Sexual
      Politics" in *The Fact of Blackness: Frantz Fanon and Visual Representation* ed. Alan Read
      (Seattle: Bay Press, 1996), 114–165.

18   Marcus Garvey, "Editorial," *Negro World* (11 September 1920), in *The Marcus Garvey
      and Universal Negro Improvement Association Papers* 3:9, ed. Robert A Hill (Berkeley:
      University of California Press, 1983), 238–245.

19   Chris Dunton, "'Wheything be Dat?' The Treatment of homosexuality in African
      literature," *Research in African Literatures*, 20. 3 (Autumn 1989): 422–448; Chantal Zabus,
      Out in Africa: Same-Sex Desire in Sub-Saharan Literatures and Cultures (Suffolk, GB: James
      Curry, 2013), first accessed as: Chantal Zabus, "'Out' in Africa," *Gboungboun: The Ponal
      magazine*, 1 (2) (November 2007), accessed February 11, 2009, http://www.projectponal.
      com/newsletter/commentary/commentaryZabus.

from his psychological complexes and from homoerotic desire. A comparative reading of *Black Skin, White Masks* proves particularly useful in understanding the place of *Chaîne* within nationalist and anti-racist discourses.

Only after Bokoum's hero has returned from alienation vis-à-vis his African Diasporic community to the heterosexual desiring of a black woman does the author allow him to rise from the depths. In this redemption of its hero, the agenda of *Chaîne* differs from that of *Black Skin, White Masks*, as *Chaîne* pre-scribes a (re)valorization of and return to blackness whereas *Black Skin, White Masks* seeks to move beyond a reliance on a prescribed black identity. Fanon affirms: "It is not the black world that governs my behavior. My black skin is not a repository of specific values."[20] Indeed, as Albert Memmi remarks, Fanon "took the position that Negritude was not the solution and in resisting the *white error*, we must not yield to the black mirage."[21] Like *Black Skin, White Masks*, *Chaîne* does not espouse Negritude, which a re-Africanized Kanaan describes as a "bavure melliflue" / mellifluous bravura, its poets "eunuques, pédants et perroquets" / eunuchs, know-it-alls and parrots.[22] For the novel's narrator, such imitation reads as a relinquishing of sexual and intellectual power and also of the will to authentic self-representation. Countering this weakness, *Chaîne* embraces a militant blackness aimed at the subject's usefulness within the Diasporic community and at saving the African from the self-destruction which results from imitating whiteness.

Chaîne begins with a dream of Noah as the father of us all, and his sons Sem, Cham and Japhet, living in the garden of Eden. His dream is inspired by Genesis 9:20–27 which tells us that Noah, having learned to grow grapes and make wine, becomes drunk, disrobes, and lays prostrate in his tent. His young-est son Cham enters Noah's tent and sees the naked body of his father, but does not avert his gaze. He then runs to tell his older brothers Sem and Japhet who, seeking not to disgrace their patriarch, cover Noah's body, but refuse to look at his nakedness. Upon awakening, Noah learns that Cham has seen his uncovered body. Angered, he banishes Cham and curses the descendants of Canaan, Cham's youngest son, condemning them to dark skin and eternal ser-vitude to the descendants of Sem and Japhet. Exegeses have encouraged the mythology that Sem and Japhet represent Middle-Eastern and (white) Western civilizations, respectively while Cham and Canaan represent the continent of

---

20   Frantz Fanon, *Black Skin, White Masks*, trans. Richard Philcox (New York: Grove Press, 2008), 202.

21   Albert Memmi, "The Impossible Life of Frantz Fanon," *The Massachusetts Review* trans. and notes Thomas Cassirer and G. Michael Twomey, 14. 1 (Winter 1973): 17.

22   Saïdou Bokoum, *Chaîne* (Paris: Éditions Denoël, 1974), 273.

Africa. Haynes (2002) reminds us of other offenses with which Cham and his descendants are charged within Christian culture: "the existence of slavery and serfdom ... the introduction of magical arts, astrology, idolatry, witchcraft and heathen religion."[23] The discourse surrounding Cham does not limit itself to Jewish and Christian traditions. Though there is no evidence of the story of Cham's transgression in the Qur'an, the myth is a part of Islamic lore. Persian historian Ja'far Muhammad Ben Ibn Jarir Al-Tabari (893–923 AD) a noted commentator of the Qur'an, describes Noah's punishment of Cham, and is careful to declare all Arabs and Persians the sons of Cham's honorable brother Sem.[24]

The significance of Cham's gaze upon Noah's naked body in Genesis 9 is hotly contested among Biblical scholars as a possible reference to castration. The debate over the meaning of "seeing a man naked" stems from difficulties of translation. Additionally, scholars often rely on interpretations provided by midrashic texts of the Hebrew Bible, which, because they imply subjective interpretation, will naturally represent points of conflict. For example, according to Graves and Patai, one midrashic convention holds that it was Cham's son Canaan, and not Cham himself who castrated Noah.[25] Another tradition states that it was actually a lion from the arc who castrated Noah and that Cham was simply a scapegoat. Though many in the Western tradition prefer to read the story of Cham's transgression as a failure to honor his father Noah, others maintain that Cham's crime was sexual in nature, taking the Biblical expression "to see a man naked" as meaning to have sexual relations with him. Eilberg-Schwartz posits that Cham violated his own father, breaking both the biblical taboo of incest and that of homoeroticism.[26] Some scholars such as Bassett believe that to see a man naked in biblical texts is to have intercourse with his wife, making Noah's wife Naamah the target of Cham's

---

23   Jarrod Hayes, *Queer Nations: Marginalities in the Maghreb* (Chicago: University of Chicago Press, 2000), 67.

24   Philippe Lavodrama, "Cham, le maudit de la Bible, Victime première," *Regards Africains*, 46/47 (Summer 2002): 47–48. See also Serge Bilé, *La Légende du sexe surdimensionné des Noirs* (Monaco: Éditions du Rocher, 2005).

25   Robert Graves, and Raphael Patai, *Hebrew Myths: The Book of Genesis* (New York, Doubleday and Company Inc., 1964), accessed Oct. 3, 2017, https://books.google.com/books?id=4sqWAwAAQBAJ&printsec=frontcover&dq=robert+graves+hebrew+myths&hl=en&sa=X&ved=0ahUKEwja9LC64NXWAhUHooMKHXfgASYQ6AEIJjAA#v=snippet&q=Ham&f=false.

26   Howard Eilberg-Schwartz, *God's Phallus and Other Problems for Men and Monotheism* (Boston: Beacon Press, 1994), 95–96.

perversions.[27] Both interpretations – that of mother-son intercourse and that of father-son intercourse – imply a homoerotic context. Even if we accept that to see a man naked suggests, but does not explicitly name, the act of having sex with his wife, and we factor in Biblical traditions in which wives are the property of their husbands, then the biblical expression of the violation of a man's wife by another man implies that the sexual act resides within the context of a masculine economy.

Kanaan's dream recreates the banishment of Cham as an expulsion from the garden of Eden by his father Noah. Cham's sexualized gaze results in the damning of his son Canaan, the namesake of Bokoum's hero Kanaan. However, *Chaîne* never names the object of Cham's gaze. Though we know that in Genesis, Cham is banished for having seen the naked body of his father, the erotic implications of this symbolic castration are too shameful for Kanaan to recount. The invocation of the Garden of Eden as a place of fertility and of origins, but which eventually expels Cham, replicates the womb of the mother from which each child is born, the location of warmth and safety which we seek to replicate throughout our lives. This nightmare suggests the origin of the black *névrose d'abandon*, to again use Germaine Guex's term as it is employed by Fanon, is the banishment of Cham, what Kanaan refers to as "la Séparation."[28] In Kanaan's dream the result of this separation is the physical and psychological enslavement of Africans.

The novel illustrates interracial desire as one aspect of Kanaan's enslavement. Early in the narrative Kanaan is romantically involved with a white Frenchwoman, Anna. Though his love for Anna seems genuine, his relationship with her is inextricably linked to the young African's obsession with "SAINT JEAN PO, dont l'orthographe est arbitraire" / SAINT JEAN PO, of which the spelling is arbitrary,[29] but which alternates in meaning with SAINT JEAN PAUL as well as with "SEINS JAMBES, PEAU." / BREASTS LEGS, SKIN.[30] Kanaan's admission of the significance of "Seins, Jambes, Peau" recalls Fanon's recounting of the racialized desires of many black men: "Je les aimais un peu: beaux seins, belles jambes, peau bien blanche." / I liked them like that,

---

27   Frederick W Bassett, "Noah's Nakedness and the Curse of Canaan, a Case of Incest?" *Vetus Testamentum*, 21. 2 (Apr. 1971): 232–237. Noah's wife is never mentioned by name in the scriptures, but is known as Naamah in the *Book of Jasher Referred to in Joshua and Second Samuel* (Salt Lake City: J.H. Parry & Co., 1887), accessed May 27, 2016, http://www.ccel .org/a/anonymous/jasher/5.htm.

28   Saïdou Bokoum, *Chaîne* (Paris: Éditions Denoël, 1974), 9.

29   Ibid., 61.

30   Ibid., 61.

beautiful breasts, beautiful legs, really white skin.[31] Kanaan has chased this synecdochic fantasy of possessing white women since his first days living in the West. His initiatory voyage to the global north takes him to the U.S. where he and his black African friends hope to fulfill their dreams of sleeping with white women:

> Enfin l'Amérique et ses Blanches allait être à nous. Et pas de négresses s'il vous plaît, on connaît ça déjà. Toubabesse, rien que des toubabesses, ces spécimens qui se raréfiaient du reste au pays depuis qu'on nous avait laissé avec notre indépendance.[32]

> Finally, America and its white women would be ours. And no Negresses, thank you very much, we already know what that's all about. White women and white women only; that specimen which has become rare in our colony since they gave us our independence.

Kanaan is equally aroused by the notion of possessing white women and by that of conquering the land of the U.S. He also fails to achieve any real connections with these women, as they are for him only examples (*spécimens*) of the signifiers of cultural, or perhaps more properly, racial capital. For Kanaan, white women represent only an objectified channel to whiteness and to white men, a way of quenching "his desire to be white, i.e., to be a man."[33] His moral failure also extends to his abandonment of the familiarity of black women, who cannot bring him the masculine prestige he desires.

Despite his attachment to Anna, Kanaan knows the racial differences which separate them are too great to overcome and he ends the affair. He also rejects the invitations by fellow Africans to become involved in their workers' unions. Depressed and isolated, he adopts the habit of passing hours in the toilettes of restaurants reading homoerotic graffiti. His shifting from the wish to mimic white men by bedding white women, to a longing to be the object of white male desires illustrates the causal relation built by the narrative between a mimetically inspired desire for white women and a passive homoeroticism. Kanaan is particularly aroused by reading messages left by strangers which allow him to identify with subaltern roles: "Jeune homme, trente-cinq ans, cherche esclave."

---

31   Ibid., 61.

32   Ibid., 79.

33   Frantz Fanon, *Black Skin, White Masks*, trans. Richard Philcox (New York: Grove Press, 2008), 190.

/ Young man, thirty-five years old, seeking a slave.[34] He also increasingly fixates on his own phallic power, which, as the flawed hero at the inception of this *Bildungsroman*, he can only identify in sexual terms:

> ... je commençais à éprouver de la frustration; une frustration suivie d'une vague curiosité: combien mesure ma verge? [...] à mon réveil vers midi ou 14 heures, je fonçais vers le lavabo, grimpais sur une chaise et inspectais mon sexe après l'avoir chauffé et mis en érection à l'aide d'une revue porno. Je restais ainsi des heures et des heures à l'évaluer sous tous ses contours.[35]

> I began to feel frustrated; a frustration followed by a vague curiosity: how long is my cock? [...] after waking up around noon or 2 pm, I would race to the toilet, I would climb on a chair and I would inspect my penis after having gotten it up with the help of a porno magazine. I did this for hours, examining each of its contours.

Having isolated himself by sleeping until the afternoon, Kanaan expresses his need for self-valorization and experiences the anxiety that this yearning produces in the obsessive measuring of his phallic value. His scrutiny of his sexual organ reproduces the trauma of society's exoticizing gaze upon the black male body. But here Kanaan is both victim and observer, as if he were donning a Fanonian white mask before measuring his black penis.

Soon Kanaan begins to leave his own messages on bathroom walls. They progress from the generally erotic to racially specific offers such as "Jeune homme noir, immense bitte." / Young black man, huge cock. Eventually he scribes "Pine noire, énormément grosse à sucer." / Black dick, amazingly huge for great sucking. He then signs his note: "Esclave noir." / Black slave.[36] The arousal he experiences while describing himself as a slave reproduces the non-valorization Fanon associates with the internalization of racist Western discourses. With these messages Kanaan again enters the erotic symbolic of European imperialism in which the black African male is both the possessor of phallic power and an object of domination. Accordingly, his erotic fulfillment increases when he is able to display his phallic capacity to a white Frenchman: "Il va voir lorsque je vais bander. Il va voir le vit d'un nègre." / I'll show *him* how

---

34   Saïdou Bokoum, *Chaîne* (Paris: Éditions Denoël, 1974), 59.
35   Ibid., 59.
36   Ibid., 60.

hard I can get. I'll show him what a Negro cock looks like.[37] This urge to exhibit
the self should not be confused with Fanon's need to make himself known as
an expression of agency following the recognition that the outside world can
only recognize him for his blackness.[38] Though it may seem buttressed by the
same sort of agency that allows Fanon to make his presence felt and to that
end, to take control of the definition of his identity, Kanaan's display only fulfills European stereotypes of the African male while maintaining the power-
structures created under slavery and colonialism in which the European is the
"agent of recognition" and the African "the object of recognition."[39] Like the
devaluation of self, brought on by an abandonment neurosis, a need to display
himself to a white male as a sexual object leads Kanaan to make himself into a
"penis symbol."[40] What Kanaan perceives as a flaunting of his sexual mastery
and a way of dominating white men reveals itself as an eroticization of the
Hegelian notion of the slave who hopes his master will recognize him.[41] This
unfulfilling reification of self is evidenced by the lack of any lasting satisfaction
from his homoerotic displays and by the constant need to up the erotic stakes.

Eventually, an insatiable craving pushes Kanaan to sodomize himself with
a knife handle clumsily sheathed with gauze and Vaseline. By becoming both
the sodomizer and the sodomized Kanaan replicates, in the Francophone context, the dilemma of double-consciousness which W.E.B. Dubois describes as
the identiary conflicts involved in being both African and American.[42] This
same crisis of identity is implied by Fanon's consideration of black skin and
white masks. Kanaan's double-consciousness reveals itself in the visual quality
of the white, destructive phallus which he has created with Vaseline and gauze,
a phallus as capable of castration as it is of penetration. However, this aspect
of *Chaîne* provides a departure from the persona of the black male presented
in *Black Skin, White Masks*, in which, as Françoise Vergès notes, "Fanon recon-
structs the black male body to evacuate any sign of vulnerability, of passivity.
He makes it a tight body, erected and immune to any form of penetration in

37   Ibid., 62.
38   Frantz Fanon, *Black Skin, White Masks*, trans. Richard Philcox (New York: Grove Press, 2008), 95.
39   Shu-mei Shih, "Global Literature and the Technologies of Recognition," *PMLA* 119.1, *Special Topic: Literatures at Large* (Jan. 2004): 17.
40   Frantz Fanon, *Black Skin, White Masks*, trans. Richard Philcox (New York: Grove Press, 2008), 137.
41   G.W.F. Hegel, *The Phenomenology of Mind*, trans. J.B. Baillie (New York: The Macmillan Company, 1931), 236.
42   W.E.B. Dubois, *The Souls of Black Folk* (Chicago: A.C. McClurg & Co., 1907), 3–4.

order to protect it against all forms of assault."[43] Rather, Kanaan seeks penetration as a physical representation firstly of his assimilation into white society and secondly, of his desire to become white.

Through his more recent erotic experiences, Bokoum's protagonist seems well aware of his vulnerability as a black man and sexual object living in post-imperial France. Perhaps as a means of compromise, auto-mutilation – and symbolic castration – is desirable to Kanaan in that it is preferable to *being* sodomized and castrated, and thus dominated by another. It represents a controlled acceptance of himself as a passive sexual object: "Je voulais m'atteindre de façon charnelle. Mais pas d'intermédiaire s'il vous plaît." / I wanted to become one with myself, carnally. But a middle man? No thank you.[44] He accepts his role as a target of desire and domination, but insists that he be in total control of the process so that in dominating himself, manipulating previous fantasies in which he is a white man's sexual slave, and then becoming both master *and* slave, he might restore the power of his own phallus. By sodomizing himself, Kanaan anticipates ridding himself of the invisible burden of the "éternelle *pénia*,"[45] which we can assume is white, and which to him represents the domination to which he is subject as an African living in the global north. But Kanaan's attempts at auto-eroticism are thwarted by the ubiquitous presence of the white male intermediary whose role as dominator he attempts to commandeer, and who is inadvertently conjured through the physical representation of the "white" phallus which Kanaan has created. His masochism might also be read as what Freud notes is "nothing more than a continuation of [...] sadism turning against one's own person in which the latter at first takes the place of the sexual object".[46] In another display of double-consciousness the subject is split between sadistic and masochistic desires. Freud believed that one possible motivation behind this sadism-turned-masochism was a fear of castration.[47] This symbolic castration is evident in Kanaan, whose chosen tool of self-mutilation seems to point to a desire to self-castrate. However, the use of the knife does not help him to produce an erection and to thus reclaim his phallic power. His sexual impotence thus symbolically reproduces his lack of power as an African immigrant living in France.

---

43   Françoise Vergès, "Creole Skin, Black Masks: Fanon and Disavowal," *Critical Inquiry* 23 (Spring 1997): 583.

44   Saïdou Bokoum, *Chaîne* (Paris: Éditions Denoël, 1974), 64.

45   Ibid., 63.

46   Sigmund Freud, *Three Contributions to the Theory of Sex*. accessed April 23, 2010, http://www.gutengerg.org/files/14969/14969-h/14969-h.htm.

47   Ibid.

His urges unsatisfied, Kanaan walks the streets of Paris and enters an arcade, where he meets a group of white teenagers from the *banlieues*: "L'un s'appelait Jean, le deuxième Popaul, le troisième Saint-Marc et un quatrième dont je ne me souviens plus le nom." / One was named Jean, the second Popaul, the third Saint-Marc and a fourth whose name I don't remember.[48] The young men befriend Kanaan and invite him on a motorcycle ride. Leaving the confines of Paris, the teenagers take the African immigrant to the woods of Fontainebleau, where Kanaan finds himself surrounded not by newfound friends but by men in balaclavas who take his shoes and clothes and proceed to sodomize him:

Je sens un acharnement, une brûlure, un déchireur.
– Hé! les gars, y desserre pas les fesses le négro!
Je sens pourtant un incendie quelque part.
– Viens Popaul, j'aime pas beaucoup, y commence à pisser du sang.

Au même moment, une vague ombre se met à danser à ma gauche. Une terrible douleur me traverse la tempe et semble s'arracher de mon œil gauche. Suit une sorte de lueur: j'émerge brutalement de ma somnolence. Où en sont-ils? Je sens une décharge. Mes entrailles qui me remontent à la bouche. Derrière moi, quelqu'un souffle comme un bœuf. C'est le temps des labours.[49]

I feel a ferocity, a burning, a tearing
– Hey guys, this Negro's keeping his butt-hole shut tight!
And yet I smell a fire burning somewhere.
– Come on, Popaul, I don't like this, there's blood coming from his ass.

At this very moment, a vague shadow begins to dance on my left, a terrible pain shoots through my temple and seems to rip through my left eye. And then a sort of glow. I snap out of my drowsiness. What are they up to? I feel a discharge. My bowels rise to my mouth. Behind me someone is breathing like a bull. It was ploughing time.

The burning Kanaan describes suggests that his violation has transported him to the mythic hell to which he dreams his forefather Cham was banished. The narrative's graphic description of Kanaan's rape expresses the significance of rape as trauma, a term which Lawrence Kritzman reminds us, indicates an

---

48   Saïdou Bokoum, *Chaîne* (Paris: Éditions Denoël, 1974), 71.
49   Ibid., 74.

"'injury' or 'wound'."[50] It allows us to see how the violence implicit in the tearing he experiences is both physical and metaphysical and "dwells in the notion of bodily autonomy, on attempts to rupture the boundaries of the self."[51] Kanaan's rape allows a penetration and a dispossession of both his body and his psyche, a violence which mirrors Stuart Hall's reading of the alienated black subject in *Black Skin, White Masks* as "a site of splitting."[52] We can compare this rape to torture, through a reading of Jean Améry, who notes:

> At the first blow [by the torturer] ... trust in the world breaks down. The other person *opposite* whom I exist physically in the world and with whom I exist only as he does not touch my skin surface as border, forces his own corporality on me with the first blow. He is on me and thereby destroys me. It is like rape, a sexual act without the consent of one of the two partners.[53]

This tearing and penetration of Kanaan shatters the border between him and his attacker – a representative of the white male persona Kanaan sought to emulate, whose own borders he initially sought to cross through consensual sexual contact. The determination of Kanaan's rapists suggests a point of no return at which whiteness will be planted inside him. Sodomy here is a highly politicized metaphor of an internalization of a culture which values whiteness. The narrative uses homoerotic rape as a warning against the destruction of the masculine self which assimilation portends. Through the violence of rape Kanaan then becomes one with the whiteness he so desires. This creates an ambiguity in *Chaîne*, which seems to implicate Kanaan in his own rape.

Though he cannot see the young men as they violate him – a vague shadow is as much as he distinguishes – they are witnesses to his shame. He, in turn, witnesses a relational shame through them, a shame which "depends on [the]

50   Lawrence Kritzman, "Ernaux's Testimony of Shame," *L'Esprit Créateur* 39.4 (Winter 1999): 139.

51   Penelope Harvey and Peter Gow, "Introduction" in *Sex and Violence: Issues in Representation and Experience*, eds Penelope Harvey and Peter Gow (New York: Routledge, 1994), 13.

52   Stuart Hall, "The After-life of Frantz Fanon: Why Fanon? Why Now? Why *Black Skin, White Masks*?" in *The Fact of Blackness: Frantz Fanon and Visual Representation*, ed. Alan Read (Seattle: Bay Press, 1996), 24. On the subject as a site of splitting see Homi Bhabha, "Signs Taken for Wonders: Questions of Ambivalence and Authority under a Tree outside Delhi, May 1817," in *The Location of Culture* (New York: Routledge, 1994), 145–174.

53   Jean Améry, *At the Mind's Limits: Contemplations by a Survivor on Auschwitz and Its Realities*, trans. Sidney Rosenfeld and Stella P. Rosenfeld (Bloomington: Indiana University Press, 1980), 28.

gaze of another ... which affects your own vision."[54] In a sense Kanaan becomes both the watcher and the watched just as he had done while observing
reflections of his erect penis in a mirror. When his perception is reduced to the
auditory, the olfactory and to the sensation of physical violation, it is their conversation that informs him that he is bleeding. As if reflecting his alienation
from his authentic, original self, he experiences a dissociative consciousness in
part through the observations of his attackers.

Following the rape Kanaan retains a telling misunderstanding about what
has been done to him: "Pourquoi me l'avoir arraché ou plutôt me l'avoir en-
foncé ainsi?" / Why would they tear it from me, or rather, force it inside me like
that?[55] Kanaan confuses castration and sodomy. He corrects his mistake mid-
sentence but expresses the connection between penetration and castration,
echoing his previous use of a white knife to sodomize himself. This underlines
the threat represented by the white phallus, which Kanaan has, nonetheless,
been so desirous of physically and symbolically possessing. And though the
narrative initially implies that his encounter with these young white men is
purely by chance, later details suggest otherwise.

For all the pain which Kanaan experiences at the hands of Jean, Popaul and
Saint-Marc, their names, which replicate "Saint, Jean, Po," and "Seins, Jambes,
Peau" suggest that his meeting them was no accident. Metaphorically speaking, Kanaan is driven and then raped, and driven to *be* raped by the things he
most desires. He later recognizes:

> Il y a pourtant une sombre préméditation dans ma vie. Depuis toujours,
> depuis les origines. Je sais qu'à l'origine, tout avait commencé par une
> gigantesque enculade. Mais il a fallu qu'avec moi ça se passât ainsi, litté-
> ralement, dans ma chair.[56]

> There has been, however, a somber premeditation in my life since the
> beginning of time. I know that in the beginning everything began as a big
> ass-fucking. But me, I needed it to happen like this, literally, in my flesh.

Here Kanaan refers to the unfair banishment and subjugation of Cham, a mythology which haunts his existence. We can compare this realization to Susan
Brownmiller's vision of the primal scene of "the first rape" as "a gang rape of

---

54   Nancy K. Miller, "Memory Stains: Annie Ernaux's *Shame*," *a/b: Auto/Biography Studies* 14.1
     (Summer 1999): 43.
55   Saïdou Bokoum, *Chaîne* (Paris: Éditions Denoël, 1974), 76.
56   Ibid., 76.

one woman by a band of marauding men" and her assertion that "if the first rape was an unexpected battle ... the second rape was indubitably planned."[57] Kanaan too relates being raped to a primal event, but unlike Brownmiller, who places blame at the feet of the perpetrators of that first rape and of those who plan subsequent rapes, Kanaan views his sexual violation as part of *his* greater plan. He seems to suggest that he sought out the sodomy to which he was subjected, that in a trajectory which began with the desire for white women and the mimicry of white men, which then progressed to erotic encounters with white men from which women were completely removed, and then to the self-mutilation in which he was both victim and violator, his final descent into hell took the form of his true desire. What he in fact yearned for was to revisit a primal scene in the creation of blackness by making himself a homoerotic object and a passive receiver of white male aggression. As part of a general trajectory, the text seems to have linked these events, so that the symbolic castration to which Kanaan is subject as a victim of rape echoes the sexual activity which precedes it. We may then view Kanaan's symbolic castration as a punishment for sexual interaction with white women. Or we might say that his castration was part and parcel of what the narrative characterizes as abnormal sexual activity for black men.

We can read the rape of Kanaan as a form of self-punishment and as part of the didactic project of *Chaîne*, which like *Black Skin, White Masks*, illustrates the dangers of a black man who fails to maintain a black, masculinist, heterosexual subjectivity. But unlike *Black Skin, White Masks*, which seeks a comprehension of the black psyche in order to create a black subject who can see beyond hierarchies of race, *Chaîne* calls for a cleansing violence which will bring its black protagonist back into the fold. In its prescription of violence, *Chaîne* is perhaps more closely related to Fanon's *Wretched of the Earth*, which proposes violence as one of the means by which the dominated and the objectified might become men.[58] But unlike *Wretched of the Earth*, which alludes to violence directed towards colonizers and capitalists, *Chaîne* directs its violence at the man who objectifies himself, and who accepts this objectification by playing an active role in his own domination. We can perhaps say that the rape of Kanaan is literal in that it is both physical and narrative. It is a narrative act of aggression meant to punish the novel's protagonist for his homoerotic

57   Susan Brownmiller, *Against Our Will: Men, Women, and Rape* (New York: Simon and Schuster, 1975), 14.

58   Frantz Fanon, *The Wretched of the Earth*, trans. Richard Philcox (New York: Grove Press, 2004), ii.

desires and, using rape as a means of catharsis, to establish a redemptive het-erosexual space within the remainder of the novel.

Before Kanaan can reintegrate himself into the African immigrant com-munity he must consider his condition as both a heterosexual African man and a victim of homoerotic rape. After the episode at Fontainebleau, Kanaan seeks the help of a psychologist with whom he eventually has the following exchange:

> Qu'est-ce que vous cherchiez la nuit? – Mais je vous l'ai déjà dit plus de cent fois : je ne le sais pas! – Pourtant, ça vous a mené à Fontainebleau. – Et alors? n'est-ce pas moi-même qui vous ai raconté cela aussi? – La coïn-cidence est troublante, vous ne trouvez pas? – Coïncidence? – Vous aviez déjà essayé avec un couteau. [...]
> Vous avez dit à la dernière séance que Saint Jean Po n'avait pas de sexe défini. – C'est un homme, mais je ne vois pas son sexe. – Mais il a des seins? – J'ai seulement dit SAINT=seins, peut-être. En tout cas, c'est un toubab. – Toubab? – Un homme blanc. Mais je ne vois pas son visage. C'est curieux, je vois à présent son sexe, il [son sexe] est noir! Soupirs.[59]

> What were you after that night? – But I've already told you a hun-dred times: I don't know! – And yet, whatever it was, it brought you to Fontainebleau. – So? That's what I told you, isn't it? – Don't you find the coincidence troubling? – Coincidence? – Well, you had already tried it with a knife [...]
> You said in our last session that Saint Jean Po had no clearly gendered genitalia. – It's a man, but I don't see his penis. – But he has breasts? – All I said was "Saint" [Seins]. This might mean breasts. Anyway, it's a cracker. – A cracker? – A white guy, but I don't see his face. But, that's weird; now I can see his penis. It's black! Gasps.

The process of the talking cure which Kanaan undergoes allows him to see the reality of his rape at the site of France's former royal hunting grounds. The epicene Saint Jean Po mirrors his ambiguous sexual desires. The text suggests that Saint Jean Po's face is hidden or perhaps masked; that at least euphemisti-cally he is wearing a white mask, but that he is really a black man. Later Kanaan realizes: "Saint Jean Po, c'était moi." / Saint Jean Po was me.[60] It is never clear if the white teenagers actually raped Kanaan. In fact, when Kanaan mentions his

59   Saïdou Bokoum, *Chaîne* (Paris: Éditions Denoël, 1974), 78.
60   Ibid., 78.

four attackers, he can only remember the names of three of them: Jean, Popaul and Saint Marc. The forth is left in the shadows of Kanaan's memory, leaving us to wonder if the forth white man was not Kanaan himself, a possibility which would render the rape a psychic form of autoerotic mutilation.

However, establishing the rape as a physical occurrence is less important than understanding that psychologically, Kanaan desired the debasement of sexual violation as a fulfillment of what for him was blackness. Even in under-standing that SaintJeanPo was a manifestation of the rejection of his African identity, Kanaan refuses an affiliation with blackness: "Ça ne finira jamais le monde noir? Eh bien, moi, je ne suis pas un Noir. Moi c'est moi." / When are we going to be done with blackness? Well, as far as I'm concerned, I'm not black. I'm just me.[61] However, realizing his failure as an immigrant in France Kanaan walks the streets of Paris and contemplates killing himself. During his wander-ing, he comes upon the site of a fire that has been set in a squat inhabited by African immigrants on la rue des Colonies. Having run in to rescue those im-migrants trapped in the blaze he comes face to face with another African:

> – Moi zé m'apèle Kanaan ... Et toi?
> – Comment ?!?
> Je suis abasourdi, Je lui demande son nom de famille [...]
> – Kouyaté. Kaman Kouyaté te dit merci.[62]

> My name is Kanaan. And you?
> What?!?
> I'm taken aback. I ask his last name.
> Kouyaté. Kaman Kouyaté thanks you.

Here Kanaan is confronted with the real horrors of immigration to France, an inferno whose location replicates European colonial projects in Africa. This symbolic journey aids Kanaan's understanding of his position as an immigrant and of the link between his present condition and colonialism. His confusion over Kaman's name reveals the beginning of his recognition of himself as an African and his reintegration into African immigrant society. When despite Kanaan's best efforts Kaman dies in the fire, the protagonist rediscovers his desire to live. Surviving the fire after attempting to help his African brothers, marks Kanaan's emergence from the hell and a recovery from an abandon-ment neurosis associated with racial alienation and homoerotic desire. As

---

61   Ibid., 81.
62   Ibid., 101.

such it also facilitates a return to Kanaan's origins, to the bosom of an African Diasporic community which acts as a symbolic womb, a place of safety and undifferentiated identity. His will to live is also a will to be useful, to be productive.

For Kanaan, productivity implies a homophobic rejection of homoeroticism, which, requires that he subscribe to a conception of personal development similar that proposed by Freud, in which the anal stage is replaced by the more productive phallic stage.[63] In *Le Désir homosexuel* Guy Hocquenghem explores the effect of such theories on society's relationship with homoeroticism:

> Tous les hommes ont un phallus qui leur assure un rôle social ... L'anus n'est pas en relation sociale, puisqu'il constitue précisément l'individu et permet par-là même la division entre société et individu ... L'anus est surinvesti individuellement parce qu'il est désinvesti socialement.[64]

> All men have a phallus which assures them a social role. The anus has no role in society, precisely because it constitutes the individual and as such permits the distinction of society and individual ... The exaggerated importance placed by individuals on the anus comes from the fact that it is socially divested.

David Caron's reading of Hocquenghem, notes the perceived lack of social productiveness of those who focus on anal desire: "What characterizes such groups is their absence of goal or social usefulness. They serve no purpose other than themselves and go nowhere in particular."[65] *Chaîne* expresses this same conviction vis-à-vis homoeroticism and acts against such desires by moving Kanaan to another symbolic stage of development. To reach this phallic and social stage Kanaan must abandon homoerotic desire and the desire to be sodomized. In doing so, he falls in love with an African woman and, in lieu of having children as a form of productiveness, he founds an African dance troupe, the Ballet Kotéba.

Kanaan explains his return to desiring black women: "Pour moi, fini de butiner à gauche et à droite [...] la prochaine ser[a] la bonne, définitivement." / For me, no more chasing booty left and right [...] the next one will be Miss

---

63   See Sigmund Freud, *Three Essays of the Theory of Sexuality*, trans. James Strachey (New York: Avon Books, 1962 [1905]).

64   Guy Hocquenghem, *Le Désir homosexuel* (Paris: Fayard, 1993), 97.

65   David Caron, "The Queerness of Male Group Friendship," in *Entre Hommes: French and Francophone Masculinities in Culture and Theory*, eds Todd W. Reeser and Lewis C. Seifert (Newark: University of Delaware Press, 2008), 254.

Right.[66] Kanaan not only describes his return to good, authentic values and to the straight-and-narrow of the African community, he also announces his straightness, a return to heterosexuality. With this comes the return of his sexual potency. He tells his new Senegalese girlfriend, Sana Arr: "tu es la première fille ... qui me fait bander en permanence [...] c'est le bonheur suprême." / You're the first girl ... who makes me hard all the time [...] it's the joy of joys.[67] After a period spent bedding white women, Kanaan finds the ultimate expression of his masculinity with an African woman. However, one could argue that his "return to blackness" through Sana, has stopped short of a return to a strict African identity. Sana is a *mulâtresse*, an avid user of make-up and wigs who Kanaan views as having "[des] fesses, un peu à la toubab, c'est-à-dire pas proéminentes comme celles de nos négresses au pays." / an ass that's a little bit like a white girl's, that is, not as prominent as those of our Negresses back home,[68] who is untrained in preparing African cuisine but well-informed regarding white female entertainers. Though Kanaan's description of Sana denies her an African and a black identity, he conceives of her – at least consciously – as an African woman. With Sana, he not only moves away from desiring white women, he also experiences a fulfillment which eluded him in his days of masturbation, self-mutilation and homoerotic encounters. The message of *Chaîne*'s narrative is clear: authentic African male sexuality can only be experienced with black women.

Kanaan further expresses his return to heterosexuality by policing Sana's desires during a conversation in which she reproaches him for his treatment of a female member of their theater group:

> – Tu es [...] méchant parfois. Je t'ai vu descendre Jacqueline à notre dernier séminaire [...] – Mais elle m'a l'air d'une gouine! Tout le temps en train de vous tripoter dans les coulisses [...] – Jalousie! Mais être jaloux d'une fille! – Et toi ne fais pas la naïve, ces filles-là sont souvent des rivales dangereuses![69]

> – You're [...] really harsh sometimes. I saw you take down Jacqueline at our last meeting [...] – But she seems like such a dike! Always fondling you and the other girls in the wings [...] – Jealous! I can't believe you're

---

66   Saïdou Bokoum, *Chaîne* (Paris: Éditions Denoël, 1974), 159.
67   Ibid., 163.
68   Ibid., 176.
69   Ibid., 163.

jealous of a girl! – Don't play naïve with me, those girls are often dangerous competition.

Kanaan follows his abandonment of homoeroticism with homophobia.
Though he may not physically touch Jacqueline, it is clear that his intentions
towards her are violent, that they mirror the punishment he received for his
own homoerotic activities. Jacqueline is threatening not only as a potential
rival, but also as a reminder of Kanaan's shame. His attitude towards her signals his acceptance of the validity of a social structure which equates blackness and heterosexuality. Further, he sees her presence as threatening to the
community, which he wishes to remain a heteronormative space.

Sana soon breaks off her engagement with Kanaan because her social-
climbing parents object to her marrying "UN HOMME DE CASTE" / A LOW-
CLASS MAN.[70] In his solitude Kanaan reflects on the sexual decadence of
Sana's mother, who had once tried to seduce him, and on a drunken confession
Sana once made to him:

> – Tu sais, un jour, j'ai voulu coucher avec Mariama [...] je ne sais pas moi
> [...] c'était l'humilier, la salir ...
> – Et tu as déjà eu ...
> – Oui, à Nice. Je sortais avec une petite. Oh! rien que deux ou trois mois!
> Elle avait des seins comme ça. Elle me dégoûtait.
> – Mais alors pourquoi sortais-tu avec elle?
> – Me venger. Oui, me venger de ma maman, de mes parents de ...[71]

> – You know, one day, I wanted to have sex with Mariama [the wife of her
> former lover] [...] I don't know, just to humiliate her, to make her feel
> dirty ...
> – And you've already ...
> – Yes, in Nice. I was going out with this chick. Oh, it was nothing, just a
> couple of months, she had these huge tits. She was gross.
> – So why did you go out with her?
> – For revenge. Yeah, to get revenge on my mother, on my family, on ...

Sana's attitude towards her own acts of homoeroticism resembles homophobia, as she makes light of her intimate relations with other women, and privileges her negative feelings towards them. She claims to have been disgusted

---

70   Ibid., 172. Original emphasis.
71   Ibid., 182–183.

by the large breasts of a former lover – indicating her disinterest in a marker of femininity – though she remained with her for a couple of months. Further, in attributing her lesbian affairs not to sexual desire but to an attempt to avenge herself upon her family, she seeks to prove to Kanaan – and to herself – that she is not a lesbian. Though Kanaan reflects on this conversation, he does not dwell on Sana's homoerotic desires and encounters, nor on her disavowal of these desires through minimization and pretext. Additionally, he does not admit that Sana's homoeroticism and homophobia might parallel his own amalgamation of desire and violence, an aspect of his personality he never shares with her. Rather, he fixates on the lack of African authenticity that Sana shares with her family: "Tout ça me fait penser à des histoires de toubabs! C'est pas croyable ce que les histoires africaines sont mêlées. Et puis ça suffit avec cette canaille assimilée." / This makes me think of white people's dramas. It's unbelievable that Africans could get caught up in this. And I've had enough of these assimilated lowlifes.[72] Kanaan is distressed by the interaction Africans have had with European and non-normative sexualities, but he projects his criticism outwards, as if SAINTJEANPO had never existed. When he pairs the words *canaille* and *assimilée* to describe Sana and her family, he excludes himself from the African losers who embrace European culture.

Later, in briefly telling the story of Adama, a waitress at the African restaurant frequented by him and his new friends, Kanaan presents his vision of an authentic African woman. Having come to France to find a way to support her family back home, Adama becomes the sexual slave of white men. She is forced into prostitution, but only accepts heterosexual subjugation: "Y'en a même un qui a voulu me payer pour que je fasse ça avec sa femme, là j'ai refusé sec! Il m'a battue …" / There was even one who wanted to pay me to do it with his wife. I said: 'No Way!' He beat me …[73] Though previously desperate enough to sell her body as a means of survival, Adama sees homoerotic activity as unthinkable. Not even a beating will break Adama's will as a heterosexual, though in her modesty she can only identify sexual activity with the pronoun "it". The refusal to engage in homoerotic acts and the violence which follows allow the narrative to cleanse Adama of her sexual sins. In this she shares with Kanaan the experience of an erotic violence which is ultimately redemptive. Unlike Sana, whose eroticism is gratuitous, self-destructive but which also seeks to destroy others, Adama is a victim of imperialism, poverty and of white men.

The end of Kanaan and Sana's relationship marks a definitive break with Kanaan's desire to emulate Europeans and an intensification of his Afrocentric

---

72   Ibid.,189.
73   Ibid., 197.

activism. While attending a party with African unionists from the ghetto Kanaan spies a beautiful black and Indian girl with thick, natural hair: Maïa, "une de ces symbioses qui donne ces joyaux, ces perles noires que l'homme blanc nous pique." / one of those racial mixes that produces those jewels, those pearls that white men steal from us.[74] As if he were engaging in a transference of racial guilt, Kanaan's first thought in seeing a beautiful black woman is that she might frequent white men. He quickly shifts from admiring Maïa's beauty to expressing a panic over white men as sexual rivals, all the while failing to remember his former quest to bed white women. His description of Maïa also creates a contrast between this new woman and Sana. Though she too is of mixed racial heritage, her hair, he notices, is not chemically treated. Unlike Sana, Maïa does not hide her hair under wigs in an effort to imitate white beauty. Maïa's personal history also sets her apart from Sana. Orphaned by her parents and raised by her grandmother she has lived a sheltered life in Martinique. And though she was once the object of an attempted rape by a *béké* or white land owner, she resisted and escaped her pursuer, her sexual purity intact. Maïa represents Kanaan's ideal black woman because she is what he has failed to be: impenetrable to white sexuality.

Kanaan is pleasantly surprised to find that Maïa is romantically interested in him. The two soon begin to plan a future together, but ultimately, he loses her in the nightmarish narrative of his dream. During a general strike in which the men and women of the Ballet Kotéba are dancing in the streets, bullets pierce the crowd and seem to take down Maïa and the other *niamas*, or female dancers: "Quatre hommes en cagoule [...] Ils ont eu nos niamas. Ils l'ont eue aussi Maïa. On me l'a tuée. On m'a assassiné." / Four men in balaclavas. They've killed our dancers. They got Maïa, they've killed my girl. They've murdered me.[75] The four masked attackers are ostensibly those who raped Kanaan in Fontainebleau, Jean, PoPaul, Saint Marc and an un-named, fourth perpetrator. Kanaan's vision of the violence of shooting a body parallels that of his rape, as both acts compromise bodily integrity. Though he first recognizes that it is the women of his community whom these masked men have violated, he quickly makes himself the object of their attack. This transference is a symbolic re-enactment of his rape which, like the shooting of Maïa, parallels all the injustices to which blacks have been subject, a "viol qui dure depuis deux mille ans" / a rape which has lasted for two-thousand years.[76] This scene of violence suggests that Kanaan's overarching vision places raped and castrated

---

74   Ibid., 210.
75   Ibid., 275, 276.
76   Ibid., 76.

black men as passive objects at the forefront of the history of white men violating blacks. The ensuing crisis of masculinity points to a conflation of gender
and homoerotic violence.

In "Male Rape: Offenders and Victims" Groth and Burgess note that a common motivation behind male-on-male rape is a need to affirm the heterosexuality of the rapist who ostensibly reproduces the insertor/insertee model of
male-female sex, and to confirm the homosexuality of the victim.[77] We can
compare this to a textual drive in *Chaîne* to dissociate Kanaan the character
in a dream from the "real" and heterosexual protagonist, Saïdou who in wak-
ing from his slumber can affirm his blackness and his heterosexuality in the
real world through political engagement.[78] And even Kanaan, the protagonist
of Saïdo's dream returns to heterosexuality after being raped by other men.
Although the narrative allows Kanaan to redeem himself by moving past homoerotic desire, his rape leaves both him and Saïdou fearful of penetration.
This culturally embedded black homophobia stems from a fear of violation by
white men, and this anxiety encourages both Kanaan's and Saïdou's nascent
political activism.

---

77   A.N Groth and A.W. Burgess, "Male Rape: Offenders and Victims," *American Journal of
      Psychiatry* 137.7 (July 1980): 806–810. See also Noreen Abdullah-Khan, *Male Rape: The
      Emergence of a Social and Legal Issue.* (New York: Palgrave Macmillan, 2008), 78.
78   On the subject of the rape of "homosexuals" as a result of homosexual panic, see DJ West,
      "Homophobia: Covert and Overt" in *Male Victims of Sexual Assault*, eds G.C. Mezey and
      M.B. King (Oxford: Oxford University Press, 1993), 17–34.

CHAPTER 7

Civil Servant Whores and Neocolonial Slum-Johns in Sony Labou Tansi's *Je soussigné cardiaque* and Williams Sassine's *Mémoire d'une peau*

> Dans ce monde de la galère où son pain ne dépend pas de soi, on est tou-
> jours pute d'une façon ou d'une autre.
>
> FATOU DIOME, *La Préférence Nationale*[1]

∵

For those who have made it their mission to rehabilitate public opinion of Europe's empire-building in Africa, perhaps the most frustrating aspect of postcolonial discourse lies in the propensity to blame Europeans for all the ills of the continent. The evidence is plentiful for those who argue that Europeans are implicated in the financial and political difficulties which many Africans face today: from the Berlin Conference of 1884 to the recruitment and subsequent abandonment of African soldiers by France; from the forced labor of men, women and children, to the neocolonial support of African dictatorships. But there is plenty of blame to go around, and one could argue for a discourse which acknowledges that European colonization of Africa depended, at least in some cases, on the collaboration of a pre-colonial African elite. Historian A. Adu Boahen provides evidence of how this ruling class prospered from the pre-colonial slave trade in his citation of a conversation in 1880 between a British consul and the Ashanti ruler Osei Bonsu, the latter lamenting the cessation of the trade:

> I cannot make war to catch slaves in the bush, like a thief ... But if I fight a king, and kill him when he is insolent, then certainly I must have his gold, and his slaves, and the people are mine too. Do not the white kings act like this?[2]

---

1 Fatou Diome, *La Préférence Nationale* (Paris: Présence Africaine, 2001), 103.
2 A. Adu Boahen, *African Perspectives on Colonialism.* (Baltimore: Johns Hopkins University Press, 1987, 2–3. Boahen cites Joseph Dupuis, *Journal of a Residence in Ashantee* (London: Frank Cass, 1966), 162–164.

Though Boahen reads this passage as an affirmation of the divergent views about the slave trade held by African elites and their European partners, one might argue that the words of Osei Bonsu illustrate how Africans and Europeans maintained similar attitudes towards conquest and exploitation. And while these principles were suitable to the pre-colonial elite as they sold their enemies to Europeans, they became problematic within the context of the cultural genocide that was the scramble for Africa.

Boahen contends that the colonization of Africa was only one aspect of European empire-building; a global phenomenon fueled firstly by a need for raw materials and for global markets and secondly by nationalist movements across the European continent and a desire to maintain a balance of power. He dismisses any notion that Africans sought to be subjects of civilizing missions or to be protected by European powers. Rather, he notes, far from displaying a desperate need for European intervention, black Africans living during the period following the end of the slave trade saw various developments which allowed for cultural, political and economic revolutions. In the latter part of the 19th century, black Africans experienced: greater stability as communities no longer raided their enemies in order to capture slaves; new kinds of trade in rubber, ivory and other materials which could be gathered by a greater portion of the society; a wider range of wealth within non-elite populations who were now producing commodities and participating in a mercantile economy.[3]

It is difficult to argue with Boahen's assertions that African's did not welcome European invasion and colonization. After all, why would any civilization accept an alien dominating force, especially at a time of relative economic and political stability? Rather than contesting his argument, I wish to examine the congruencies between the European subjugation and exploitation of Africans and the exploitation of Africans by the continent's own elite. Surely neither tradition is blameless, though both seem to justify their actions in a discourse of "might makes right". And yet, we tend to judge them differently, to declare the sale of one's neighbor into slavery is part of a tradition, all the while proclaiming that colonial conquest is inhuman. Have we convinced ourselves that atrocities committed by one civilization outweigh those of another? And if so, how do we negotiate this double-standard? What can we learn from a comparative study of European imperialists and African collaborators?

This chapter performs such a study, specifically within the domain of sexual commoditization and exploitation in the postcolony. In this reading of Sony Labou Tansi's *Je soussigné cardiaque* (1981) and Williams Sassine's *Mémoire d'une peau* (1998) I theorize the sexualization of corruption, collaboration and

---

3   A. Adu Boahen, *African Perspectives on Colonialism*. (Baltimore: Johns Hopkins University Press, 1987), 4–8.

neo-colonial exploitation. This study firstly observes the propensity in both texts to refer to many African women as whores and to the country itself as a brothel. While I acknowledge the presence in both texts of female characters engaged in traditional forms of sexual self-exploitation, the chapter focuses primarily on a homo-eroticized political prostitution in which the male players offer themselves up to be exploited by other men. These male protagonists, both civil servants, view their own self-exploitation with attitudes ranging from acceptance, anxiety and rejection. Additionally, the chapter examines the actions and motivations of the slumjohns of both the novel and the play, European neocolonialists who seek sexual gratification through the exploitation of the degraded.

In *Mémoire d'une peau* protagonist and narrator Milo Kan, a once orphaned African albino, becomes a killer and womanizer. Though unrepentant, Milo, an amateur novelist, yearns to write and live the perfect love story. After a life of meaningless sexual encounters and an unfulfilling marriage, Milo finds true love with Rama, an African who is ambiguously gendered and possibly intersexed or hermaphrodite, but also with her white French husband, Christian. Rama and Christian arrive in an unstable, unnamed postcolonial state as wealthy transients. The narrative, which is set within one twenty-four-hour period, recounts Milo's lovemaking with Rama and later, his homoerotic encounter with Christian. Though Rama never confirms or denies her sexual ambiguity, slips of the tongue and the narrator's confused observations tell us that her gender lies between the traditional male-female dichotomy. Christian and Rama eventually leave Milo's country and Milo learns of Christian's plans to hijack an airplane carrying African ministers. Milo reunites with his wife and returns to the normalcy of his life before his encounter with Christian and Rama.

Je soussigné cardiaque, whose absurdist title, literally translates to "I, the undersigned cardiac," is set in 1960 in the fictional country of Lebango – also the name of actual towns in Gabon and Congo Brazzaville. The play presents the struggle for dominance between Mallot Bayenda – a teacher – and Perono – a "colon espagnol," who has lived in Lebango for thirty years and who is now a citizen of the postcolonial state. When Mallot arrives for his new teaching assignment in a village controlled by Perono, the two engage in a violent but erotically-charged war of words, the result of Mallot's refusal to grovel before his wealthy and powerful rival. Perono, who is dying of heart disease, promises to persecute Mallot from beyond the grave, and urges the African to beg for forgiveness before it is too late, but the latter defies him. For the sake of avoiding the interminable transfers from town to town which Perono has promised as punishment for the teacher's insolence, Mallot visits Dr. Manissa and seeks a letter affirming that he suffers from a grave heart and lung condition. Manissa at first refuses, but then capitulates. However, the doctor's assistance cannot save the teacher from a subsequent imprisonment at the bidding of Perono. After attacking Béla Ébara, the Minister of Education who has been bribed by Perono, Mallot is sentenced to die. Before he is put to death, his fictional illness transforms into a reality as his body is ravaged by a persistent cough and ever-increasing physical tics. Even so, he prefers this fate to prostituting himself as a public servant in the postcolony.

As this analysis of *Je soussigné cardiaque* and *Mémoire d'une peau* will show, defining and theorizing prostitution can prove challenging, because multiple permutations of the act of selling sex provide us with varied points of view. Perhaps the most comprehensive definition of prostitution is the engagement in sexual activity in exchange for payment. This general definition allows consideration of agency but also of exploitation. Those who view prostitution as exploitive often compare it to rape. While this is the case for victims of trafficking, according to Julia O'Connell Davidson, the issue is more complex:

> First, prostitution differs from rape in that it is an institution which allows men to *contract* for sexual use of bodies, rather than taking those bodies by force, and social relations which are imagined and organized as (either implicit or explicit) contractual *exchanges* are sustained by and reproduce more complex forms of power than are implied by the term 'domination'. Second, the mastery clients attain within prostitution is not conferred by the performance of any particular sex act, but by the fact that they can contract for powers of sexual command over the prostitute.[4]

Davidson thus views the attraction customers experience towards prostitution as the result of an economic and class gratification, such as one might have while buying a new car or checking in at the Ritz Carlton. And as Davidson notes, likening prostitution to domination risks imposing a reductive label to the relation between the sex worker and his or her client, who both stand to gain from the interaction. Still, we may think of prostitution as contracted domination, especially in situations in which the prostitute's choices for basic survival remain limited. It seems that the domination of prostitution begins in the moment of negotiation, when the prostitute and his or her client assign monetary value to highly personal sexual acts, behaviors which erase the lines of separation and personhood between one individual and another. To assume

---

4   Julia O'Connell Davidson, *Prostitution, Power and Freedom* (Ann Arbor: University of Michigan Press, 1998), 124.

that such an erasure can be commoditized and that the price paid by the client will suffice already surrenders the body to domination.

Whether viewed as a business person, or as a victim, the prostitute is almost always imagined as female, but barely so. The prostitute often fails to fulfill the biological and social imperatives of producing offspring, having "more sex but fewer children than women in stable families."[5] She shares the designation of a non-producer with homosexuals whose sexual activity bears no fruit. In this line of thinking, the prostitute is an anti-woman and her womb a graveyard. Like all women when they are labeled as destined uniquely for childbearing, the prostitute devolves into "disembodied sexual organs"[6] and becomes something less than human. Further, she remains a non-being because her identity is either veiled or irrelevant to her customers.[7] The prostitute is adaptable; a survivor who exploits available resources in tough times. As such we can consider the agency of a prostitute who recognizes the monetary value of a sexuality divorced from the burdens of marriage, reproduction and homemaking.

The prostitute is generally motivated by profit, but the notion of profit should not be confused with that of wealth. Profit might simply mean having a modest income where there once was none as a prostitute may consider selling her body as a last resort under desperate and precarious economic circumstances. As Nils Johan Ringdal reminds us:

> Prostitution has by no means been equal at all times and in all places. It flourishes most extensively in evolutionary intermediary phases of history, during which a country or region is marked by a rapid upsurge in the population, urbanization, migration, and economic transformation. Prime examples have been the emerging Roman Empire, Western Europe in the 1800s, the Wild West of the United States, Japan in the 1700s and Southeast Asia today.[8]

To this list of eras and spaces in which prostitution has flourished one might add colonial and postcolonial black Africa. In colonial Africa, "mariages à la mode du pays," temporary couplings between European colonials and African

---

5 Nils Johan Ringdal, *Love for Sale: A World History of Prostitution.* (New York: Grove Press, 2004), 2.

6 Julia O'Connell Davidson, *Prostitution, Power and Freedom* (Ann Arbor: University of Michigan Press, 1998), 140.

7 Ibid., 134, 141.

8 Nils Johan Ringdal, *Love for Sale: A World History of Prostitution* (New York: Grove Press, 2004), 6–7.

women which often produced children, but which ended once the European returned to his country, represented for some a form of prostitution, or at the very least, of *concubinage*. But this practice allowed some women to survive and even flourish under a system which weakened their social and economic status. Additionally, colonization made possible economic relationships between European adventurers and their male porters or houseboys such as those described by André Gide in *Voyage au Congo*, which sometimes involved sexual encounters, and which might be viewed at least in part as a kind of opportunistic sexual tourism. Prostitution in postcolonial black Africa seems also to be facilitated by systems of political instability. This is evidenced in what Paulette Beat-Songue, writing on Yaounde, Cameroun, calls "semi-prostitution," in which "la prostitution n'est pas la seule activité de l'intéressé(e), ou la seule source de revenus." / prostitution is not the individual's only activity, nor is it her only source of income.[9] Further, as Beat-Songue explains, the semi-prostitute is generally more selective of her clients and might base her choices on the criteria of physical attractiveness, social class, and reputation.[10] She notes that semi-prostitution in the so-called developing world differs from prostitution in the west:

> Elle est le lot de personnes qui dans la vie courante sont engagées dans une activité autre que celle de la prostitution, et mènent de front les deux, simultanément ou à titre secondaire. Il s'agit d'étudiants, d'employées de maison, de bureau, ou encore travaillant au sein d'établissement en rapport direct avec la prostitution: les bars, dancings, hôtels.[11]

> Semi-prostitution is the lot of those who in today's [developing] world are engaged in an activity other than that of prostitution, and who either prioritize both activities equally or for whom one activity is secondary to the other. Those in question are generally students, household servants, office workers, or those working in establishments with direct links to prostitution: bars, dancehalls, hotels.

Many factors may motivate the semi-prostitute and it would be irresponsible to assume she or he always lives in abject poverty and thus practices the trade as a mode of survival. However, Beat-Songue's description suggests that

9   Paulette Beat-Songue, *Prostitution en Afrique: l'exemple de Yaoundé* (Paris: L'Harmattan, 1986), 11.
10   Ibid., 11.
11   Ibid., 15.

semi-prostitution might be prevalent in market economies in which opportunities for mainstream employment might exist but remain somewhat limited or unpredictable.

Those who consider the prostitute or semi-prostitute a victim thus point to her as subject to the whims of her exploiters as well as to socio-historic instabilities. In a reading of Orlando Patterson (1982) O'Connell Davidson argues that prostitutes can be compared to slaves because as non-beings existing in a form of social death, they lack the ability to demand respect and protection from their customers.[12] In *Decolonization and the Decolonized* (2006) Albert Memmi describes a postcolonial system of abuse which recalls the slavery-like conditions of forced labor in the colonial era but which also closely mirrors the exploitation of bodies that defines prostitution:

> In the colonies it was said, sarcastically, that the job of the sheiks, local leaders recruited from the ranks of the colonized, was to grab the goats by the horns so they could be milked more easily, goats here symbolizing the colonized. The new sheiks appointed by their government after independence serve their leaders in that same capacity.[13]

Memmi's description presents two modes of exploitation, the first performed during the colonial era by African elites who then answer to European colonizers, the second by postcolonial elites belonging to a constantly self-perpetuating ruling class. Even without taking this depiction of colonial and postcolonial domination literally, it is difficult to avoid the physical aspects of the confrontation in which the goat, like the prostitute, is allowed a nominal existence, so long as it continues to give of its body. By including the character of the colonial-era sheik in his anecdote Memmi also allows us to consider precolonial African elites who sold those they had conquered to Europeans, only to be conquered themselves. This notion of one who exploits others only to be exploited himself can be compared to the role of the postcolonial subject who collaborates, who seeks to profit from neo-colonization even though he risks also falling victim to corrupt regimes.

With this confluence of theories of prostitution and of what can be called "the colonized subject who accepts" we confront the gendered nature of both

---

12   Julia O'Connell Davidson, *Prostitution, Power and Freedom* (Ann Arbor: University of Michigan Press, 1998), 134. Orlando Patterson, *Slavery and Social Death* (Cambridge, M.A.: Harvard University Press, 1982).

13   Albert Memmi, *Decolonization and the Decolonized*, trans. Robert Bononno (Minneapolis. University of Minnesota Press, 2006), 4.

discourses. Colonized and decolonized subjects are generally portrayed as masculine, a tendency which implies that colonized women had no ability to either contest or accept colonial domination, or that their reactions to imperialism are negligible. As for prostitution, societies often assume that men cannot participate in the trade despite much evidence to the contrary. Read together, these theories create an opposition of the (female) prostitute and the (male) colonized subject. This opposition rejects any equation of sexual self-exploitation and masculinity and assumes that real men, though they might be politically and economically dominated, would never sell their bodies. The supposed impossibility of men selling themselves seems largely a question of honor. As O'Connell Davidson notes:

> There are some things which people cannot honourably sell to the highest bidder. Thus people who sell their children, their military capabilities or their friendships have traditionally been viewed as people who are willing to betray ties of community and kinship for personal gain and so as people without honour, and the prostitute is censured for attaching a monetary value to something which, like a man's capacity to bear arms in defence of his king and country, is somehow constitutive of honour.[14]

This theory suggests that there is no automatic conception of women as dishonorable, and that women are just as capable as men of achieving honor by refusing to sell what should not be commoditized. But if we admit the generally gendered conception of the prostitute, we can posit that while society believes women to be capable of achieving honor by refraining from selling themselves as sexual objects, they are generally perceived as more likely than men to prostitute themselves. It then follows that men who betray their honor through self-exploitation, be it in an explicitly sexual manner or not, are comparable to the dishonored woman who has sold her body.

Just as the role of the prostitute is gendered, so too is that of the customer. The customer is not only generally considered a male, but any male. That is, any male is potentially a customer of a prostitute because of the dominant role implied by the use of prostitutes and the manner in which that use replicates societal and economic hierarchies and heteronormative relations. It is no coincidence then that Anglophones generally refer to the customer as a "John". Because like a John Doe, he is potentially every man. Though there are various terms used in the francophone context, one typically refers to the John

---

14   Julia O'Connell Davidson, *Prostitution, Power and Freedom* (Ann Arbor: University of
        Michigan Press, 1998), 128–129.

as *le client*, underlining the economic aspect of the sex trade as well as the anonymity which money can buy. The myth of the client as singularly male is informed by the traditionally masculine ability to purchase goods and services. As a buyer, the client remains blameless in the exploitation of the prostitute because his purchase results from a mutually agreed-upon transaction, and also because some believe that prostitution potentially acts as an alternative to rape. That is, the tradition of prostitution acts as a release of social pressures, and allows men to fulfill their functions as brothers, husbands and fathers without abusing society's legitimate women.

Although the client is seen as almost universally male, his appetites are varied. This chapter focuses its analysis on what I call the "Slumjohn". I define Slumjohns as customers who seek out the most tainted of prostitutes, and for whom the major aspect of erotic pleasure issues from sexual contact with the most vulnerable members of society. Julia O'Connell Davidson seems to refer to such a customer in her description of men who seek out:

> [...] the pornographic fantasy of the 'dirty whore' to be embodied in the person of a woman whom they perceive as utterly degraded (street walkers tell of 'bag ladies' and tramps on their 'patches' who do brisk trade), or in street walkers who appear to be particularly vulnerable (visibly bruised, drug addicted or pregnant, for example.)[15]

Although one could imagine that the physical marks on the bodies of these women – dirt, bruises, puncture wounds – would excite the slumjohn who seeks to engage in the erotic domination of the prostitute, it is equally possible that his interest stems from the thrill of sex with a partner who is unclean and possibly diseased; that the slumjohn might be driven by curiosity and by a need to commune with the abject.

Whatever the motivations of slumjohns, O'Connell Davidson also notes that the desires of such clients are often racialized:

> I have interviewed procurers in South Africa, Latin America and the Caribbean who say that white American, German and British men ask them to find 'really dark, dark, black women', often specifying that women should not be successful professional girls; in one case the client even explicitly asked for a 'dirty, unwashed, poor, very black girl'.[16]

---

15   Ibid., 143.
16   Ibid., 143–144.

In these cases, the blackness of the prostitute's skin performs as a signifier in the same manner as the bag lady's physical filth or the drug user's track marks. The racial, cultural and economic implications of these client-prostitute relations re-create the colonizer-colonized power dynamic. We might thus conclude that like Albert Memmi's colonizer who accepts, these slumjohns engage in an acting-out of imperial power on the bodies of the global south. They may compensate for unexceptional access to power in their home countries by exercising white privilege in sexualized postcolonial contexts. But again, their motivation may not be to dominate, but rather to experience an erotic rush fueled by personal values that hold sex with theses racial others as taboo. The rush in this scenario would come from the risk of being found out, from the prostitute leaving a trace of herself on his body, or even from the pleasure of breaking societal rules. Or perhaps their desire is mimetic, and sex with poor black women allows them to feel that they are also poor, black and female; that they can escape the constraints and responsibilities of wealth and whiteness, until the end of their encounter when they return to their privileged lives. Whatever his inspiration, the slumjohn's brief coupling with the degraded prostitute is thus not so much sex with another individual as it is sex with a husk.

Both *Je soussignée cardiaque* and *Mémoire d'une peau* associate prostitutes with filth and engage in a discourse which labels most, if not all women in the postcolony as prostitutes. The only exception is the wife of Labou Tansi's protagonist, Mwanda, who is also the mother of his children. Her practice of these traditional forms of femininity make her exempt from being labeled a prostitute. However, the childless secretary, Hortense is portrayed as exploiting her sexuality for non-productive ends. In *Mémoire* Milo Kan refers to most women as whores, even Mireille, his wife with whom he has several children. And after Christian discovers Rama's infidelity he refers to her as "ma pute" / my whore, who is satisfied with life "Pourvu qu'elle ait son chéquier." / as long as she has her checkbook.[17] Further, both texts describe the postcolony itself as part of the mechanism of prostitution. Labou Tansi's Bayenda equates his country to a "putainerie" or a whorehouse and suggests it is the cause of all his suffering.[18] In *Mémoire*, Rama acknowledges that African women seek out white men but suggests they are motivated by the fact that African men have already sold out the continent[19] and Kan's narration displays a movement from the subject of African *coups d'états* to that of prostitution: "On parla du Bénin,

---

17   Williams Sassine, *Mémoire d'une peau* (Paris: Présence Africaine, 1998), 138.
18   Sony Labou Tansi, *Parenthèse de sang suivi de Je soussigné cardiaque* (Paris: Hatier, 1981), 83.
19   Williams Sassine, *Mémoire d'une peau* (Paris: Présence Africaine, 1998), 171.

du Nigeria, du Togo. Les avis étaient partagés, les dates confuses, les noms des auteurs contestables. Une pute me faisait de l'œil de l'autre côté, [...] du bar." / At the bar we spoke about Benin, Nigeria, and Togo. Opinions were divided, dates were confused, the names of the actors disputable. A whore was giving me the eye from across the room [...].[20] The slippage from a conversation on African politics to one about sexual self-exploitation is no accident, and the anonymity of both the prostitute and the postcolonial actors indicates the banality of endless and invariable instances of sexual and political exploitation.

Acts of prostitution in both *Je soussigné cardiaque* and *Mémoire d'une peau* present a fusion of the sexual and the political, and point to a pessimistic observation of the limited forms in which women participate in public life. Labou Tansi and Sassine develop prototypes of the postcolonial prostitute whose sexual trade is built upon the economic and political fortunes of the continent. Hortense of *Je soussigné* and Rama of *Mémoire* both seem to practice semi-prostitution. As such, neither woman sells her body in a bordello or on the street. Semi-prostitution as it is illustrated by Sony Labou Tansi and Williams Sassine reflects the constraints of postcolonial capitalist societies in which women's bodies continue to be commoditized, their increased capacity for earning capital outside the sex trade notwithstanding. But the authors go further, blurring the lines between selling sex as a prostitute and participating in those trades deemed more respectable, specifically, when such professions involve collaboration with postcolonial regimes.

Rama first meets Sassine's protagonist, Kan in a bar, where he assumes she is there to sell herself to white men. Despite her denials of prostitution, Rama does admit that her reasons for marrying Christian, her former teacher, came from a desire for financial gain: "C'est Christian qui m'a libérée. Il m'a donné sa nationalité, son nom, sa confiance, son chéquier. Je viens d'un pays de merde de l'autre côté de l'Afrique ..." / It was Christian who freed me. He gave me his nationality, his name, his trust, his checkbook. I come from a shithole on the other side of Africa ...[21] Rama also gives herself to Christian in exchange for what we might call civic capital, a chance to trade her place in the global south for French citizenship.

While Rama leaves her home to be with Christian, Labou Tansi's Hortense is content to remain in Lobango, where her work as a secretary and mistress affords her cars and villas. She first encounters Bayenda, Sony Labou Tansi's hero, in the office of a man who is both her boss and her client, and seems, initially,

---

20   Ibid., 48.
21   Ibid., 117.

to extoll the advantages of selling sex. However, she soon admits her disgust at her self-exploitation:

> Je le déteste. Mais surtout je me déteste. Je suis devenue très amère à moi-même. Oh, si vous saviez combien. Tous ces baisers puant qui vous éparpillent la peau! Tous ces gestes louches! Cette odeur de salive! Ces mouvements crasseux! Quand je sors de ses mains, je me lave fortement – je frotte, je rince, je gratte.[22]

> I hate him, but I hate myself more. I've become very bitter towards myself. If only you knew. All those stinking kisses all over your skin! All those sleazy moves! That smell of saliva! Those filthy motions! When it's over I wash myself hard. I rub, I rinse, I scratch.

Hortense's sexual encounters with her employer alienate her from herself and make her an observer of her own prostitution. She describes the sexual act as if it were happening to someone else. She even removes her boss/customer from the scene, reducing him to touches, kisses, movements and bodily fluids. She returns as a subject only in her vain attempts to purify herself.

Although Hortense mistakenly believes that Bayenda is incapable of comprehending her life as a semi-prostitute, she unknowingly describes his own experiences as a collaborator of the state, which have driven him to madness. As a teacher and government employee Bayenda finds himself at the mercy of the caprices of his superiors. Though, ultimately, he becomes a victim of the state, during his life he enjoys the benefits of acting as its representative. He owes his career as a schoolteacher to a centralized system which, like its model in nineteenth century France, guarantees governmental control of student educational and political development, and disseminates a dogma created by a dictatorship. If, in Bayenda's country, the government supports teaching children to read, it is only to assure that citizens will be able to understand and obey the laws generated by its president-for-life.

Bayenda's choice of a career in teaching seems inspired by a misguided faith in his country's system of governance, but also by a desire for greater cultural capital. After all, he describes his father as a simple "planteur d'ignames" / yam farmer, who, in order to feed his family "se mettait à genoux pour supplier les gros messieurs d'Hozana de lui acheter ses queues de persil." / got on his knees

---

22   Sony Labou Tansi, *Parenthèse de sang suivi de Je soussigné cardiaque* (Paris: Hatier, 1981), 138.

and begged those bigshots in Hozana to buy his bunches of parsley.[23] Though
Bayenda never aspired to positions of power, he viewed teaching as a manner
of both making a living and gaining the respect of his countrymen. But when
he becomes a victim of Lobango's political system Bayenda begins to see the
corrupt country as "le plus grand consommateur mondial des putains." / The
world's largest consumer of whores.[24] In the universe of *Je soussigné cardiaque*,
the whore represents the most abundant natural resource of the postcolony;
a recyclable raw material, both feeding and being fed by the same perverted
system for which it becomes an emblem.

   While Sony Labou Tansi's hero revolts against a corrupt postcolonial regime,
Milo Kan, the protagonist of *Mémoire d'une peau* provides an even more convincing example of selling out. Although his true aspiration is to write a great
novel, in his function as a state employee he monitors the press and enforces
a subtle, implicit censorship. One can imagine that his corruption of the nation's press transforms the institution into something "insipid and colorless,
poorly selective" and "reduced to a handful of repeated topics."[25] For Kan, news
articles are either good or bad based on their portrayal of the government. He
recounts what seems a typical day of contacting a newspaper editor to cite:
"[...] quelques passages des articles 'mauvais' en lui soulignant que le chef de
l'État ne voulait plus de censure mais de la clarté." / A few passages from the
"bad" articles, stressing to him that our leader no longer sought censorship,
but rather, clarity.[26] As Michel Foucault suggests in his commentary on sexual
prohibition: censorship takes the form of "affirming that such a thing is not
permitted, preventing it from being said, denying it exists."[27] As such censorship is a policing of reality, and Kan, at the bidding of the state, contributes to
maintaining a system of unreality. In his quest for 'good' articles and his rejection of 'bad' articles, he perpetuates the postcolonial regime as "the organizer
of public happiness."[28] As a censor in this state-constructed reality he keeps
in check all those who would peel away the layers of simulacrum protecting
illegitimate regimes. He then attempts to reform the offending journalists,

23   Ibid., 127.
24   Ibid., 133.
25   Albert Memmi, *Decolonization and the Decolonized*, trans. Robert Bononno (Minneapolis. University of Minnesota Press, 2006), 14.
26   Williams Sassine, *Mémoire d'une peau* (Paris: Présence Africaine, 1998), 37.
27   Michel Foucault, *The History of Sexuality Volume 1: An Introduction*, trans. Robert Hurley (New York: Vintage Books, 1990), 84.
28   Achille Mbembe, *On the Postcolony*, trans. A.M. Berrett. (Los Angeles: University of California Press, 2001), 30.

corralling independent voices and, as Dominic Thomas might say, engineering a national press.[29]

Kan's interest in working as a state censor is, no doubt, motivated by money and status. But his selling out also speaks to an attraction, present since his childhood, to the power of postcolonial dictatorships, represented in one passage of the novel by a description of Ethiopia's "Roi des Rois," Haile Selassie: "Je dormais à l'époque avec une de ses photos là où il donnait à bouffer à ses Dobermans dans des plats d'or, pendant que son peuple crevait de faim." / At the time I used to sleep with one of his pictures, the one of him feeding his Dobermans from gold plates while his people were starving to death.[30] The narrative seems to reference the Wollo famine in Ethiopia, between 1972 and 1974, which killed tens of thousands. Selassie, known for his great love of dogs, and for leading an opulent lifestyle, seemed to react to the famine "with a disregard that bordered on disdain."[31] When Kan shares his bed with the image of a dictator who, despite the dysfunction of his country, remained a revered international figure, he yearns not only to resemble Selassie physically, but also to emulate his vision of power:

> Déjà je savais que les pauvres sont des emmerdeurs, on devrait les jeter dans un trou, je rêvais d'un monde riche et clair comme ma peau. Déjà je voulais ma petite bombe pour les faire tous sauter, ces mendiants handicapés et les idiots. Je les aurais tous réunis sur une place et Boum![32]

> Even back then I knew that the poor were troublemakers; that they should just be thrown in a ditch. I would dream of a world that was richness and that was lightness like my skin. Even then I dreamt of having a little bomb to blow them to pieces, all those handicapped beggars and retards. I would have gathered them in the town square and boom!

Since as an African albino Kan must, each day navigate a society in which he is an outsider, his desire for normalcy in the postcolony implies he must turn against those who in their degraded states might remind him of his own

---

29   See the chapter "National Conferences and Media Decentralization" in Dominic Thomas, *Nation-Building, Propaganda, and Literature in Francophone Africa* (Bloomington: Indiana University Press, 2002), 160–192.

30   Williams Sassine, *Mémoire d'une peau* (Paris: Présence Africaine, 1998), 56–57.

31   Peter Woodward, *The Horn of Africa: Politics and International Relations* (New York: I.B. Tauris, 1996), 89.

32   Williams Sassine, *Mémoire d'une peau* (Paris: Présence Africaine, 1998), 56–57.

vulnerability. We can read Kan's selling out as a reaction to his revulsion vis-à-vis poverty and disability, though as an albino, he often fell into the same category as his country's most defenseless citizens. As a censor, he finds safety within the current postcolonial regime, one that chooses to employ him rather than arrest him. He is thus perfectly suited to his profession of controlling independent thought, and maintaining a dictatorial power structure which protects him from harm becomes his *raison d'être*.

Because, as public servants, both Bayenda and Kan allow themselves to be exploited, they reflect conflicted relationships with the postcolonial dictatorships under which they serve. Their doubts about selling out manifest in a sexual panic in which each man invokes a gendered discourse of prostitution which is often represented as a feminized, feminizing and dishonorable activity. But the similarities end there as Sony Labou Tansi's protagonist expresses a closer and perhaps more lucid comparison of himself to the traditional prostitute than does Sassine's hero. His meeting with Hortense justifies this comparison and strengthens his resolve to leave his job under the Ministry of Education and to "démissionner de la fonction publique des putains." / quit the public service of whores.[33] For Bayenda, honor is not a concept, but rather a physical embodiment akin to the sexual organs of a prostitute. And so, in losing his honor by serving a dictatorship, Bayenda can see no difference between himself and Hortense, as both submit to being screwed, as it were, by the powerful postcolonial and neocolonial elite.

Unlike Bayenda, Kan endeavors to draw contrasts between his professional behavior and that of the female prostitutes of the text. His tendency to label most of the women he meets as whores, even in jest, suggests an attempt to deflect the implications of his political activities and points to a crisis of gender in Kan. Unable to conceive of selling oneself as anything other than a purely female activity, Kan remains blind to his own self-exploitation, particularly as it implies participation in a political arena which is almost exclusively male and in which

> les politiciens servaient bien encore après trente ou quarante années, rhumatisants dans leurs opinions, se trompant souvent de camp, performants qu'à la troisième mi-temps, toujours copains avec le nouvel arbitre.[34]

---

33   Sony Labou Tansi, *Parenthèse de sang suivi de Je soussigné cardiaque* (Paris: Hatier, 1981), 111.

34   Williams Sassine, *Mémoire d'une peau* (Paris: Présence Africaine, 1998), 22.

politicians were still in office after thirty or forty years, entrenched in their ideas, often playing for the wrong team, sitting out until the third quarter, always friends with the new referee.

The functionaries of Kan's professional world readily sell themselves to the highest bidder, in the hopes of securing a posting which requires little of them. These are the members of the postcolonial pseudo-bourgeoisie made up of paper-pushers and intellectuals and "which turns its country virtually into a bordello for Europe."[35] Like the prostitute, their skill lies in attracting, pleasing and bending to the will of their benefactors. If Kan remains in his job as a "tailleur de papier" / a paper clipper[36] in one corrupt postcolonial regime while Mallot Bayenda refuses to continue teaching in the national school system of another, it is surely because the latter recognizes he has compromised his ability to respect himself, while the former censors the truth of his professional selling-out.

Participation in these postcolonial regimes implies engaging not only the African elite, but also Europeans with neocolonial intentions. Here too we can speak of exploitative relations and both Sony Labou Tansi and Williams Sassine liken them to the association of a prostitute and a client. Perono, the villain of *Je soussigné cardiaque* and Christian, the left-wing revolutionary of *Mémoire d'une peau* represent two distinct kinds of slumjohns, the former engaging in an explicit, racialized erotic violence, and the latter inspired by a yearning for intimacy with a postcolonial Africa which both attracts and repulses him. Salvator Perono manifests in the postcolony, the worst of what Memmi calls the "Colonizer who accepts". He fully embraces the privileges that whiteness affords in the postcolony, which he perceives as God-given. As his first name suggests, Perono believes the postcolony cannot survive without him. But as the play on words that is his family name – "pero no" / but no – indicates that this savior is maleficent, a consumer and destroyer of worlds. He takes as proof of his beliefs the Hamitic Hypothesis, which he uses to explain the neocolonial world order to his houseboy Karibou:

> "Qu'il soit l'esclave de l'esclave de ses frères." Peut-être crois-tu que ça sort de moi seulement. Eh ben, non. C'est depuis la Genèse. Ça vient tout droit de Dieu. Vous descendez de Cham. Maudits pour de bon.[37]

---

35   Frantz Fanon, *The Wretched of the Earth*, trans. Richard Philcox (New York: Grove Press, 2004), 102, 118, 119.

36   Williams Sassine, *Mémoire d'une peau* (Paris: Présence Africaine, 1998), 21.

37   Sony Labou Tansi, *Parenthèse de sang suivi de Je soussigné cardiaque* (Paris: Hatier, 1981), 91.

"A slave of slaves shall he be unto his brothers." Maybe you think that this is just coming from me. Well, not at all. It's been this way since Genesis. It comes straight from God. You're descended from Cham. Cursed for good.

Perono's religious conformation of the degradation of Africans also binds them to him in perpetuity. This bond of domination and submission be-comes eroticized when Bayenda challenges the neocolonizer's claim to power. Perono, excited by the challenge, chooses to perform a ritual of negotiation which resembles that of a client and a prostitute and during which he informs Bayenda that he will take his virginity.[38] In another attempt to humiliate the African, Perono throws a wad of bank notes on the floor and orders Bayenda: "Ramassez. Ça me ferait un gros plaisir de vous voir baisser la tête." / Pick it up. It will make me extremely happy to see you bow your head.[39] Though Perono already believes himself superior to Bayenda, he seeks the joy of a humiliation in which his interlocutor can be paid to further degrade himself and he de-lights in testing the limits of this self-exploitation. From Perono's point of view Bayenda's acceptance of cash in exchange for a display of his subservience would be a double indictment of the African. And it is indeed the pleasure found in the spectacle of domination and submission that interests Perono. This dance provides an iteration of living for the other, in which the exertion of power means nothing without a witness. Additionally, Perono enjoys the plea-sure of commanding capital, celebrating his ability to buy the physical actions of another man and in turn, to manipulate that man's identity.

When Perono fails to bend the African to his will, he warns Bayenda that he can easily destroy him by calling upon his many cronies in the postcolonial state who are paid to do his bidding:

> Là-bas, au large du Lebango, j'ai des gens. Trois ou quatre qui accepteront mes dix millions et qui te donneront l'enfer [...] Tu vas croire que tu me coûtes cher. Pas du tout. J'ai acheté du plus sale à des prix plus élevés.[40]

> I have people all over Lebango. Three or four who'll accept my ten million francs and who will make your life hell [...] Think you're costing me a lot? Not at all. I've spent even more money than this on people who were even filthier.

---

38   Ibid., 103.
39   Ibid., 100.
40   Ibid., 106.

Perono's language is one of commerce and it reveals an individual for whom everything is for sale. But beyond that, it is the purchase of filth that most moves him and for Perono, nothing is filthier than black bodies. There is a certain decadent luxury in the ability to spend one's money on that which is abject and then to transform the abject into the practical; to draw pleasure from it.

Williams Sassine presents a more complex neocolonial slumjohn in Christian, whose name, like Sony Labou Tansi's antagonist, suggests that a European God complex underpins some neocolonial activities in black Africa. Whereas Perono fulfills his desire in the eroticized humiliation of Africans as well as in the spectacle of his purchasing power, Christian arrives on the continent with dreams of saving it from itself. But his conditional love of Africa replicates the crisis of conscience of the colonizer who refuses, described by Albert Memmi as suffering from "humanitarian romanticism."[41] I take humanitarian romanticism to entail the creation of myths about the capacity of the visitor to transform countries in need, if only their inhabitants would subscribe to the hegemonic cultural and political traditions offered to them. The bedfellow of poverty porn and slum tourism, humanitarian romanticism is undergirded by an intense desire for emotional fulfilment via the acknowledgement of one's status as savior. Because its continued existence and proliferation are based on the ongoing degradation of subaltern populations, humanitarian romanticism is torn between helping and harming.

Christian's humanitarian project functions on both a micro and macro level, manifesting firstly in his travelling to Africa to teach those living in abject poverty, secondly, in rescuing Rama and thirdly in his plan to hijack an airplane full of African ministers. Intent on creating the closest possible bond with the African he encounters, Christian compares himself and Rama to Kan after the latter recounts his difficult life as an African albino: "Peut-être qu'on est des albinos. On nous montre du doigt partout où on passe ..." / Perhaps we too are albinos. Everyone points at us wherever we go.[42] Christian's comparison of his personal trials as a white European and closeted homosexual to those of an albino citizen of a postcolonial African state demonstrates a desire to slip into a subaltern identity, if only temporarily. Christian experiences slumming through erotic intimacy and imagined mimicry, first with Rama and then with Kan. He is drawn to them by the foreignness of their degradation, by a need to comprehend, to embrace and to become the epitome of the abject. But this

41   Albert Memmi, *The Colonizer and the Colonized*, trans. Howard Greenfeld (London: Earthscan Publications, 2003), 65.
42   Williams Sassine, *Mémoire d'une peau* (Paris: Présence Africaine, 1998), 148.

conveniently temporary transformation reveals Christian's hypocrisy, for no amount of going native can erase whiteness as the ultimate of privileges.

Christian's brief erotic encounter with Milo Kan allows the latter a glimpse at the underlying motivations of the Frenchman's fantasies of revolution. But their mutual homoerotic desire creates an opportunity for the African and the European to meet on an equal footing, and denies the replication of the prostitute-slumjohn paradigm that we have seen in other neocolonial relations. In a letter to Christian, Kan wonders if the Frenchman's "homophile" tendencies were not proof of a disinterest in Rama as a sexual partner and of his use of her skin color as a prop, a signifier of his "antiracism."[43] Milo Kan thus recognizes these exploitive tendencies in Christian and challenges him to reconsider his relationship with the continent:

> [...] *je n'aime pas ceux qui veulent nous 'aider'. C'est à cause d'eux que nous ne savons pas où nous en sommes. Je n'aime pas non plus ceux d'entre vous qui cherchent à limiter leur 'dégâts'. Et je n'aime surtout pas les plus aimables qui nous pondent nos héros en nous demandant de les couver.*[44]

> [...] I don't like people who want to 'help' us. It's because of them that we're all mixed-up in the first place. I also don't like those of you who are trying to limit their 'damages'. And I really don't like the nicest among you who lay our heroes like eggs and then ask us to hatch them.

For Kan, attempts by outsiders to help Africa seem motivated by a selfish need for emotional gratification. Helping Africa entails an implicit social contract in which Africans will first display the pathos of their condition in order to elicit the pity of outsiders. Pity in this context augments the desire and the pleasure of the helper. Outsiders then proceed to execute their own conception of the solution to Africa's problems, forcing it on the continent, often as a condition of economic aid. Although these solutions often aggravate already fragile situations, helpers never face these consequences. They are free to leave the continent, assured that they have contributed to its future development.

The soft power of the neocolonial slumming described in *Mémoire d'une peau* in which a desire to help is in fact a desire to control and dominate may in fact be more dangerous than the direct, unapologetic display of power that we observe in *Je soussigné cardiaque*, which portrays a neocolonizer who readily admits his hatred of Africans. In Sony Labou Tansi's play, neocolonial power

---

43   Ibid., 160.
44   Ibid., 160.

shows itself clearly, openly insists on African inferiority and demands that Africans of the postcolony prostitute themselves thus participating in their own domination. However, Williams Sassine's novel presents an insidious neo-colonialism which replicates the lies of the colonial *mission civilisatrice*; a paternalist domination whose self-serving goals are disguised as altruistic.

CHAPTER 8

The Space Between: Bisexuality, Intersexuality, Albinism and the Postcolonial State in *Mémoire d'une peau*

> – the special frisson of being somewhere between inside and out, be-
> tween hidden and revealed, partly expansive and partly enclosed. This is
> the pleasure of the socially sanctioned secret.
>
> GARGI BHATTACHARYYA, *Sexuality and Society: An Introduction*[1]

∴

The postcolonial subject does not know his place. In the imagination of the global north he represents a stubborn problem. For although he is easily recognized through the gaze of exterior observers as inhabiting the postcolonial space, he lacks what Anthony Giddens calls a "reflexivity of the self"[2] that would allow him to fully recognize his place in the postcolonial sphere. We can see him for what he is, but he, like a goldfish in a pond, remains blind to the greater socio-political context in which he exists.[3] Despite the far-reaching notion distinguishing the global north from the global south – that mythology disseminated in this modern age by world media – what we call "the postcolonial subject" does not see himself as such. One of the difficulties of the term "postcolonial" then, is its application by exterior forces. Though much ink has been spilt in the name of the postcolonial, we nonetheless fail to make this Other respond to the designation we have given him. We fail to fully convince him to declare, in a gesture of lexical colonization: "I am postcolonial;" to relinquish his right to identity formation and self-determinacy.

Another problem with the notion of the postcolonial subject and thus with that of the postcolonial state, is our tendency, even without uttering the word

---

1   Gargi Bhattacharyya, *Sexuality and Society: An Introduction* (New York: Routledge, 2002), 145.
2   Anthony Giddens, *Modernity and Self-Identity: Self and Society in the Late Modern Age* (Stanford: Stanford University Press, 1991).
3   This concept of fish in a pond, unaware of the world above them is inspired by Michio Kaku's discussion of string theory in *Physics of the Impossible* (New York: Doubleday, 2008), 234.

"postcolonial," to treat it as a monolithic geo-political signified. As such, every postcolonial or "third world" country becomes the same, distinguished from others only by a crude racial taxonomy. So, while Phil Mickelson is that golfer from the US, VJ Singh, from Fiji, is that Indian golfer. And while Charles de Gaulle was from France, Patrice Lumumba was from Africa. We benefit from the inefficiency of this over-generalized way of viewing the world firstly, because it allows us to participate in a grammar in which distinct identities are reserved for countries in the global north, secondly, because it ensures that those identified as Africans or Indians continue to learn their place in a global hierarchy, and thirdly, because it helps citizens of the global north to define what they are not. As Achille Mbembe asserts:

> [...] it is in relation to Africa that the notion of 'absolute otherness' has been taken the farthest. It is now widely acknowledged that the idea of Africa has historically served, and continues to serve, as a polemical argument for the West's desperate desire to assert its difference from the rest of the world.[4]

This idea of "absolute otherness" can be found in the work of Belinda Edmondson, who writes about the postcolonial in a Caribbean context. Edmondson considers the notion that the West Indies – a region which owes its name to an error by Christopher Columbus – has long been defined by a quality of "'somewhere elseness' ... with its attendant notion that the *space* of the West Indies is more metaphorical than material."[5] A similar belief about the African postcolony exists in our imaginations, in critical discourses and in literary fiction that describes a postcolony whose name is invented or absent, and whose precise location is often withheld; a space which, like the West Indies, lies in-between the real and the imaginary. The postcolony, located in the so-called "third world," exists upon another plane, in another dimension.

A third problem related to postcolonial discourse is its imposition of a limited temporality upon postcolonial spaces and subjects alike. A postcolony is no longer a colony, under the rule of some external force, but nonetheless continues to wait at the doors of legitimate nationhood. The postcolony is never an England or a United States, or a France, though all these countries have colonial pasts. Recounting the history of France requires acknowledging the

---

4   Achille Mbembe, *On the Postcolony*, trans. A.M. Berrett (Los Angeles: University of California Press, 2001), 2.
5   Belinda Edmondson, *Making Men: Gender, Literary Authority and Women's Writing in Caribbean Narrative* (Durham: Duke University Press, 1999), 20.

country's origin as a colony of the Holy Roman Empire. We are aware of the historical events that have shaped the nation, but to think of France in colonial terms seems unnatural. However, like Britain and the U.S., France has made the global epistemic shift from colony to country, both politically, and culturally. It controls its own existence in a continually evolving time and space, convincing outside observers of its place in the First World. Were France a fish in a pond, it would look up and return our gaze.

Unlike France the postcolony is not simply a nation "following the colonial period," but rather and evocation of the binary of the Occident and its Other, particularly with regards to perceptions of sovereignty. Thus, for example, while Australia is not considered a postcolony, the nation of Kenya is. The two nations were both part of the British Empire, Australia only severing ties with Britain in 1942, twenty-one years before Kenya declared its own independence. That, of the two, only Australia maintains Queen Elizabeth II as its monarch, does not change the notion that Australia, as the more politically and economically stable country is considered a more legitimate nation while Kenya remains a postcolony.

As the term suggests, the postcolony can never really be "post," burdened as it is by its colonial past. The stakes for those who inhabit nations that are considered less legitimate are astronomical. For if Australia is a more legitimate nation than Kenya, then it follows that Australian citizenship is more legitimate than Kenyan citizenship. This idea of legitimacy burrows like a worm to the core of the human experience and allows us to justify viewing inhabitants of the "third world" as less human than those of the "first world". Mbembe notes the perception of Africa as a postcolony stuck in time, observing representation of "the African human experience ... [as] ... incomplete, mutilated, and unfinished."[6] In this mythology created and disseminated by the global north, physical, intellectual and temporal underdevelopment are linked to a lack of humanity. These states preclude self-reflexivity, so that like fish in a pond, the African remains unaware of his post-colonial and pre-human state, unaware of his limited plane of existence and of his lack of access to more legitimate dimensions of space and time.

We can compare the deployment of the term "postcolony" to the sociopolitical choice that is labeling individuals by race, gender and sexual preference(s), an exercise which proves useful firstly because it aids in defining normative societal default positions, namely whiteness, maleness and heterosexuality and secondly, because characterizing these identities as in-between,

6   Achille Mbembe, *On the Postcolony*, trans A.M. Berrett (Los Angeles: University of California Press, 2001), 1.

incomplete states, allows us to both define and isolate them. Further, like the marking of certain geographical spaces with the term "postcolony" labels of race, gender and sexuality allow those who live outside these spaces to define what they imagine they are not.

In what follows I explore the concept of the postcolonial space, whose geo-political indeterminacy I compare to equivocal expressions of homoerotic desire in Williams Sassine's novel *Mémoire d'une peau* (1998). The novel presents singular postcolonial encounters, framed by ambiguous race, gender and sexuality and invites us to consider representations of the in-between space of the postcolony as a location of gender-bending, of ambiguous eroticism, and of uncertain racial and national identities.

Though the narrative, looking at the nation from the inside, never uses the term "postcolony," the fictional country of Milo Kan typifies what we have come to know as the postcolonial state: constantly in political flux, never recovering from its colonial past and re-creating that past in the form of corruption and violent coups d'état. Milo lives in a nation that is always becoming, but never is. The in-between space of a postcolony echoed in the textual tropes of bisexuality, intersexuality and albinism forms a foundational theme in Sassine's novel, as does the notion of self-reflexivity. The normative world visions that mark this postcolonial state as an ambiguous, in-between, unfinished space also denote and devalue the racial and sexual "deviants" within the text. To be black is to rest outside of the valued racial norm. But to be an albino, physically white but ethnically ambiguous, implies inhabiting an extra-human space. To identify or be identified as homosexual can invite the weight of societal rejection. But to be bisexual is to occupy an impossible space of desire, to reside ostensibly "*between* the categories homosexual and heterosexual."[7] Despite protestations that bisexuality "is systematically related to differences *within* the category heterosexual," a bisexual identity can indicate an exile for which heterosexuality *and* homosexuality become normative alternatives.[8] Finally, the intersexed individual is often viewed as imperfect and unfinished. Allowing the intersexed to officially exist, is to threaten the stability of the male-female binary and of the larger phallocentric project. The difficulty an intersexed individual faces arises from the societal construct of the "hermaphrodite" as "not really the combination of a whole man and a whole woman, but as of

---

7   Janet E Halley, "The Construction of Heterosexuality," in *Fear of a Queer Planet: Queer Politics and Social Theory*, ed. Michael Warner (Minneapolis: University of Minnesota Press, 1993), 83.

8   Ibid., 83.

parts of each and ... thus neither."[9] Further, as Alice Domurat Dreger notes, the "phenomenon of sex sorting," which often takes the form of biomedical interventions with a goal of establishing either a male or female, has historically been motivated by the threat that intersexuality poses to heterosexuality, and even to homosexuality. For many who find intersexuality disturbing, the assumption is "if you don't know who is male and who is female, how will you know whether what you've got is a case of heterosexuality or homosexuality?"[10] While working from Anne Fausto-Sterling's conviction that "labeling someone a man or a woman is a social decision"[11] allows for facile comparisons of the labeling of gender and those of race and desire, the intersexed merit close consideration as they upset traditional taxonomies and frustrate dominant modes of decision making. They are the exiles, the square pegs of a dialectical gender system that has no place for them.

Because for many, the intersexed, like homosexuals, bisexuals and colonized subjects, are incomplete and thus less than human, they have also long been excluded from the protection of the law. Michel Foucault observes that "For a long time hermaphrodites were criminals, or crime's offspring, since their anatomical disposition, their very being, confounded the law that distinguishes the sexes and prescribed their union."[12] Additionally, if, as Gaurav Desai suggests, "heteronormativity was a necessary accomplice to the workings of colonial authority"[13] we can imagine that the colonial project placed "sexual deviants" within the same category as the "uncivilized native" defining both intersexuality and bisexuality as residing outside of the laws of nature and the laws of men.

Discourses which exclude albinos, bisexuals and the intersexed from more normative states signal the potential of these sexually and racially exiled individuals who, by their ambiguous natures replicate Mikhail Bakhtin's notions of "the grotesque body"[14] to participate in the destabilization of the static bound-

---

9   Simone de Beauvoir, *The Second Sex*, trans. and ed. H.M. Parshley (Paris: Gallimard, 1949), xxvii.

10 Alice Domurat Dreger, *Hermaphrodites and the Medical Invention of Sex* (Cambridge: Harvard University Press, 1998), 9.

11 Anne Fausto-Sterling, *Sexing the Body: Gender Politics and the Construction of Sexuality* (New York: Basic Books, 2000), 3.

12 Michel Foucault, *The History of Sexuality Volume 1: An Introduction*, trans. Robert Hurley (New York: Vintage Books, 1990), 38.

13 Gaurav Desai, "Out in Africa," in *Post-Colonial Queer: Theoretical Intersections*, ed. John C. Hawley (Albany: State University of New York Press, 2001), 147.

14 Mikhail Bakhtin, *Rabelais and His World*, trans. Hélène Iswolsky (Bloomington: Indiana University Press, 1984), 230.

aries of heterosexuality and homosexuality, of male and female, and of black and white. In the same manner, a de-ghettoization of history which removes the postcolony from the caste of the grotesque and the untouchable, which encompasses and contextualizes the development of *all* postcolonial states and which abandons the unspoken goal of "deny[ing] African societies any historical depth"[15] might destabilize the discourse of the imagined political and societal hierarchy which supports the idea of a First and a Third World.

However, in *Mémoire d'une peau* there are no overt challenges issued to normative dominant discourses on the place of African countries within history and no explicit contestations of the barring of marginalized identities from participation in global society. Milo Kan's country is what Mbembe refers to as a *régime du simulacre*, "a hollow pretense, a regime of unreality."[16] In such a country only dissimulation, avoidance and hiding in plain sight – in short, refusals of self-reflexivity – make these neither-nor existences bearable. Characters hide not only from the eyes of others, but also from their own gaze, refusing even private ontologies. The veracity of the resultant narrative is thus always questionable as the reader becomes aware of the unreliability of the narrator's confessional.

As a black-African albino, Milo Kan is a paradox. While he presents Negroid hair and physiognomy, his albinotic skin bars him from technically being black. But he is also not considered racially white. Milo, whose name is also that of an albino grain grown in West Africa, is regarded as "colorless" in a world that values distinct racial divisions. A letter from a former female lover confirms this perception of Milo's colorlessness: "Milo, ombre de Blanc, négatif de Nègre, violeur de sentiments". / Milo, shadow of the white man, negative of the Negro, violator of emotions.[17] Milo is described as a shadow, a negative, but never a color. Though his skin is white – as if it were the negative of a photograph – Milo could never possess the social or racial capital of a white man. His albinism is likened to criminality. As an albino Milo represents a dangerous, undefined state: "C'est très dur [être albinos] au début ... Chez nous un albinos serait le croisement d'un diable et d'une femme qui se dénude sans certaines précautions. Nous servons de sacrifices dans certaines régions d'Afrique." / It's very difficult [being an albino] at first. In my country albinos are considered the offspring of the devil and of a woman who bares her body

15   Achille Mbembe, *On the Postcolony*, trans. A.M. Berrett (Los Angeles: University of California Press, 2001), 11.

16   Ibid., 108.

17   Williams Sassine, *Mémoire d'une peau* (Paris: Présence Africaine, 1998), 124.

without taking certain precautions. We are used as sacrifice in certain parts of Africa.[18] In a system that relies not only on racial binaries but also on clear divisions between the human and the nonhuman, the albino represents a precarious blurring of distinctions, a reminder of the polarized positions that he/she straddles. The belief that albinos are the result of unnatural sexual practices between the human and the nonhuman relegates them to the margins of society. Because they are marginalized, because they "lack a champion," albinos provide the perfect opportunity for the collision of "violence and the sacred."[19] As René Girard notes:

> If we look at the extremely wide spectrum of human victims sacrificed by various societies, the list seems heterogeneous, to say the least. It includes prisoners of war, slaves, small children, unmarried adolescents and the handicapped ... what we are dealing with, therefore, are exterior or marginal individuals, incapable of sharing the social bonds that link the rest of the inhabitants.[20]

To this list of social outcasts Girard could surely add albinos, who Voltaire believed were "une classe d'être intermédiaires remplissant l'intervalle entre l'homme et les animaux." / a class of intermediary beings, a missing link between man and animals.[21] For the albino, issues of humanity precede those of race. Although the black African slave who Voltaire's Candide encounters in Suriname is considered a "pauvre homme" / unfortunate man[22] the albino in Voltaire's mind is not legitimately human. This link to the sub-human which creates in the albino a perfect sacrificial lamb also makes his condition a metaphor for that of the postcolony, a space which still bears the mark of colonialist discourses "based on a very simple equation: there is hardly any difference between the native principle and the animal principle."[23]

Like the albino, the postcolony connotes a subhuman phenomenon, incapable – even after decades of independence – of establishing a lasting, civilized

18   Ibid., 133.
19   René Girard, *Violence and the Sacred*, trans. Patrick Gregory (Baltimore: Johns Hopkins University Press, 1977), 13.
20   Ibid., 12.
21   Robert Aquaron and Luc Kamdem, "Regards sur les Albinos Africains," in *L'Autre et Nous: "Scènes et Types"*, eds Pascal Blanchard, Stéphane Blanchoin, Nicolas Bancel, Gilles Boëtsch, Hubert Gerbeau (Paris: ACHAC and SYROS, 1995), 89.
22   Voltaire, *Candide* (Paris: Librairie Larousse, 1970), 78.
23   Achille Mbembe, *On the Postcolony*, trans. Steven Rendall (Los Angeles: University of California Press, 2001), 236.

peace. The postcolony is a sacrificial victim of global proportions, a marginal state whose political and historical purgatory valorizes the identities of stronger nations by showing them what they are not. The sacrifice of the postcolonial state to neocolonial powers is a major factor in guaranteeing peace among stronger nations and keeping the postcolony on the edge of the world. And yet the postcolony does not consider itself a postcolony. It knows it is no world power, but hides from this damning category behind the deployment of what Mbembe calls "fetishistic power". This mask of power that "turns the postcolonial autocrat into an object that feeds upon applause, flattery, lies."[24] is also at play in the parades and independence celebrations of postcolonial states.[25] In *Mémoire* it can be compared to Milo's use of cosmetics in an effort to look "normal": "Regarde-moi. Je me teins les cheveux en noir, j'ai des crèmes pour ma peau et j'utilise même des trucs pour mes lèvres, alors au lieu de rester ce que je suis, je ressemble de loin à un métis." / Look at me. I dye my hair black. I have skin creams and I even use stuff on my lips, so instead of remaining what I am, from far away, I look like a mulatto.[26] Milo's albinism is no secret, and yet he engages in a type of "passing," seeking to hide his color from the knowing gaze of others. In this exercise in futility he aims to remove himself from the margins of African society by inserting himself into a racial category. Though he cannot hope to look black, he is satisfied with giving the impression – at least from afar – that he is a *métis* rather than a colorless African. And even though he knows he must eventually submit to a close physical inspection by those who mistake him for bi-racial, the lie involved in "making himself up" allows him to believe, on some level, that he really is black. Indeed, as a child he would, upon seeing another albino, say: "Papa, voilà un albinos,"[27] displaying a kind of dissociative amnesia in which he ceases to recognize his own white skin and forgets the past traumas associated with his condition. These instances of non-recognition represent an upheaval of Frantz Fanon's recounting of identity formation through the gaze of the other. In *Mémoire* the subject, who engages in defining those who resemble him does so while remaining unconscious of his own physical identity.

Milo's albino identity makes him a kindred spirit for Christian and Rama, both living on the margins of society, and in in-between sexual spaces.

---

24   Achille Mbembe, *On the Postcolony*, trans. Janet Roitman and Murray Last (Los Angeles: University of California Press, 2001), 111.

25   See Lydie Moudileno, *Parades postcoloniales: la fabrication des identités dans le roman congolais* (Paris: Éditions Karthala, 2006).

26   Williams Sassine, *Mémoire d'une peau* (Paris: Présence Africaine, 1998), 146–147.

27   Ibid., 134.

Christian likens their condition to Milo's: "Peut-être qu'on est des albinos. On nous montre du doigt partout où on passe." / Perhaps we too are albinos. Everyone points at us wherever we go.[28] To be sure, interest in Christian and Rama might be due to their interracial coupling, but there is also a curious sexual dimension to each of them. Milo first notices this in Rama: "Trop plate physiquement pour moi. On dirait un garçonnet. Une pute à Blancs probablement." / Too flat-chested for me. Like a little boy. Probably a prostitute catering to whites.[29] He determines she is either a boy or a female prostitute at the service of white men. This pronouncement not only points to Milo's vision of the ambiguous desires of white men, it is also loaded with an innocent, unconscious discovery of Rama's intersexuality. Nevertheless, Milo's inner voice – his true self – soon tells him he must possess Rama: "La petite voix était là: 'Milo Kan, il te faut une femme exceptionnelle. Rama, avec cette somme de tout ce que tu n'aimes pas chez une femme, sera peut-être ton unique amour." / The little voice was there again: Milo Kan, you need an exceptional woman. Rama, even with all those qualities that turn you off in a woman, might be your one true love.[30] What Milo seems to seek in Rama is not an exceptional woman in the sense of one who is superior to all others, but rather in the sense that she deviates from the norm. He can love her, not *despite* the fact that she possesses none of the attributes he looks for in a woman, but *because* she identifies as female while resembling a young boy. What Milo experiences with Rama, might be called male homoeroticism, were it not for the ambiguous nature of the latter's sexuality. Again, intersexuality not only denotes the in-between space of sex, but also connotes desires that are difficult to define.

When they do make love, Rama mentions to Milo: "Fais doucement j'ai été opérée d'un bouton sur la raie." / Be careful, I've had an operation for a growth on my vaginal folds.[31] Though this passing comment is not enough evidence to prove that Rama is intersexed, it is common for intersexed individuals who have had procedures such as clitorectomies to have vaginal rugae (*raie*) created where there had previously been none. There are, however additional textual clues that suggest Rama is intersexed. Though Milo perceives Rama as a woman, he is confused by aspects of her anatomy: "Je voulais lui dire: 'C'est bizarre ton sexe est tout à fait en arrière,' mais elle éclata en sanglots." / I wanted to say to her: 'It's strange that your vagina is totally backwards,' but she broke

---

28   Ibid., 148.
29   Ibid., 50.
30   Ibid., 69.
31   Ibid., 113.

into tears.[32] As in this passage in which Rama begins to cry before Milo can make an observation about her genitalia, all those which refer to Rama's sex are interrupted by diversions, dissimulations and half-truths:

> Je réembobinais en vitesse tout le film de notre rencontre ...
> – Pourquoi t'a-t-on coupé dans le sexe? lui demandai-je. Pas de petites lèvres. Clitoris inexistant ... On pratique encore cette barbarie dans ton pays?
> – On ne m'a rien enlevé. Tu n'as pas fait attention. Tu as été si vite, si fort! Je reboutonnais ma chemise. Elle me ferma ma braguette.[33]

> I quickly replayed the film of out tryst ...
> – Why did they cut your vagina? I asked her. No labia. No clitoris at all ... Do they still have that barbaric practice in your country?
> – No one took anything from me. You weren't paying attention. You were so fast, so strong!
> I was buttoning up my shirt. She zipped up my pants.

Rama denies she has undergone female excision, but insists that nothing has been taken from her body. If we chose to believe both Milo's observations and Rama's affirmations, then the latter is an intersexed individual, who, though representing herself as a woman, does not possess all the physical determinants of a female. As such their erotic encounter might more properly be defined as bisexual. But like Milo's ethnicity, lovemaking with Rama escapes categorization, in part, because Rama diverts the conversation by describing Milo's sexual performance and closes the subject when she zips up his pants. We, like Milo are left replaying and re-reading the scenes of their lovemaking in an attempt to find some definitive clue about Rama's sex.

The presence of a child, Awa, in Rama and Christian's home does nothing to concretely determine Rama's sex. Rather, the child's origins are shrouded in half-truths. Christian is the first to announce to Milo that he and Rama "avons une petite fille" / have a little girl.[34] The child's identity becomes vague when Rama mentions casually "ma petite sœur [est] avec nous." / my little sister is with us.[35] Though we might deduce from this last statement that Rama is not the child's biological mother and that she in fact, has no children at all, the

---

32   Ibid., 105–106.
33   Ibid., 117–118.
34   Ibid., 51.
35   Ibid., 117.

narrative does not offer any definitive clues of familial relation. A physical description might be instrumental for inferring that the child was a product of Rama and Christian's bi-racial coupling. But even in meeting the child, Milo omits this detail.

Rather than clearly defining Rama's reproductive status, the narrative obsessively presents the notion of Rama as a bearer of children, all the while suggesting that she has not had and cannot have a child: "Et quand je découvris son bas ventre tout plat mais couvert de vergetures, je calculai le poids d'imagination pour oublier ces coups de griffure de l'enfantement." / And when I uncovered her stomach, completely flat but covered with stretch marks, I calculated how much imagination it would take to forget theses scars of childbirth.[36] Milo assumes that Rama's stretch marks are from child-bearing, but the imagination he requires is perhaps not for the purpose of forgetting these scars, but in order to believe that the woman he desires – "sans fesses, sans nichons" /flat-bottomed, flat-chested – is capable of having a child.[37] For although inter-sexuality takes on various forms, and though it is theoretically possible for some intersexed individuals to have children, sterility is common.[38] Christian too, plays along with the lie of Rama as child bearer, even in broaching the subject of her disturbing genitalia with Milo:

– Je ne comprends rien. Comment as-tu trouvé son sexe?

....

– Comme toutes les femmes sans beaucoup de fesses, elle est bien ouverte. Il paraît que quand tu l'as déflorée, elle n'a pas senti grand-chose, comme à son accouchement d'ailleurs

– Tu m'emmerdes.[39]

I don't understand. What did you think about her vagina?

....

– It was the same as with all flat-bottomed women. She was pretty wide open. Apparently, when you deflowered her, she didn't feel much, just like when she was giving birth, by the way.

– You're so annoying.

---

36   Ibid., 92.

37   Ibid., 55.

38   Anne Fausto-Sterling, *Sexing the Body: Gender Politics and the Construction of Sexuality* (New York: Basic Books, 2000), 51–52.

39   Williams Sassine, *Mémoire d'une peau* (Paris: Présence Africaine, 1998), 142.

Milo responds to Christian's un-ease vis-à-vis Rama's genitalia by diverting the conversation. Rather than questioning Rama's sexuality, Milo challenges Christian's virility. But how are we to take Milo's assumption that Rama felt nothing while giving birth when he has already revealed his knowledge of the young child's origins, if not as a cynical recognition of Rama's inability to have a child? And why is the notion of Rama as child bearer so important to all three? We might say that believing Rama can have children, guarantees her femininity as well as the heterosexual quality of the love each man has for her. Like Milo's mulatto make-up, Rama's euphemistic mask of pregnancy is a quest for "normalcy" in which all three are implicated, but which does not survive close, outside scrutiny.

Just as Milo goes to great lengths to perform race, Rama performs the feminine. In Rama's absence, Christian slips into her role. After having pinned him to an armoire in an amorous position, Milo admires Christian's simulation of Rama: "Tu as bien imité tout à l'heure. C'était ta femme. Il suffisait de fermer un peu les yeux. – Quand je le veux je peux être une femme, Milo." / You imitated her very well just now. It was exactly like your wife. One just had to close one's eyes a little. – When I want to I can be a woman, Milo.[40] Christian's belief that being a woman is a choice, echoes the ambivalence of Rama's self-representation as a woman and underlines Judith Butler's argument of gender as drag; "a performance that *produces* the illusion of an inner sex or essence or psychic gender core."[41] The dissimulations produced by each character in conjunction with the testimony of an unreliable narrator result in an overarching theme of illusion in *Mémoire*. And though facts are presented in the narrative, singular truths, like singular races and sexualities are elusive. Suitably, Milo discovers his love for both Christian and Rama, who, as performers of gender, become interchangeable for him. All this adventure requires is self-deception and the creation of illusion.

Both men must close their eyes in order to attain what they both ultimately desire: each other. Rama serves as a vehicle for this desire. When Milo first meets Rama, he finds her uninteresting. Only after a European man sits next to her does he begin to desire Rama. But this desire is not exclusive. His little voice urges: "Milo, tu dois les prendre." / Milo, you must take them, the "les" being both Rama and Christian.[42] Thus, when Milo makes love to Rama, Christian is metaphysically present. The final section of the narrative breaks

40   Ibid., 138.
41   Judith Butler, *Bodies that Matter: On the Discursive Limits of "Sex"* (New York: Routledge, 1993), 317.
42   Williams Sassine, *Mémoire d'une peau* (Paris: Présence Africaine, 1998), 56.

down the triangle. By physically removing Rama from their presence the narrative throws Milo and Christian together in a power outrage caused by a storm:

> – Je viens de coucher avec elle, lui dis-je. Il s'est tu. Je me suis encore rap-
> proché de lui. – Tu sais que j'ai peur du tonnerre? fit-il simplement. J'avais
> un bras sur son épaule. Il sentait le parfum, le corps de Rama. J'attirai sa
> tête et l'embrassai comme on embrasse une femme interdite, fragile. Il
> s'abandonna ... – Il faut que je parte, Milo. Je suis saoule et je me sens
> fatigué d'un coup.
>
> Je le retins encore un peu en le caressant. Je me découvrais des en-
> vies de voyage, des amours de l'inconnu, de virginité, de conquête d'un
> autre monde. – Tu embrasses mieux que ta femme. Et je lui donnai des
> détails qui l'aidèrent à s'abandonner pour lui ressembler. – Milo, je t'en
> prie, laisses-moi partir. Il se leva, se réajusta pour redevenir 'monsieur
> Christian'.[43]

> – I just slept with her, I told him. He fell silent. I moved closer to him. –
> Did you know, I was afraid of thunder? he said. I had my arm around
> his shoulders. He smelled of Rama, of her perfume. I brought his head
> towards me and kissed him as one kisses a forbidden, fragile woman. He
> gave in ... – I have to go, Milo. I'm drunk and suddenly I feel tired.
>
> I held him close for a moment, caressing him, discovering within my-
> self a desire for voyages, a love of the unknown, of virginity, of the con-
> quest of another world. – You kiss better than your wife. And I gave him
> details that would help him let go so that he might be more like her. –
> Milo, please let me go. He got up and readjusted himself in order to once
> again become 'Mr. Christian'.

Milo's announcement of his tryst with Rama transports Christian to the scene
of their love-making. What follows is a transformation of Christian, which each
man perceives is a feminization and which allows them to imagine their subsequent kiss is heterosexual. In this moment in which homoeroticism hides in
plain sight, Christian becomes an innocent female virgin while Milo indulges
in a colonial fantasy of sexual conquest. What Milo as narrator recounts next
is an example of Sassine's innovative use of language to suggest the ambiguity of the narrative in *Mémoire*. Telling Christian the details of his lovemaking
with Rama is meant to help Christian "s'abandonner," but this too complicates
the meaning of the passage. Certainly, *s'abandonner* has an erotic connotation,

43   Ibid., 122–123.

often used to denote a woman who has given herself over to desire. It could also signify letting oneself go, relaxing. But one might interpret it as Milo's wish that Christian literally abandon his masculine identity by relinquishing his inhibitions; that he become more like Rama. But because readjusting himself suggests an unnatural capitualtion to normative visions of the world, Christian essentially straightens himself out. And because leaving Milo's side allows Christian to become a *monsieur* again, we can assume that – at least in Milo's imagination – Christian's sexual contact with him meant the feminization of the latter.

This feminization of Christian allows him to take the place of Rama, who, from the time of Milo and Christian's kiss to the end of the narrative, is almost always physically absent. Having locked herself in her room after discovering that Milo has betrayed her confidence, she leaves the two men alone in the salon of the home she shares with Christian, allowing the men to once again express their desire for one another. And yet, in the midst of their homosocial and homoerotic bonding, Rama is often the subject of an exchange that displays the erotic potential of language in Sassine's novel:

> Le festin ne venait que de commencer. Le corps de Rama, sa vie, ses petits secrets devaient être mis au nu, dépecés, et nous savions que chaque mot nous aiderait à la dépecer davantage, chaque verre à la dépouiller, les silences à se la partager. Elle nous avait appartenue.[44]

> The feast had only just begun. Rama's body, her life, her little secrets had to be stripped bare, dismembered, and we knew that each word would help us to cut her up even more, each glass of wine to skin her, the silences to split her between the two of us. She had belonged to us.

If we read *festin* here as a gastronomic event of extreme *jouissance*, we can imagine that Rama's naked body serves as a main course. The verbs *dépecer* and *dépouiller* support such an interpretation and emphasize the animalization of Rama in Milo's narrative. This *festin*, in which socially-mediated "ho(m)mosexuality" displaces genital homosexuality,[45] represents the symbolic meeting of two hunters who share a common imaginary quarry. The temporal construction of the scene points to Milo and Christian's use of fantasy to attain *jouissance*. There are three verbs tenses used here to describe the *festin*:

---

44   Ibid., 131.

45   Luce Irigaray, *This Sex Which is Not One*, trans. Catherine Porter (Ithaca: Cornell University Press, 1985), 117.

the *imparfait*, the *conditionnel* and the *plus-que-parfait*. While the first two relate what is actually happening to an "already dead" Rama and what they imagine will happen to her body, the *plus-que-parfait* foregrounds the scene and allows us to imagine Rama still alive, as she is split in two by her lovers. This is a crucial point in reading the triangular homoerotic desire that brings these men together. We must also consider the use of "nous" or "us" in this phrase. The eroticism of possessing Rama is deepened by the fact that Milo and Christian have shared her. The sexual arousal of each man results from images of Rama's body as it relates to that of the other, to the other's penis and semen.[46]

The *festin* in which they partake can also be read as recreating a wedding feast: the passing of a female between her father and her husband, a celebration whose culmination occurs at the moment in her passage from one male to another, when she is equidistantly between them. As in the wedding ceremony the *festin* does not formalize a bond "between men and women, but between men and men by means of women, who are merely the occasion of this relationship."[47]

Rama's physical absence from the *festin*, the fact that she can only be present in the imaginations of men who desire to rip her apart and share her, and that she lacks the ability to look back at her ravishers, make the power of the erotic inaccessible to her. The "twin mechanisms of fetishism and voyeurism"[48] at play during the *festin* rely, firstly, in the fetishistic mode, on "the physical beauty if the object transforming it into something satisfying in itself,"[49] and then, on voyeurism, which "has a sadistic side, and is involved with pleasure through control or domination, and with punishing the woman."[50] This scene exemplifies the larger role of sadism in *Mémoire* where sexual pleasure is linked not only to a giving over of oneself to different desires, but also to submitting to pain and domination. Milo knows he desires a composite Christian-Rama

---

46   For more on homoerotic elements in multiple-partner relationships see Julia O'Connell Davidson, *Prostitution, Power and Freedom* (Ann Arbor: University of Michigan Press, 1998), 141.

47   Claude Lévi-Strauss, *The Elementary Structures of Kinship*, ed. Rodney Needham, trans. James Harle Bell, John Richard von Sturmer, and Rodney Needham (Boston: Beacon Press, 1969),16.

48   Ann E. Kaplan, "Is the Gaze Male?" in *Powers of Desire: The Politics of Sexuality*, eds Ann Snitow, Christine Stansell and Sharon Thompson (New York: Monthly Press Review, 1983), 312.

49   Laura Mulvey, "Visual Pleasure and Narrative Cinema" *Screen* 16. 3 (Autumn 1975): 14.

50   Ann E. Kaplan, "Is the Gaze Male?" in *Powers of Desire: The Politics of Sexuality*, eds Ann Snitow, Christine Stansell and Sharon Thompson (New York: Monthly Press Review, 1983), 312.

because he yearns to dominate both of them. His sadomasochistic affair with Rama pleases not only Milo, but also, Christian, his new mistress, who is both aroused and wounded by Milo's account of his and Rama's lovemaking.

Despite the erotic *jouissance* Milo and Christian experience during their *festin*, we can describe the role that is forced upon Rama as one of a conjured object of pornography, itself a "direct denial of the power of the erotic" and representing "the suppression of true feeling."[51] The erotic is also absent in the "relation" between each man and the image he creates of Rama because there is no mutual participation of desiring (feeling) subjects. Perhaps we can also conclude that the homosocial bonding that Christian and Milo experience with each other during their *festin* is more akin to the pornographic than it is to the erotic because their ritual represents a suppression of the true feelings of desire between them. That is, they position Rama between themselves and, in so doing, mask their desire for one another.

Milo and Christian's sadistic *festin* is an expression of the pleasures of homosocial company in which, Rama – still the focus of their conversation – is only a bridge connecting the two men, a unit of exchange flowing between them, which allows them to enjoy moments of sensuality in each other's presence while fantasizing the infliction of pain. And as partners of exchange, Christian and Milo are endowed with a "quasi-mystical power of social linkage."[52] Their vision of Rama allows the two to become one, thus the repetition of *nous* / we – and the absence of *je* / I and *il* / he in this passage. Later, Milo tells Christian: "Notre femme a ma montre." / Our woman (wife) has my watch[53] and likens himself and Christian to "des frères siamois" / Siamese twins.[54] This further comparison to bodies lying outside normative categories also refers to the Maninke tradition of Haute-Guinea in which albinos and intersexed individuals are considered twin beings, linked to the god Faro, an albino and hermaphrodite who gave birth to the first set of twins through self-impregnation.[55] This homoerotic coupling and fusion of Milo and Christian produces yet another

---

51   Audra Lorde, "Uses of the Erotic: The Erotic as Power," in *Black Feminist Cultural Criticism*, ed. Jacqueline Bobo (Malden, MA: Blackwell Publishers, 2001), 286.

52   Gayle S. Rubin, "The Traffic in Women: Notes on the Political Economy of Sex," in *Toward an Anthropology of Women*, ed. Rayna Reiter (New York: Monthly Review Press, 1975), 93.

53   Sassine, Williams, *Mémoire d'une peau* (Paris: Présence Africaine, 1998), 142.

54   Ibid., 143.

55   G.H. Imperato, and P.J. Imperato, "Beliefs and Practices Concerning Twins, Hermaphrodites and Albinos Among the Bamana and Maninka of Mali," Department of Preventive Medicine and Community Health, State University of New York, accessed May 1, 2016, http://www.ncbi.nlm.nih.gov/pubmed/16830507?itool=EntrezSystem2.PEntrez.Pubmed. Pubmed_ResultsPanel.Pubmed_RVDocSum&ordinalpos=5.

in-between identity, a hybrid individual who cannot be defined by markers of race or nationality.

Although the two men eclipse Rama, she remains a necessary element in their homoerotic relation. As the female in the group she helps, even in her absence, to justify the recounting of sexually explicit acts between men. And though she is initially the subject of conversation, she soon becomes the object of imitation:

> [Christian:] combien tu donnes à Rama en amour ?
> Je balançai une main de gauche à droite avec une moue.
> – ... Elle adore se faire prendre par derrière.
> Il se leva et dans le salon s'appuya contre le haut buffet.
> – Les jambes en retrait, bien écartées et les reins creusés.
> Il m'obéissait au fur et à mesure. Sa posture devenait délicieusement éro-tique et pleine d'attente. Je revoyais sa femme. Je bandais à nouveau. Et soudain ce fut la catastrophe. Le buffet commença à vaciller sous son poids et finit par tomber dans un bruit épouvantable. Pendant qu'il se relevait, le gardien accourut. Le chien aboya.[56]

> [Christian:] how would you rate Rama in bed.
> I moved my flat hand from side to side, pouting.
> – ... She loves to be taken from behind.
> He got up and leaned on the breakfront in the living room.
> – Her legs set back, nice and wide, her back arched.
> He obeyed me with each detail. His stance became deliciously erotic and inviting. I could see his wife in him. I got hard again. And then suddenly all hell broke loose. The breakfront began to sway under his weight and finally toppled over with a crashing noise. While he was getting back on his feet, the security guard came running. The dog began barking.

Milo's ability to see Rama in Christian again throws into doubt the genders of the husband and wife as well as Milo's sexuality. If a feminized Christian resembles his wife is it because of his feminine qualities or because of her mas-culinity? And if neither Christian nor Rama can be assigned a fixed gender, are Milo's relations with them not bisexual? As for Christian, his initiation of a conversation about sex requires that he first make Rama the subject of scrutiny before moving to his real concern: Milo's sexuality. Though Rama is his wife, it seems he can only discover her sexually through Milo's eyes. And the goal of

---

56   Williams Sassine, *Mémoire d'une peau* (Paris: Présence Africaine, 1998), 137–138.

his inquiry is not to renew his intimacy with Rama, but rather to better imitate her so that he might take her place as Milo's partner. In doing so, Christian becomes a submissive ready to obey Milo's orders. In this postcolonial inversion of the master-slave dichotomy, the imperial guilt which Christian bears seems to feed his erotic impulses and his desire to be possessed by Milo.

Like his attraction to Rama, Milo's desire of Christian is mixed with a yearning to inflict pain upon the other. Milo as narrator describes their first meeting and recounts: "Je voulais déjà te faire mal, Christian." / I already wanted to hurt you, Christian.[57] Milo's sadistic attraction to Christian may be read through the Hegelian lens as inspired by his need as a marginal member of society to be recognized by another, to become the lord to Christian-as-bondsman.[58] Christian, as a white European male and a signifier of power, proves a perfect target for Milo's aggression, because of the social capital he possesses. To be recognized by Christian would allow Milo to transcend the societal barriers erected before him as a result of his albinism, his bisexuality and his position as a postcolonial subject. Milo insures that Christian will recognize his existence through the deployment of erotic power and cruelty. His recounting of his sexual relations with Christian's wife suggests Milo's potency, but also exposes his dependency on Christian to validate his existence. As Jessica Benjamin explains, "Violence is a way of ... establishing one's own autonomy and negating the other person's. It is a way of repudiating dependency while attempting to avoid the consequent feeling of aloneness."[59] So while Milo's recognition of Rama and Christian as fellow "albinos" suggests his desire for fellow outcasts, the pain he wishes to cause them is underpinned by his need for supremacy over others. And though we are trained by the discourse born of colonial domination to envision the African man as the victim of the European's quest for recognition and power, in *Mémoire* it is Christian, the post-imperial European, who becomes the tool of an imperious African. He allows Milo to master him and fully takes on what he perceives is the persona of the dominated subject by becoming a woman.

Milo readily accepts Christian's transformation into Rama, making his sexual excitement acceptably heterosexual. But again, Milo's narrative conveniently interrupts this possible moment of truth when the two might have faced each other without the veil of heteronormativity. The sudden fall of the breakfront,

---

57   Ibid., 53.
58   G.W.F. Hegel, *The Phenomenology of Mind*, trans. J.B. Baillie (New York: The Macmillan Company, 1931), 236.
59   Jessica Benjamin, "Master and Slave: The Fantasy of Erotic Domination" in *Powers of Desire: The Politics of Sexuality*, eds Ann Snitow, Christine Stansell and Sharon Thompson (New York: Monthly Press Review, 1983), 285.

the noise this creates, the arriving watchman and the barking dog all function as distractions, not only for Christian and Milo, but also for the reader of
Milo's narrative. One sees in these all-too-coincidental occurrences a possible
attempt on the part of Milo the narrator to deceive, so that the reader will
never be privy to the true relation between Milo the protagonist and Christian.
Indeed, the novel ends after their brief homoerotic encounter and any possible
continuation of the affair is precluded by Christian's terrorist acts. The resolu-
tion of the narrative restores heteronormativity to Milo's world. Christian and
Rama, who threaten Milo's persona as a heterosexual, are removed from the
postcolonial stage and Milo re-unites with his wife.

The end of the novel and Milo's return to heterosexuality take place on the
morning after his affair(s) with Christian and Rama. In the light of day Milo ostensibly becomes a heterosexual again, but to the reader the dawn of this new
day exposes his ambivalence towards homoeroticism and bisexuality. While,
on the previous night, Christian openly admits his bisexuality, this subject is
the only one in the narrative that frightens Milo:

> – on a déjà été un peu trop loin, Christian. C'est vrai, j'ai peur. Peur de
> franchir la limite.
> – Ne me raconte pas que tu n'as jamais essayé.
> – Quand j'étais élève. Des attouchements. On se comparait la grosseur, la
> longueur ...
> – Est-ce que tu dis tout à ta femme?
> – Oui et non. Chaque fois que je la trompe, quoique je n'aime pas le mot
> tromper. Disons que je ne la trompe pas puisque je ne lui cache pas me
> coucheries, mais je ne dévoile pas l'identité des personnes ...[60]

> – We've already gone a bit too far, Christian. It's true, I am afraid. Afraid
> of crossing the line.
> – Don't tell me you've never tried it.
> – In my student days. Some touching. We would see who was bigger,
> longer ...
> – Do you tell your wife everything?
> – Yes and no. Each time I cheat on her, even though I don't think of it as
> cheating, *per se.* Let's just say that I don't really cheat on her because I
> hide noting from her, even my affairs, except I don't reveal the identities
> of the people.

60   Williams Sassine, *Mémoire d'une peau* (Paris: Présence Africaine, 1998), 138–139.

Although Milo freely recounts his heterosexual adventure with Rama, and fearlessly embraces Christian-as-Rama, he is ill at ease while providing concrete details about his relationship to bisexuality, as if the creation of a discourse around this particular yearning would force him to confront the reality of his desires. He can close his eyes and engage in a veiled homoeroticism in which his male partner performs the feminine, but he can never accept the sight of himself as a bisexual, that is, as one who knowingly and openly desires both genders. As with his albinism, Milo chooses to cover up his true self in hopes of achieving normalcy in his own eyes and in the eyes of others. His tactic in speaking of his homoerotic tendencies is the use of vagueness and half-truths. He admits that he fears crossing boundaries, but never says what those boundaries are. Christian is equally elusive, perhaps in recognition of Milo's reticence. His first question to Milo conveniently has no named object, so that one cannot say precisely what it is Milo has tried. Milo does admit to touching the genitalia of his male schoolmates, but quickly justifies his homoerotic activity by claiming an amateur interest in phalloplethysmography, the measurement of genitals during arousal. Such a competitive activity can easily masquerade homoeroticism by espousing the machismo of hyper-masculinity, and can be normalized by the allusion to a scientifically provable outcome. And while Milo does tell his wife whenever he has cheated on her, the fact that he never reveals the identity the *people* involved might be Milo's indirect manner of admitting to regular homoerotic encounters. The neutrality of this conversation and the minimizing of his schoolboy activities allow Milo to dissimulate his sexual tendencies. This permits a self-representation that bows to the normative structures of the society he inhabits.

Dissimulation, or "passing" is thematically linked to other individuals in *Mémoire* outside of the Milo-Rama-Christian triangle. Sadou, the deaf-mute who works as Milo's houseboy pretends to listen to the radio, in order to "ressembler aux autres" / look like others.[61] Hadja, the respected, pious Muslim who becomes the mistress of the young Milo behind closed doors, is also the former mistress of Milo's deceased father, Charles. Milo always refers to his father as "Monsieur Charles," naming him between quotation marks, as if his father, like "Monsieur Christian" were in some way an imposter who must constantly be re-created through the speech act. And though Milo affectionately remembers "Monsieur Charles" as a lover of many women, he also discovers, at the beginning of the narrative, that "Monsieur Charles" was sterile. The quotations around his father's name seem to assert Milo's newfound

---

61   Ibid., 152.

consciousness of the persona his adoptive father maintained in order to portray a virility which he did not possess. The quotations suggest that both "Monsieur," denoting masculinity and "Charles," which signifies "virile man"   ᵿ belie the reality of his father's condition, but, like his womanizing, allowed him to appear to be something he was not.

Sterility masquerading as fecundity defines "Monsieur Charles" and possibly Rama, whose status as mother is doubtful, but also applies to Milo as a citizen of a postcolonial state. Milo earns his living clipping, reading and sorting periodical articles in which the current government is mentioned and then lobbying the directors of national journals for positive press. As the manager of his department within a "régime qui hurlait la mort" / regime that screamed death[62] he creates memorandums that he knows no one will read. An aspiring author, he describes the texts he writes while at his government job as offspring: "Je voulais devenir écrivain comme on veut devenir papa. Mais je sentais que je n'avais pas assez de couilles pour fabriquer un enfant." / I wanted to become a writer in the manner that one wishes to become a father. But I suspected that I didn't have the balls to produce a child.[63] Though he has an urge to create, Milo's deficient masculinity is implicated in the production of "des romans avortés, des poèmes plagiés, des contes inachevés" / aborted novels, plagiarized poems, unfinished stories, texts that like the postcolonial space, are never realized.[64] If he continually asks his secretary to retype these confirmations of a failure to create, it is, in part, as an act of false mastery, accomplished through surrogacy and meant to maintain the appearance of productivity within a sterile environment.

As his symbolic children, Milo's novels are abandoned, unfinished, inauthentic works. In this they imitate their albino creator, an African who has no pigmentation and is thus both racially "unfinished" and inauthentic, and who was also abandoned as a child. But they also echo the traditional European myth of Africans as "inachevé" / incomplete, unfinished and as "hommes en devenir" / developing men, read: on their way towards becoming men.[65] As such, another possible reason for Milo's continued attempts at writing is the promise of an authentic creation, one that surpasses the mediocrity of his past attempts at literary production. Here literary production, like race, gender and

---

62   Ibid., 162.
63   Ibid., 39.
64   Ibid., 37.
65   Philippe Dewitte, "Le 'Noir' dans l'imaginaire français," in *L'Autre et Nous "Scènes et Types"*, eds Pascal Blanchard, Stéphane Blanchoin, Nicolas Bancel, Gilles Boëtsch, Hubert Gerbeau (Paris: ACHAC and SYROS, 1995), 28.

sexuality, becomes a metaphor for the postcolony's struggle for authenticity under postcolonial regimes that are built upon death.

Milo accepts the environment of his country as "une forme de démocratie" / a form of democracy[66] but his "petite voix" compares the condition of this postcolony and of other African postcolonies to that of the unproductive characters of *Mémoire*: "Beaucoup d'Africains ne rêvent plus [...] L'Éthiopie est devenue un pays d'albinos, l'Afrique ne serait-elle un paradis qu'à condition qu'il n'y ait pas d'Africains?" / Many Africans no longer dream [...] Ethiopia has become a land of albinos; can Africa only become a paradise if there are no longer any Africans there?[67] Dreaming here does not only suggest the psychological act of seeing a different reality, but also implies self- reflexivity: the act of truly seeing oneself, which allows one to desire and to strive for other planes of existence. Dreaming here is a projection of the self into possible futures. It is creative; an act of autogamous procreation, which would allow Africans a place among the "productive" peoples of the world. Its implications are spatial and temporal because dreams exist outside of space and time and are thus subject to neither. But Milo's internal voice complains that Africans, like fish in a pond, cannot see past their immediate realities, cannot return the gaze that defines them as less than human. Like Milo, they are continually frozen in a postcolonial present in which every day is the same. If in the protagonist's deepest vision of the postcolony, Africans – represented synecdochically by Ethiopians – are the albinos of the world, then we can imagine that Milo sees all Africans as he sees himself and as he sees the intersexed Rama and the bisexual Christian: as unproductive outcasts within a larger global society, tortured by their inability to be "normal" and attempting to "make themselves up" so as not to appear out of place.

The erotics of *Mémoire d'une peau* occupy a space between violence and what Milo Kan calls love. Though he remembers a time not long before meeting Rama and Christian when "L'amour autant que la mauvaise conscience [lui] était inconnus." / Both love and guilt were unknown to him[68] meeting the husband-and-wife pair seems to answer Milo's dream of finding true love: "J'ai vraiment envie d'écrire une histoire d'amour." / I have such a yearning to write a love story.[69] Milo's desire to write about love is really a desire to encounter love. The emotions he experiences during his bisexual affairs with

66   Williams Sassine, *Mémoire d'une peau* (Paris: Présence Africaine, 1998), 37.
67   Ibid., 177.
68   Ibid., 59.
69   Ibid., 18.

Rama and Christian lay in a space between the destructive desire to dominate another and the possibly productive longing to give oneself to another. And though, when Rama and Christian leave, Milo again finds himself without true love, Williams Sassine's narrative acknowledges the possibility of a productive postcolonial eroticism.

CHAPTER 9

Must *la victime* Be Feminine? Postcolonial Violence, Gender Ambiguity, and Homoerotic Desire in Sony Labou Tansi's *Je soussigné cardiaque*

Est-ce mon époque ou mon espace qui me tue?

V.Y. MUDIMBE, *Entre Les Eaux*[1]

∴

The scholarship which has, in recent decades, sought to create a dialogue be-tween Queer Studies and postcolonial African literatures, has produced read-ings of homoeroticism and gender-bending in African contexts by critics such as Chris Dunton (1989), Guarav Desai (2001), and Chantal Zabus (2009, 2013). The compelling nature of this critical work results, in part, from its contesta-tion of the still unyielding taboo of imagining a queer Africa. Though several African literary texts can be read for homoeroticism and gender-bending, most of the continent's authors do not dare to speak explicitly of queerness. And yet, queerness is a crucial aspect of African postcolonial literature, firstly, because so much of the African cosmologies which inform these texts depends on gen-der-bending and intersexuality, and secondly, because in these texts, stepping outside of established sexual and gender norms is concomitant with political movement, be it that of the revolutionary or of the tyrant.

This chapter seeks to explore the potential of queerness, specifically ho-moeroticism as well as slippages between masculine and feminine personas, as a driving force within African postcolonial literature through a reading of Congolese author Sony Labou Tansi's 1981 play *Je soussigné cardiaque*. This study joins an on-going discussion of violence and power in the works of Labou Tansi, initiated by critics such as Elieen Julien (1991) who writes on rape in *La vie et demie* (1979), Roger Ravet (2007) who focuses on narcissism and sexual violence, also in *La vie et demie*, and Dominic Thomas (2002) who considers phallocratic power and sexual violence in Labou Tansi's oeuvre. What I wish to add to this discourse, which already acknowledges the position of women

---

1 V.Y. Mudimbe, *Entre Les Eaux* (Paris: Présence Africaine, 1973), 72.

as objects of sexual abuse in Labou Tansi's work, is an exploration of the male homoerotic elements disguised in these texts as heterosexual economies. I also hope to provide a consideration of how men display political capital through gender-bending. Further, my reading of *Je soussigné cardiaque* is informed by feminist discourses on gender-bending as well as by the specific queer Kongo context expressed in Labou Tansi's treatment of the gendered body. While Thomas has already indicated the struggle over phallocratic power in sonyien literature as occurring between males who struggle for primacy in the public sphere,[2] I wish here, through a queer reading of this play, to expose, firstly, the sexual implications of this struggle to claim the phallus, and secondly, how a man's need to possess the phallus may reveal a desire to engage in homoerotic violence.

In *La Jeune Née* (*The Newborn Woman*), Hélène Cixous reflects on two disparate modes for conceiving gender: a unisex and uniquely male reproduction portrayed in patriarchal mythology and *bisexualité*, which would allow individuals to experience both genders, to recognize the potential for feminine men and masculine women, and would derail the phallocentric project threatening both men and women. Cixous notes that the phallocentric ideal of unisex fecundity erases the woman, but retains the vessel or Great Mother function of the feminine: "And dreams of filiation that is masculine, dreams of God the father issuing from himself in his son – and no mother then."[3] This description of a womanless reproduction coincides with Danielle de Lame's portrayal of patriarchal colonial and postcolonial African societies in which African women are often subordinate to "Le Père et le Fils, autant que le colonisateur" / "The Father and the Son, as well as the colonizer."[4] The Christological trinity to which de Lame alludes enacts not only a subordination, but also an obliteration of African womanhood. The relationships within the trinity are wholly male, each feeding into the other, each giving birth to the other.

One may contrast the male dominance in the reproductive sphere described by Cixous and De Lame, with the crucial role of women in traditional Bântu-Kongo cosmology as described by Kimbwandende Kia Bunseki Fu-Kiau in *African Cosmology of the Bântu-Kôngo: Tying the Spiritual Knot: Principles of*

---

2 Dominic Thomas, *Nation-Building, Propaganda, and Literature in Francophone Africa* (Bloomington: Indiana University Press, 2002), 65.

3 Hélène Cixous, Catherine Clément, *The Newly Born Woman*, trans. Betsy Wing (Minneapolis: University of Minnesota Press, 1986), 65.

4 Danielle de Lame, "Que sont mes amis devenus? Se Re-créer des rapports de genre," in *Changements au féminin en Afrique noire*. Vol 1., eds Danielle de Lame and Chantal Zabus (Paris: L'Harmattan, 1999), 30.

Life and Living. By way of a proverb, Fu-Kiau illustrates the importance of the woman in Kongo culture:

> As long as there is a female "shoot" within the community, it cannot be annihilated. The presence of a female in the community is the symbol of continuity of life in that community, and on the contrary, her absence is the symbol of its end. The feminine is life (God) in and around us.[5]

Contrary to de Lame's notion of the unisex trinity in colonial and postcolonial life and Cixous' description of the patriarchal dream, this traditional Kongo proverb acknowledges the role of women in reproduction and implies a normative male-female vision of the world.

Though Fu-Kiau makes clear the importance of heterosexual coupling in the *Bântu-Kongo* tradition, the queerness of *Bântu-Kôngo* cosmology is revealed through the ubiquity of intersexuality. Fu-Kiau refers to a genderless life-creating energy known as the "V" or "the basis of all realities," conceived of in four cyclical stages from conception to death and re-birth.[6] The first stage, "Vângama," is one of a "pregnancy" which can be both physical and intellectual, and which designates neither a male nor a female element as its catalyst. Fu-Kiau explains that, "In this sense, ideologically, we all get pregnant" that is, we all give birth to ideas, to works of art, and to ourselves.[7] Similarly, in *Death and the Invisible Powers*, Simon Bockie notes that Kongo cosmology commences with god's creation of a being who reproduces asexually:

> BaManianga believe that the first man God created was called Mahungu, from the verb *hunga*, 'to carry away.' He was a bisexual being, able to procreate by himself. He was *muntu wahunga* – a complete being to whom God entrusted the management of the whole creation. He was more powerful than the ancestors, for God's will was to make him *alter sui* – 'another himself.'[8]

---

5 Kimbwandende Kia Bunseki Fu-Kiau, *African Cosmology of the Bântu-Kôngo: Tying the Spiritual Knot: Principles of Life and Living* (New York: Athelia Henrietta Press, 2001), 104.

6 Ibid., 129.

7 Ibid., 138.

8 Simon Bockie, *Death and the Invisible Powers* (Bloomington and Indianapolis: Indiana University Press, 1993), 36.

We can take Bokie's use of the term "bisexual" to mean an individual possessing both male and female reproductive organs rather than as an indication of sexual desire. This bisexuality described by Bokie is, in fact intersexuality. Yet, though Mahungu is intersexed, Bokie's language leads us to believe that, like his creator, this first human's persona was that of a "he" and not of a "he/she," that Mahungu's intersexuality is a means towards achieving asexual reproduction rather than the basis of an identity which rejects gender distinction. These observations demonstrate that while Kongo cosmology relies heavily on queer sexualities, its post-cosmological belief system holds fast to normative gender distinctions.

The queerness of a Kongo cosmology that accepts as possible both intersexuality and masculine, asexual reproduction informs significantly the discourse of Sony Labou Tansi. This is evidenced, not only in *Je soussigné cardiaque*, but also in his 1990 article "Lettre aux Africains sous couvert du parti punique" / "'An Open Letter to Africans' c/o The Punic One-Party State" in which the author deftly equates the tradition of the one-party dictatorship and the rejection of diversity which such a system demands, to the notion of the male as the singular agent of procreation:

> Let it be said that the word 'founding father' carried with it a magical halo that tragically suggested the idea of a shameless founding father endowed with patriotic, national and procreative powers; powers that in turn carry a hint of the notion of the fatherland as the product of an act of birthing.[9]

Labou Tansi's allusion to a singular being crowned with a "magical halo" echoes the myth of Mahungu, recorded by Bokie, and precedes Achille Mbembe's description in *On the Postcolony* of the monotheistic god who "is his own genesis."[10]

Mbembe's suggests a link between "the biblical phantasm of the One" and "concepts of kingship and sovereignty."[11] He describes "the One" as "both father and son," but, wherein the narrative of the Mahungu myth and Labou Tansi's description of the one-party state evacuate the woman's role in reproduction, Mbembe theorizes that the process of reproduction within the phantasm

---

9   Sony Labou Tansi, "'An Open Letter to Africans' c/o The Punic One-Party State," trans. John Conteh-Morgan, *African Literature: An Anthology of Criticism and Theory*, eds Tejumola Olaniyan and Ato Quayson (Malden, MA: Blackwell, 2007), 273.

10   Achille Mbembe, *On the Postcolony*, trans. Steven Rendall (Los Angeles: University of California Press, 2001), 214.

11   Ibid., 218.

of "the One" does require the woman as a vessel: "the son is realized in the mother."[12] However, Mbembe concludes that within sovereign power structures the son, and ultimately "the One," is created *in* a woman, but not *by* a woman, so that this birthing nevertheless wrests the agency of creation from the woman. For his part, Labou Tansi criticizes such a system by removing the woman from his prose, perhaps hoping the reader will grasp the irrationality of a discussion of childbirth in a context where the man is the sole agent. Ultimately Labou-Tansi attempts to link this absurdity to that of a single-party dictatorship. Labou Tansi concludes his letter by describing the idea of "a supreme insemination of the fatherland by the sole father of the nation" as "beyond ridiculous"[13] a conviction that seems to warn of the threat dictatorship poses to all Africans in much the same manner as Cixou's *La Jeune Née* treats phallogocentrism as a menace to both men and women.

In what precedes, we can note an ambivalence in Kongo belief systems towards intersexuality and asexuality, which, though both essential to Kongo cosmology, are perceived as unnatural when they exist in contexts beyond the creation of the first woman. Within contemporary contexts they become archaic and perverse. Where these queer sexualities were once essential aspects of spirituality, they are now metaphors for personal and political corruption. This ambivalence also resounds in *Je soussigné cardiaque*, where queerness symbolizes both personal agency and indignity.

Labou Tansi wrote his open letter nine years after the publication of *Je soussigné cardiaque*. Although none of the characters of the play are physically intersexed, the play's male hero, like the dictators Labou Tansi criticizes in his "Open Letter," fantasizes about giving birth to himself. However, unlike Labou Tansi's dictators who see their own masculine insemination as the sole manner of reproduction, the hero of *Je soussigné cardiaque* adopts a feminine persona in his struggle towards spiritual and political rebirth. As Edwige Gbouablé (2008) has suggested in a reading of *Je soussigné cardiaque*, when present in the oppressed, a struggle for re-birth and, more specifically, for self-birthing – "[un corps qui peut] se refaire" / "a body which can re-create itself" – can be read in Labou Tansi as a sign of agency and hope.[14] Gbouablé's interpretation of self-birthing parallels what Wyatt MacGaffey notes is the BâKongo

---

12   Ibid., 220.

13   Sony Labou Tansi, "An Open Letter to Africans' c/o The Punic One-Party State," trans.
      John Conteh-Morgan (trans). *African Literature: An Anthology of Criticism and Theory*, eds
      Tejumola Olaniyan and Ato Quayson (Malden, MA: Blackwell, 2007), 273.

14   Edwige Gbouablé, "Langage du corps et voix d'auteur dans le théâtre de Sony Labou Tansi:
      une écriture de l'alibi," *L'Esprit Créateur*, 48.3 (Fall 2008): 20.

"reciprocating universe" in which "the dead are recycled through this world."[15] Additionally, giving birth to the self reflects Fu-Kiau's description of the powerful force of the "Vee," a cyclical process, which indicates rebirth:

> Kôngo cosmology tells us, the dual soul-mind [...] is ready to reincarnate (rebirth or re-re [...] birth) in order to rise again in the upper world [...] This is demonstrated in a continuum of rebirth after rebirth, meaning incarnation after incarnation.[16]

Like the rebirth within the "Vee" cycle, the reincarnation suggested in Gbouablé's reading of *Je soussigné cardiaque* suggests that personal rebirth depends not on masculinity or femininity, but rather on masculinity *and* femininity; on the will of the individual, intersexed subject.

One might be satisfied with such an interpretation of gender in *Je soussigné cardiaque*, were the instances of men taking on feminine personas uniquely life-affirming. Instead, while the motif of men re-imagining themselves as women permeates the text, these men do not embrace the feminine. Rather, in this play the feminine becomes a location of suffering and a casualty in a battle of words and wills between two men: Mallot, a black man living in an African postcolony, and Perono, a Spanish neocolonizer. Each man relies on language to feminize the other and to simulate the erotic violation of that other. The two rivals thus engage in a male encounter disguised as a violent heterosexual coupling in which the feminized male is always the receptor of erotic violence. In what follows I consider the gendering of sexual violation in *Je soussigné cardiaque* through an examination of the use of the feminine in the homoerotic encounter between Perono and Mallot, specifically as the conjuring and debasement of the feminine is the principal tool in their implicit denial of reciprocal homoerotic desire and domination.

Mythologies of autogamic reproduction can be found in various works by Labou Tansi. Emmanuel Yewah provides an apt example of a dictator's dream of self-creation in his reading of *L'Etat honteux*:

> When [the dictator Martillimi Lopez] declares that "je suis Martillimi Lopez, fils de Maman Nationale," we can try to understand his origins by studying his genealogy by using his mother as a point of reference. But

15 Wyatt MacGaffey, *Religion and Society in Central Africa: The BaKongo of Lower Zaire.* (Chicago: University of Chicago Press, 1986), 63.
16 Kimbwandende Kia Bunseki Fu-Kiau, *African Cosmology of the Bântu-Kôngo: Tying the Spiritual Knot: Principles of Life and Living* (New York: Athelia Henrietta Press, 2001), 35.

such effort is impossible because "Maman Nationale" is actually a metaphor for the whole nation which, of course makes Lopez "fils de la nation"
and ultimately "père de la nation." In that capacity he becomes some sort
of mythic being with ubiquitous powers.[17]

Yewah's observation that the female element in Lopez's genealogy is nothing
but metaphor, that is, that the woman never really exists, and that the reproductive function of the feminine is co-opted by a man, is crucial in understanding how some of Labou Tansi's male characters conceive of the feminine and of
women. This notion of woman as metaphor helps us to question instances in
sonyien literature in which the feminine might be present, but women are not.

   Je soussigné cardiaque represents the feminine as an archetypal object rather than, as Simone de Beauvoir recommends, as "the present state of education and custom."[18] Rejecting an essential or "eternal" feminine, de Beauvoir
espouses a more constructive vision of "individual feminine existence," which
entails a conscious acknowledgement of real women.[19] In *Je soussigné cardiaque*, however we witness the imposition of a static grammar of the feminine
whose parameters are both dictated and performed by men.

   Of course, there are female characters in the play: Mwanda (Mallot's pregnant wife), Hortense (Minister Ébara's secretary), and Nelly (Mallot's young
daughter). But these female characters are never present during the at once violent and erotic encounters between Mallot and Perono in which the feminine
is portrayed as a victim. Despite the absence of real women in these scenes
of erotic violence, the text reveals a symmetry between Mallot and Perono's
gendered fantasies and the identities of these three female characters. For
the male adversaries of *Je soussigné cardiaque*, the feminine is invariably a
mother – "Il faut que j'arrive à accoucher de moi." / I must find a way to give
birth to myself,[20] a sexual object – "Tout le monde me saute." / Everybody's
jumping my bones,[21] or a young girl – "Je vous fatigue comme une fille." / I'm
wearing you out like you're a little girl.[22] The feminine is often symbolized

17   Emmanuel Yewah, "Sony Labou Tansi and his Unstable Political Figures," *The French
      Review*, 67.1 (Oct. 1993): 98.
18   Simone de Beauvoir, *The Second Sex*, trans. and ed. H.M. Parshley (Paris: Gallimard, 1949),
      xxx.
19   Ibid., xxx.
20   Sony Labou Tansi, *Parenthèse de sang suivi de Je soussigné cardiaque* (Paris: Hatier,
      1981), 111.
21   Ibid., 132.
22   Ibid., 102.

by genitalia and signified by what Gbouablé calls "mots-segments,"[23] which, like the subject of the medieval *blason anatomique*, have been conceptually disengaged from a whole female body – "le sexe endolori de la putain" / the prostitute's aching vagina.[24] In short, in the play's conjuring of the feminine, women are invariably absent. We shall see below that when women are presented in the play they predictably enact the feminine as Mallot and Perono conceive it.

The text tends to associate Mallot, the dominated African subject, with the feminine. Still, this propensity for feminizing the African should not be confused with Cixous' association of the African continent with the feminine, in that both are victimized by "the white continent."[25] The attitude of the principal characters of *Je soussigné cardiaque* suggests that while the victim *might* be African, that victim is *always* inherently feminine. In contrast, Cixous, like de Beauvoir, does not propound the existence of essential identities. Rather she considers, firstly, the manner in which one represents the self, secondly, the perception of an individual by another, and finally, how one might internalize those external perceptions. While Cixous acknowledges that both the African continent and the woman suffer victimization, there is, in *La Jeune Née*, no suggestion of an innate victimhood where either Africa or femininity is concerned. In fact, for Cixous, phallogocentrism is an "equal-opportunity" victimizer. It is a structure that subjugates both men and women, as well as people of all ethnicities. Conversely, Labou Tansi's hero believes that the *logos* threatens only those who are truly feminine. In Doctor Manissa's office he describes his feminization as a victim of his country's laws: "Figurez-vous que moi j'ai été déviergé, transgressé avec des lois. Ils m'ont saccagé." / Can you believe it? I've been de-virginized, violated by laws. They've ravaged me.[26] Though the past participles *déviergé, transgressé*, and *saccagé* indicate that the object of violence in the phrase is masculine rather than feminine, both *dévierger* (to de-virginize) and *saccager* (to ravage) traditionally denote a feminine rather than a masculine object.

23   Edwige Gbouablé, "Langage du corps et voix d'auteur dans le théâtre de Sony Labou Tansi: une écriture de l'alibi," *L'Esprit Créateur*, 48.3 (Fall 2008): 20.

24   Sony Labou Tansi, *Parenthèse de sang suivi de Je soussigné cardiaque* (Paris: Hatier, 1981), 78.

25   Hélène Cixous and Catherine Clément, *The Newly Born Woman*, trans. Betsy Wing (Minneapolis: University of Minnesota Press, 1986), 68.

26   Sony Labou Tansi, *Parenthèse de sang suivi de Je soussigné cardiaque* (Paris: Hatier, 1981), 124.

Despite Mallot's conception of the feminine as a victim of logocentric violence, he imagines childbirth as a convenient strategy of revolt. However, his
notion of childbirth is a queer one in that it is either asexual and/or intersexed as it would require only *his* will, rejecting the participation of any other:
"Il faut que j'arrive à accoucher de moi pour les vaincre." / I must find a way to
give birth to myself so that I can defeat them.[27] Mallot believes that in order to
resist becoming a victim of Perono's appetite for domination, and further, in
order to become a dominator himself, he must recreate his life by giving birth
to himself, recalling the "Vee," or self-creating force found in Kongo cosmology.
By re-creating himself, Mallot hopes to secure an existence otherwise threatened by Perono. Nonetheless, in spite of the self-creation that this symbolic
childbirth promises, *Je soussigné cardiaque* also treats pregnancy as a conceiv-
able result of having a body that is penetrable to domination. Thus, later in the
play, a subjugated Mallot finds himself fighting what he feels is Perono's name
growing inside of him: "Perono! Je porte ce nom comme une grossesse. Il bouge
dans mes côtes, il ébranle mes reins. Je vais le mettre au monde." / Perono! I'm
carrying this name like a pregnancy. It's stirring in my rib cage, it's shattering
my loins. I'm going to give birth to it.[28] In a perversion of the "Vee" within a
modern African subject, Mallot can no longer impregnate himself, nor can he
be pregnant *with* himself. The queer asexual agency implied in the "Vee" of
Kongo cosmology is thus co-opted by the neo-colonizer who dominates, pen-
etrates and impregnates his victim with the spoken word. As such, this victim
loses his potential for both being and becoming. This internalization of the
logos of an oppressor represents the negative potential of all postcolonial subjects: a domination so complete that the subject not only internalizes but also
reproduces it.

There are thus two modes of metaphysical pregnancy in Labou-Tansi's play:
positive, asexual self-creation; and a heterosexual coupling in which the role
of the woman is also the role of the victim. Still Mallot's adoption of a feminine persona is useful within the play as gender-bending allows him to experience and describe his violation at the hands of male dominators. This gender
ambiguity is expressed in another description of Mallot's suffering within the
postcolonial machine:

---

27   Ibid., 78.
28   Ibid., 98.

Je suis leur homme, tu comprends? Leur chose. Et il faut que je leur ar-
rache ça. J'enrage d'être un chiffre dans leurs vilains calculs. Un chiffre
qu'on pousse, qu'on bastonne, qu'on bouscule.[29]

Do you understand that I'm their man? Their thing. And I have to wrest
that away from them. I'm infuriated at being a pawn in their wicked
schemes. A pawn that they push, that they beat, that they knock around.

Mallot initially affirms his masculinity, through the use of the term *homme*
and with the phallic implication of a *chose* – literally a "thing," but also a sexual organ, which he plans to grab onto and retrieve. However, the description
of his status as a dominated, postcolonial subject veers toward the feminine,
firstly as a castrated man and then as whore and victim. Though the verb *bas-
tonner* literally means "to beat or punish," it also suggests the use of a prostitute. Furthermore, *bousculer*, or "to turn over or bother" also signifies taking a
woman sexually.[30]

Mallot decides to reclaim his masculine power and realizes that he must
kill his violator in order to do so. But because Perono is out of reach – having
forced Mallot and his family to quit the region – Mallot must take revenge on
Ébara, who, as the Minister of Education has participated in persecuting the
school teacher. Mallot believes that by killing Ébara, he will bring himself into
existence. Once again, the protagonist becomes a man-woman in order to give
himself a new life, but he attempts to thwart victimhood by refusing to possess
feminine reproductive organs: "Exactement comme ma mère, moins le vagin."
/ Exactly like my mother, minus the vagina.[31] Though Mallot chooses to give
birth to himself while rejecting the feminization implied by a vagina, he does
imagine, in his fantasy of killing Ébara, that his rival possesses female genitalia:

ÉBARA: Ne me tuez pas.
MALLOT: Non? Et pourquoi donc? Pour vous faire plaisir, n'est-ce pas?
Oh! Vous ne voulez pas que j'existe un peu? Vous ne savez donc pas qui
vous êtes pour moi? Le vagin. Et le chemin. Il faut que je vous traverse. Là.
(*Il lui crache à la figure.*)[32]

---

29   Ibid., 110.
30   Albert Doillon, *Le Dico du sexe* (Paris: Fayard, 2002), 67, 106.
31   Sony Labou Tansi, *Parenthèse de sang suivi de Je soussigné cardiaque* (Paris: Hatier, 1981),
      145.
32   Ibid., 145.

ÉBARA: Don't kill me!

MALLOT: No? And why not? Just to make you happy? Oh! Don't you want me to exist just a little? Don't you know what you are to me? The vagina. And the path. I've got to go through you. Right there. (*He spits in his face.*)

Mallot conceives of Ébara as the feminine whose death – in childbirth – will allow him to be born, an example of Jean-Marie Kouakou's observation of killers in sonyien narrative who can only be truly alive once their victims have ceased to exist. This scene provides a more literal example of Kouakou's assertion as Mallot hopes that Ébara will literally give birth to him. The phlegm, which Mallot spits onto the face of his rival/mother, connects the two men like a viscous afterbirth. Assigning Ébara the role of the feminine and the mother, allows Mallot to experience an intimate violence, which is sexual – in the strictest biological sense – without being obviously sensual. Ultimately, what is crucial for Mallot is that this feminine presence be destroyed so that he might live.

Ébara, for his part, conceives of the state's domination as a feminization of Mallot, threatening, during a confrontation with the latter: "Je te ferai arrêter, fusiller, castrer … Je te ferai ronger un morceau de ta viande de putain." / I'll have you arrested, shot, castrated … I'll have them cut off a piece of your goddamn flesh.[33] Emasculating – read feminizing – Mallot through castration is analogous to annihilating him, as in *arrêter* and *fusiller*. Cutting off (*rogner*) a piece of his meat – another threat of castration – will reveal Mallot's true feminine character. Further, the term *viande*, a common element in Labou Tansi's lexicon (for instance in *La Vie et Demie*, *L'Anté-Peuple*, and *L'État honteux*) may be defined as the body of a person and, in the sonyien context, can be understood as a decomposing body.[34] Additionally, in erotic contexts, *viande* commonly denotes a woman or a girl.[35] The implication here is that Mallot can only be dominated in the in-between space of intersexuality in which he can be partly feminine. But while he becomes a man-woman, his attackers remain fully masculine. Despite his best attempt to regain his masculinity by feminizing and thus victimizing his foes, Mallot cannot contest his own victimhood, and thus must remain at least partially feminine. Ultimately, the performance

33   Ibid., 149.

34   Martin Mégevand, "Le corps et la pathologie du pouvoir dans le théâtre sonyien," in *Sony Labou Tansi à l'œuvre*, eds Papa Samba Diop and Xavier Garnier (Paris: L'Harmattan, 2007), 81.

35   Albert Doillon, *Le Dico du sexe* (Paris: Fayard, 2002), 383.

of the feminine in a phallocentric construct allows for a veiling of the homoeroticism within the desire shared by Mallot and Perono.

In their designation of the feminine as victim both men maintain normative
gender constructs and confuse the notion of a passive and "insertee" role with
that of the feminine. Nevertheless, it might be possible to separate Mallot and
Perono's notion of the feminine in *Je soussigné cardiaque* from their relationship to actual women, so that perhaps the characters' casting of the feminine
as victim or, more precisely, their victimization of the feminine, is simply the
result of the crudeness of their vocabularies. Perhaps they misunderstand not
only the meaning of womanhood – because they assume the victim is always a
woman – but also the condition of masculinity – because they cannot imagine
a male as a victim, because they cannot conceive of a male as penetrable to desire and violence. Indeed, it seems unlikely that the homosocial bonds in a play
where the female presence is fleeting would produce any great understanding
of the feminine. Despite an early reference to Perono as "très très gynécologue"
/ very, very [knowledgeable about female genitalia][36] – an innocent error in
speech by a young child who means to say "généreux" – the Spaniard lives
alone in a large villa with only his houseboy. Mallot's wife, Mwanda, though
a supportive, nurturing presence, is only of incidental consequence in the
drama and is relegated to the home, away from the "phallocratically controlled
public space" of the postcolony inhabited by Perono and Mallot.[37] Though
her pregnancy suggests heterosexual relations between the two, and though
Mallot specifically mentions in one instance "on fera l'amour." / we will make
love.[38] this future action never occurs within the margins of the play. In fact,
Mwanda's rapport with Mallot provides no evidence of heterosexual desire
within the couple. Her function seems solely as an aid in the exposition of the
intrigue. Twenty-seven phrases in the play are spoken by Mwanda, many of
which are two-word utterances dedicated only to the progression of Mallot's
narrative:

---

36   Sony Labou Tansi, *Parenthèse de sang suivi de Je soussigné cardiaque* (Paris: Hatier, 1981), 86.
37   Dominic Thomas, *Nation-Building, Propaganda, and Literature in Francophone Africa*
       (Bloomington: Indiana University Press, 2002), 67.
38   Sony Labou Tansi, *Parenthèse de sang suivi de Je soussigné cardiaque* (Paris: Hatier,
       1981), 112.

MWANDA : Qui il?
MALLOT : Perono.
MWANDA : Qui est Perono.
MALLOT : La loi d'ici.
MWANDA : La loi?
MALLOT : Tu te rappelles? Il y a quatre mois, on nous a chassés de Kwamou. Parce que j'ai dit la vérité au chef régional et parce que j'ai montré au gouverneur qu'il trompait les analphabètes, qu'il était un simple tueur de whisky.
MWANDA : Oui je me rappelle. Et bien?[39]

MWANDA: Who, he?
MALLOT: Perono.
MWANDA: Who's Perono.
MALLOT: The law around here.
MWANDA: The law?
MALLOT: You remember, don't you? Four months ago, they chased us out of Kwamou. Because I told the regional director the truth, and because I showed the governor that he was cheating the illiterate, that he was just another lush.
MWANDA: Yes, I remember. And so?

Because her character is never revealed in dialogue, and never developed beyond its general functions as wife and mother, Mwanda exercises gendered but not erotic force. This observation is by no means intended to debase Mwanda's maternity, which, from an African feminist point of view, is a strong signifier of social status and which, with its reference to future generations, is perhaps the solitary source of hope in the text.[40] Rather, considering the roles given to Mwanda provides insight into how *Je soussigné cardiaque* portrays women and men, and into how the play represents heterosexual and homoerotic relations. The play does, in one instance, reference Mwanda's physicality, but here there

---

39   Ibid., 108–109.
40   On maternity in African Feminism see Helen Cousins, "Nothing Like Motherhood: Barrenness, Abortion and Infanticide in Yvonne Vera's Fiction," in *Rites of Passage in Postcolonial Women's Writing*, eds Pauline Dodgson-Katiyo and Gina Wisker (New York: Editions Rodopi, 2010) 21–40; Filomina Steady, "African Feminism: A Worldwide Perspective," in *Women in Africa and the African Diaspora*, eds Rosalyn Terborg-Penn, Sharon Harley & and Andrea Benton (Washington D.C.: Howard University Press, 1987), 18–19.

is no suggestion of a sexual relationship with Mallot. Rather, their dialogue is a tender exchange in which she persuades an agitated Mallot that they have nothing to fear:

> MALLOT : Qu'est-ce qu'on a fait ma chérie?
> MWANDA : *doucement* Nous? On n'a rien fait.
> MALLOT : (*Il l'embrasse*) Tu es sûre qu'on n'a rien fait? Sûre de ton corps de femme?
> MWANDA : Oui, de tout mon corps. Sûre.
> ....
> MWANDA : Personne ne nous traque.[41]

> MALLOT: What did we do honey?
> MWANDA: *sweetly* Us? We haven't done anything.
> MALLOT: (*he kisses her*) You're sure we haven't done anything? Do you feel it in that woman's body of yours?
> MWANDA: Yes, I feel it in my body. I'm sure of it.
> ....
> MWANDA: No one's stalking us.

Though Mwanda's feminine intuition is incorrect and lacks an understanding of the political system that rules her life, this passage expresses the import of her maternal position. Nevertheless, her rapport with her husband is more maternal than sensual and their dialogue lacks the sexually charged vocabulary present in the exchanges between Perono and Mallot.

Mwanda's "*corps de femme*" is juxtaposed with that of Hortense, the secretary and mistress of Minister Ébara. Suitably, Hortense uses her charms to secure a meeting for Mallot with Ébara.[42] While Mwanda's sexuality is linked to the maternal, Hortense is a corporal being who knows only "Ma chaleur. Mon odeur. Et le froissement de mon corps de femme." / My warmth, my scent. And the rustling of my feminine body.[43] Though Hortense's "knowledge," makes her more aware than Mwanda of the political web in which she is caught, the secretary is just another whore of the postcolony. Her encounter with Mallot provides her an opportunity to explain the effects of her life as Ébara's sexual

---

41   Sony Labou Tansi, *Parenthèse de sang suivi de Je soussigné cardiaque* (Paris: Hatier, 1981), 111.

42   Ibid., 134.

43   Ibid., 137.

plaything. And believing they have bonded over their shared experiences as exploited postcolonial subjects, Hortense invites Mallot to make love to her:

> HORTENSE: Je veux passer le week-end avec vous dans ma villa. D'accord? ...
> MALLOT: Je refuse ...
> HORTENSE: Je parie que vous êtes vertueux.
> MALLOT: Pas du tout. Mais je ne veux pas que ça se fasse comme dans un film ... Vous m'avez rendu un gros morceau de moi. Je ne veux pas que ça se casse.[44]

> HORTENSE: I want to spend the weekend with you in my villa. OK?...
> MALLOT: I refuse ...
> HORTENSE: I guess you must be virtuous.
> MALLOT: Not at all. But I don't want it to happen like in a film ... You've given me back a huge part of myself. I don't want to spoil it.

Mallot's rejection of Hortense owes nothing to his familial commitment. As he clarifies, virtue is not a quality he possesses. Rather, Hortense repulses him because he fears that any contact with her would expose him to her corruption as a postcolonial subject who readily exploits her sexuality for material gain. It is as if Hortense's social condition and her attitude towards her sexuality were a communicable illness. Thus, whereas Mallot becomes the victim of symbolic homoerotic violation at the hands of Perono because he has dared to speak out against domination and corruption, Hortense has given herself to her boss, Minister Ébara and created the conditions for her own victimization. Though Hortense has given Mallot a small victory by securing him a meeting with Ébara, Mallot's gratefulness does not extend to granting her sexual favors. For him this would imply a prostitution of himself similar to Hortense's misuse of her own sexuality, when she allows herself to be the passive object of Ébara's desire. For Mallot, giving into Hortense's sexual advances would be no different from accepting the passive role in which Perono has cast him. Ironically then, in rejecting Hortense's request Mallot protects his own masculinity, as it is his refusal of this heterosexual encounter that allows him to feel that he has rejected a feminization of himself. Again, the "feminization" here is one of his own construction, one defined by the same passive sexuality he is forced to experience as a symbolic receiver of Perono's sexual aggression.

---

44   Ibid., 139.

Despite the fact that Mallot rejects her advances, Hortense reappears immediately before his execution, bringing the other females of the play, Mwanda,
Nelly, and the newly born Lahla, to the prison and into the official space of
what Achille Mbembe calls the *commandement*, a self-defined "cosmology,"
whose "purest expression ... is conveyed by a total lack of restraint."[45] In en-
tering the phallocratic space of the prison, the women themselves remain
restrained; speechless, save for a brief song, which Nelly repeats after being
instructed to do so by her father. Mwanda and Hortense's silence and Nelly's
role as an object of ventriloquism are emblematic of the lack of agency associated with femininity and the scarcity of meaningful interaction between men
and women in *Je soussigné cardiaque*.

Though the actual women of Labou Tansi's play are more often observers
than participants in the politics of the postcolony, for the male rivals in *Je soussigné cardiaque*, their own femininity is a socio-political condition which one
might have the misfortune to occupy, but which may be escaped, through possession of oneself and/or of others. When Mallot and Perono first meet, the
cordiality between them suggests that despite their racial and economic differences, they nevertheless accept each other's masculinity and can thus treat
each other with respect. As their battle intensifies and Mallot descends into
the feminine, a class distinction also becomes apparent:

> PERONO : Tout à l'heure vous avez failli me faire croire qu'il y a des pyg-
> mées spéciaux. Non. Vous n'êtes qu'un pygmée comme tous les pygmées
> du monde. Vous puez un peu. Vous respirez le caca [...] Tout à l'heure
> quand vous me crâniez dans le dos, je vous admirais. Je me disais: ça n'est
> pas de la pacotille, ce gosse. Tu étais imprenable à un certain moment. Je
> vais t'annuler, salaud.[46]

> PERONO: You almost convinced me just now that there was such a thing
> as an exceptional pygmy. But no. You're nothing but another pygmy, just
> like all the pygmies of the world. You know, you smell a little. Your breath
> smells like caca [...] Just now when you were showing off to me, I ad-
> mired you. I said to myself: he's not just for show, this kid. There was a
> time when you were impregnable. Now I'm going to annihilate you, you
> bastard.

---

45   Achille Mbembe, *On the Postcolony*, trans. Janet Roitman and Murray Last (Los Angeles:
     University of California Press, 2001), 108, 111.
46   Sony Labou Tansi, *Parenthèse de sang suivi de Je soussigné cardiaque* (Paris: Hatier, 1981),
     106.

In addressing Mallot, Perono moves from the formal "vous" to the informal "tu" to mark this pivotal moment in the development of their relation. Though Perono's description of Mallot's "showing off" suggests a false courage on the part of his rival, he nonetheless admires the machismo displayed in the attack. For though he will never consider Mallot his equal, any perceived aggression confirms the African's masculinity. Perono describes the masculine as "*imprenable*," a term which, drawn from the verb *prendre* (to take) and closely related to the verb *imprégner* (to impregnate) suggests firstly that one could not seduce Mallot and secondly that he is impermeable to violence. But when Mallot falters, Perono can no longer see him as a man. This shift in the hero's status from "*imprenable*" to "*prenable*" or "penetrable" signals Perono's conception of the African as feminine. This change from masculinity to what both men describe as femininity represents a shift in social capital.

Their mutual disdain for the perceived weakness of the feminine reveals a projection of their own masculine insecurities. Mallot and Perono collaborate in a portrayal of the feminine which conceals their greatest fear, namely that the archetypal victim might be masculine. I make no claim here as to the existence of an archetypal victim, masculine or feminine. Rather I wish to indicate the operation of such a logic in the minds of Perono and Mallot, who are motivated by an aversion to the idea of the masculine as passive and penetrable. Their conception of the feminine as a victim, a receptacle for sexual aggressions with no aptitude for actancial expression, heightens their own fear of losing what they imagine to be masculinity – be it the phallus or an active, impenetrable body – and their obsessive desire to possess it.

Mallot's gender identification remains unclear until his execution, but his discourse suggests that impenetrable masculinity is his ultimate goal. When Lebango's leader gives Mallot the choice between a firing squad and the hangman, the hero chooses death by hanging. As a radio announcer in the final scene of the play informs us: "Nous vous rappelons, frères et sœurs, que les quinze condamnés à qui le guide avait offert de choisir entre la corde et le peloton ont tous choisi le peloton à l'exception de Mallot Bayenda qui, lui, a préféré la corde." / We remind you, brothers and sisters, that the fifteen convicts, to whom our guide has offered a choice between the hangman and the firing squad, have all chosen the firing squad, with the exception of Mallot Bayenda, who preferred to be hung.[47] Mallot's choice of a rope over a bullet further exhibits his wish to affirm his masculinity by avoiding – even in death – the penetration of his body by all forms of violence. Though he has been

---

47   Ibid., 153.

lumped in with other victims of the postcolony, he exercises the little agency
he retains by choosing what he perceives as the more masculine death. To be
sure, hanging, in the postcolonial context might be compared to the lynching
of the post-civil-war U.S., which like rape, was a form of subordination.[48] For
Mallot, however, hanging represents a way to maintain his "bodily integrity,"[49]
signifying in the swaying of his corpse "the sexual organ itself swinging at the
end of a rope."[50] His death becomes a solitary performance of masculinity as
resisting the desire of the phallocracy.

In the moments before his death Mallot reaffirms his masculinity: "J'ai dis-
loqué l'univers. Homme. Moi. Vierge. J'ai disqualifié le vide." / I've pulled the
universe off its hinges. Man. Me. Virgin. I've put the void to shame.[51] Even with
the knowledge of his impending death, Mallot is comforted by his status as
"vierge," convinced of the failure of those who wished to violate him. However,
Mallot's earlier confrontation with Perono suggests a desire on both their parts
to symbolically violate each other. They express this desire through the feminization of the other, ostensibly eliminating the possibility of reading a homoerotic economy in an exchange that might be compared to a mating ritual:

> PERONO: Voyez-vous, depuis longtemps je n'ai jamais eu que du vide
> devant moi. Du vide en face. Un vide vierge. C'est énervant, le vide […]
> Vous êtes le seul qui allez m'obéir parce que je commande. Les autres,
> mon Dieu, c'est la foutaise. Ils m'obéissent par paresse. Vous, je vous fête.
> J'en aurai au moins un, oui, au moins un qui m'obéira par conviction,
> donc tendrement.
> MALLOT: *Amusé.* Je ne sais pas obéir.
> PERONO: Rassurez-vous, vous apprendrez et c'est là que ça devient
> séduisant.[52]

> PERONO: You see, for a long time I've had nothing but a void before me.
> I've been facing a void. A virgin void. It's troubling, the void […] You are

---

48   Jacquelyn Dowd Hall, "'The Mind that Burns in Each Body': Women, Rape and Racial
     Violence," in *Powers of Desire: The Politics of Sexuality*, eds Ann Snitow, Christine Stansell
     and Sharon Thompson (New York: Monthly Press Review, 1983), 311.
49   Ibid., 342.
50   Hélène Cixous and Catherine Clément, *The Newly Born Woman*, trans. Betsy Wing
     (Minneapolis: University of Minnesota Press, 1986), 25.
51   Sony Labou Tansi, *Parenthèse de sang suivi de Je soussigné cardiaque* (Paris: Hatier, 1981),
     153–154.
52   Ibid., 95.

the only one who will obey me because I command it. The others, my God, the others are just full of shit. They obey me out of laziness. But you, I celebrate your presence. I'll have at least one, yes, at least one who will obey me out of conviction, and thus tenderly.
MALLOT: *Amused*. I don't know how to obey.
PERONO: Don't worry. You will learn, and that's where it becomes appealing.

Mallot's "virginity," his political purity, seduces Perono, as does the postcolonial subject's confident resistance of domination. Like a dangerous, unsown land, Mallot challenges Perono's ability to claim him. Perono's conviction that authority over Mallot will produce affection on the part of the African is another reminder of the paternalist discourse found among new colonizers. Underlying this discourse is the sexual tension present in the dichotomy of the hunter and the hunted. Perono's wish to command and to teach Mallot indicates a quest for sexual hegemony. The Spaniard's excitement is heightened by an imagined ritual that will result in mastery over the African: the struggle that will necessarily ensue and the reward which will come in the form of the subdued and weary Mallot, who must finally give himself to his new master. The force of this erotic ritual lies not in physical violation, but rather, in the ritual's social violence. As Wyatt MacGaffey has suggested, "The significance of sexuality in ritual [is in part] connected with social organization as an arena of regulated competition for productive capacity [...] The erotic is not sex but socialized sex."[53]
Conscious of the implications of the erotic ritual into which Perono has drawn him, Mallot attempts to turn the tables on his pursuer, but nonetheless, retains the role of the dominated:

MALLOT : ....vous m'obsédez d'une obsession délicieuse. Vous me remuez. Vous êtes une ordure pure. Or moi, j'ai un petit faible pour la pureté, le plein ... Vous m'avez infligé un coup de foudre.[54]

MALLOT. I'm obsessed with you and it's a delicious obsession. You arouse me. You're pure filth. Now, the thing is, I have a weakness for purity, for fullness. You've made me fall in love with you.

---

53   Wyatt MacGaffey, *Religion and Society in Central Africa: The BaKongo of Lower Zaire* (Chicago: University of Chicago Press, 1986), 159, note.

54   Sony Labou Tansi, *Parenthèse de sang suivi de Je soussigné cardiaque* (Paris: Hatier, 1981), 98.

As the title *Je soussigné cardiaque* suggests, the notion of illness figures heavily in this work. More than that, a fusion of disease and desire defines the relationship between Perono and Mallot. The latter's speech vacillates between fascination and disgust, attraction and repulsion, but he affirms that he has been – in some measure – seduced, though his "coup de foudre" is more viral than romantic and has been violently imposed ("infligé"). The verb "remuer" is equally ambiguous here, as its usage could indicate an arousal resulting from either physical penetration and/or a spiritual inspiration. And indeed, it seems that Perono's violation of Mallot inspires the revolt of the latter, who can only find satisfaction in imagining a heterosexually framed scenario of domination between himself and the Spaniard:

> MALLOT : Je vous fatigue comme une fille. Je vous dissous ... Je vous défais le nombril et l'anus. Je vous mets des bulles de merde dans le cerveau [...] J'ai forniqué avec vous.[55]

> MALLOT: I'm wearing you out like you're a little girl. I'm dissolving you [...] I'm breaking apart your belly button and your anus. I'm putting bubbles of shit in your brain. I've fornicated with you.

Here is a form of torture that "merges the carnal act of love with violence."[56] Mallot expresses a desire to cast Perono as a passive receiver of his sexual aggression. Perono thus receives every transitive action of the passage. In a sparagmos-like ritual, Mallot carves holes in Perono's body to emphasize the latter's status as a receptacle of sexual violence. He feminizes Perono, firstly to remove what he perceives is the power of his masculinity and to replace it with what he believes is the weakness of the feminine and, secondly, to ensure that his imagined sexual act remains heterosexual. His fantasy also includes depriving Perono of his senses and, in turn, of his subjectivity and autohegemony, by filling his head with excrement. Read in company with the Lacanian notion of the phallus as the signifier in which language is joined to desire in the symbolic order, Mallot's scatological fantasy can be described as an attempt to deprive Perono of speech and, by extension, of phallic power.[57]

Regardless of their erotic discourse, both men reject explicit homoerotic acts even as each fantasizes aloud about violating the other. While they implicitly

55   Ibid., 102, 103.

56   Frank Graziano, *Divine Violence: Spectacle, Psychosexuality & Radical Christianity in the Argentine "Dirty War"* (San Francisco: Westview Press, 1992), 153.

57   Jacques Lacan, *Ecrits: A Selection*, trans. Alan Sheridan (New York: W.W. Norton, 1977), 220.

agree that their encounter will be defined in traditional heterosexual terms, they cannot come to an understanding that the dominated postcolonial subject will play the role of the feminine. Perono promises to have his way with Mallot: "Je vous déviergerai." / I'm going to de-virginize you.[58] While Mallot refuses the role which has been allotted him, protesting that he is "imprennable" or impossible to possess sexually. Despite this logistical conflict, they can deny neither the existence of a mutual attraction nor their desire to penetrate and dominate the other. They also concur that the feminine is indispensable as an imagined facilitator for the (non)expression of their homoerotic desire. And it is because the feminine here is imagined, that it (she) can be so one-dimensional and so bereft of all notions of power and agency.

Mallot and Perono's conjuring of the feminine serves as a bridge of heterosexuality between them. Through the Girardian lens of triangular desire the feminine here might be viewed as the object or mediator.[59] And, we might go further, concluding that the feminine does not figure in this triangular desire at all, not even as an object. Rather, the object of desire in the Mallot-Perono encounter is masculinity. This "eminently contagious" metaphysical desire, in which two subjects become consumed by a need to both mimic and possess each other, first spreads from Perono to Mallot in their initial encounter and mirrors the transfer of Perono's physical cardiac disease to Mallot's invented malady.[60] The question of possession first arises when Perono proclaims to Mallot: "Posséder, la seule réalité de ce monde. Nous sommes deux groupes d'homme sur cette terre, oui, deux: ceux qui possèdent et ceux qui cherchent à posséder." / Possessing, the only reality in this world. There are two groups of men on earth, yes two: those who possess and those who seek to possess.[61] This life lesson, which Perono shares as if he were his rival's mentor, later becomes a part of Mallot's personal philosophy: "Posséder. Je suis venu au monde pour posséder." / Possess. I was born to possess.[62] Mallot speaks not specifically of owning himself (self-possession), but of possession in general. This statement signifies a passage from a desire to possess oneself, to engage in a self-creation

58   Sony Labou Tansi, *Parenthèse de sang suivi de Je soussigné cardiaque* (Paris: Hatier, 1981), 104.

59   René Girard, *Deceit, Desire and the Novel: Self and the Other in Literary Structure*, trans. Yvonne Freccero (Baltimore: Johns Hopkins Press, 1965), 17.

60   Ibid., 96.

61   Sony Labou Tansi, *Parenthèse de sang suivi de Je soussigné cardiaque* (Paris: Hatier, 1981), 104.

62   Ibid., 140.

similar to that of the "Vee" mentioned above, to a yearning to possess the other. Mallot's declaration reveals his position as desiring subject to Perono's mediator, but in truth, their battle of wills is a reciprocal mediation in which they are "opposed but alike, and even interchangeable," in which they "are partners, but they agree only to disagree."[63] Each feeds upon the challenge represented in the other. Mallot knows this instinctively when he says: "Nous sommes faits l'un pour l'autre." / We're made for each other.[64] The feminine is present in their encounter only as a token, a justification for the violent desire each inspires in the other. The feminine also represents the one thing between them about which they can agree, for creating and destroying the feminine allows them to fabricate an erotic mythology within which they may justify the homoerotic nature of their relationship.[65] Within this mythology each desiring subject assigns the role of the feminine to the other, so that he might keep his gender identification intact within a normative heterosexual framework. This construction of desire also allows for the imagined deployment of phallic power in the manner in which Mbembe envisions it: "the individual male's ability to demonstrate his virility at the expense of a woman" in order to "obtain its validation from the subjugated woman herself."[66] The ritual in *Je sous-signé cardiaque* in which men victimize the feminine, and which we may call a symbolic gynæcolonization,[67] diverges from Mbembe's description only in that the "woman" in question, who is both the object of violence and a potential authenticator of her attacker's masculinity, is in fact a feminized male.

The interaction between Mallot and Perono situates both of them among those who seek to possess, to dominate. This common goal unites both men as erotic subjects, each desiring the other, and is a basis for theorizing the ambiguity of their assumed racial, social, and national differences. Both the "homosexual panic" incited by their first encounter and their inability to move beyond the struggle of the Hegelian master-slave dialectic makes their

---

63   René Girard, *Deceit, Desire and the Novel: Self and the Other in Literary Structure*, trans. Yvonne Freccero (Baltimore: Johns Hopkins Press, 1965), 103.

64   Sony Labou Tansi, *Parenthèse de sang suivi de Je soussigné cardiaque* (Paris: Hatier, 1981), 96.

65   Frank Graziano, *Divine Violence: Spectacle, Psychosexuality & Radical Christianity in the Argentine "Dirty War"* (San Francisco: Westview Press, 1992), 154–155.

66   Achille Mbembe, *On the Postcolony*, trans. A.M. Berrett (Los Angeles: University of California Press, 2001), 13.

67   Roger Little, "Blanche et Noir aux années vingt," in *Regards sur les littératures coloniales, Afrique Francophone: Approfondissements*, ed. Jean-François Durand (Paris: L'Harmattan, 1999), 19 note.

invocation of the feminine as a victim indispensable.[68] In this postcolonial context, the notion of a victim who must always be feminine springs from a phallogocentric definition of the feminine condition and a self-deceptive repudiation of homoerotic desire. In denying the possibility of a vulnerable masculinity, Mallot and Perono fail to understand that as participants in a phallocracy we are all – masculine or feminine – subject to physical and intellectual violation. Additionally, implicit denials of homoerotic desire in the homosocial space of the postcolony cannot but ring false in cases where the feminine serves only as a counterfeit mediator of desires. This reading of *Je soussigné cardiaque* attempts to take up the challenge issued in Sony Labou Tansi's text, which dares us to venture beyond the superficial strength of the dueling protagonists in order to witness the weakness of character they attempt to hide behind the scapegoat of femininity. Ultimately, though, it is the strength of the feminine that prevails through endurance in *Je soussigné cardiaque*. When the *cardiaque* Perono has disappeared from the stage and Mallot has been hung, the female characters are still standing.

---

68   Eve Kosofsky Sedgwick, *Between Men: English Literature and Male Homosocial Desire* (New York: Columbia University Press, 1985), 19.

Works Cited

Abdullah-Khan, Noreen. *Male Rape: The Emergence of a Social and Legal Issue*. New York: Palgrave Macmillan, 2008.

Adler, Alfred. *The Individual Psychology of Alfred Adler*, edited by H.L. Ansbacher and R.R. Ansbacher. New York: Harper Torchbooks, 1956.

Aldrich, Robert. "Colonial Man." In *French Masculinities: History, Culture and Politics*, edited by Christopher E. Forth and Bertrand Taithe, 123–140. New York: Macmillan, 2007.

Alonso, Ana Maria and Maria Teresa Koreck. "Silences: 'Hispanics,' AIDS, and Sexual Practices." In *The Lesbian and Gay Studies Reader*, edited by Henry Abelove, Michèle Aina Barale, David M. Halperin, 110–126. New York: Routledge, 1993.

Améry, Jean. *At the Mind's Limits: Contemplations by a Survivor on Auschwitz and Its Realities*. Translated by Sidney Rosenfeld and Stella P. Rosenfeld. Bloomington: Indiana University Press, 1980.

Apter, Emily. *Gide and the Codes of Homotextuality*. Saratoga, CA: Anma Libri, 1987.

Apter, Emily. *Feminizing the Fetish: Psychoanalysis and Narrative Obsession in Turn-of –the-Century France*. Ithaca: Cornell University Press, 1991.

Apter, Emily, ed. *Fetishism as Cultural Discourse*. Ithaca: Cornell University Press, 1993.

Aquaron, Robert and Luc Kamdem. "Regards sur les Albinos Africains." In *L'Autre et Nous "Scènes et Types,"* edited by Pascal Blanchard, Stéphane Blanchoin, Nicolas Bancel, Gilles Boëtsch, Hubert Gerbeau, 89. Paris: ACHAC and SYROS, 1995.

Bair, Barbara. "Remapping the black/white Body: Sexuality, Nationalism and Biracial Antimiscegenation Activism in 1920s Virginia." In *Sex, Love, Race: Crossing Boundaries in North American History*, edited by Martha Hodes, 399–419. New York: New York University Press, 1999.

Bakhtin, Mikhail. *Rabelais and His World*. Translated by Hélène Iswolsky. Bloomington: Indiana University Press, 1984.

Barthes, Roland. *La Chambre Claire: Note sur la Photographie*. Paris: Cahiers du cinéma, Gallimard, Seuil, 1980.

Barthes, Roland. *Camera Lucida: Reflections on Photography*. Translated by Richard Howard. New York: Hill and Wang, 1980.

Bassett, Frederick W. "Noah's Nakedness and the Curse of Canaan, a Case of Incest?" *Vetus Testamentum*, 21. 2 (Apr. 1971): 232–237.

Baudelaire, Charles. *Les Fleurs du mal*. Paris: Librairie Générale Française, 1972.

Beat-Songue, Paulette. *Prostitution en Afrique: l'exemple de Yaoundé*. Paris: L'Harmattan, 1986.

Beauvoir, Simone de. *The Second Sex*. Translated and edited by H.M. Parshley. Paris: Gallimard, 1949.

Benjamin, Jessica. "Master and Slave: The Fantasy of Erotic Domination." In *Powers of Desire: The Politics of Sexuality*, edited by Ann Snitow, Christine Stansell and Sharon Thompson, 280–299. New York: Monthly Press Review, 1983.

Benjamin, Walter, *Illuminations*. Translated by Harry Zohn, edited by Hannah Arendt. New York: Schocken Books, 1969.

Berger, John, *Ways of Seeing*. New York: Viking Penguin, 1972.

Berliner, Brett A. *Ambivalent Desire: The Exotic black other in Jazz-age France*. Amherst: University of Massachusetts Press, 2002.

Bertrand, Jean-Pierre et al., eds. *Histoire de la Littérature Belge Francophone 1830–2000*. Paris: Fayard, 2003.

Beynon, John. *Masculinities and Culture*. Philadelphia: Open University Press, 2001.

Bhabha, Homi. *The Location of Culture*. New York: Routledge, 1994.

Bhattacharyya, Gargi. *Sexuality and Society: An Introduction*. New York: Routledge, 2002.

Bilé, Serge. *La Légende du sexe surdimensionné des Noirs*. Monaco: Éditions du Rocher, 2005.

Binet, Alfred. *Études de psychologie expérimentale*. Paris: Octave Doin, 1888.

Blair, Dorothy S. *African Literature in French: A History of Creative Writing in French From West and Equatorial Africa*. New York: Cambridge University Press, 1976.

Blanchard, Pascal and Nicolas Bancel. "Quelques réflexions sur les représentations du corps des tirailleurs sénégalais (1880–1918)." *Africultures*, 25 (Feb. 2000): 41.

Blanchard, Pascal, Nicolas Bancel and Éric Deroo. *Le Paris Noir*. Paris: Hazan, 2001.

Boahen, A. Adu. *African Perspectives on Colonialism*. Baltimore: Johns Hopkins University Press, 1987.

Bockie, Simon. *Death and the Invisible Powers*. Bloomington and Indianapolis: Indiana University Press, 1993.

Bokoum, Saïdou. *Chaîne*. Paris: Éditions Denoël, 1974.

Boone, Joseph. "Mappings of Male Desire in Durrell's *Alexandria Quartet*." In *Displacing Homophobia: Gay Male Perspectives and Culture*, edited by Ronald R. Butters, John M. Clum, and Michael Moon, 73–106. Durham: Duke University Press, 1989.

Boone, Joseph. "Vacation Cruises; or, The Homoerotics of Orientalism." *PMLA* 110.1 (Jan. 1995): 89–107.

Boone, Joseph. *The Homoerotics of Orientalism*. NYC, NY: Columbia University Press, 2014.

Bourdon, C.H. "Les Romans." *Revue des lectures*. 13. 1 (Jan. 15, 1925): 26–27. Accessed May 1, 2016. http://gallica.bnf.fr/ark:/12148/bpt6k574335on/f32.image.r=revue%20 des%20lectures;%201925,%20Bourdon%20Romans%20mauvais%20Mille%20 Demaison%20homme%20nu.

Brownmiller, Susan. *Against Our Will: Men, Women, and Rape*. New York: Simon and Schuster, 1975.

Butler, Judith. "Imitation and Gender Insubordination." In *The Lesbian and Gay Studies Reader*, edited by Henry Abelove, Michèle Aina Barale, David M. Halperin, 307–320. New York: Routledge, 1993.

Butler, Judith. *Bodies that Matter: On the Discursive Limits of "Sex"*. New York: Routledge, 1993.

Camara, Laye. *Dramouss*. Paris: Librairie Plon, 1966.

Capécia, Mayotte. *Je suis martiniquaise*. Paris: Corrêa, 1948.

Caron, David. 'The Queerness of Male Group Friendship." In *Entre Hommes: French and Francophone Masculinities in Culture and Theory*, edited by Todd W. Reeser and Lewis C. Seifert, 251–266. Newark: University of Delaware Press, 2008.

Chalaye, Sylvie. *Du Noir au nègre: l'image du Noir au théâtre: de Marguerite de Navarre à Jean Genet (1550–1960)*. Paris: L'Harmattan, 1998.

Charcot, Jean-Martin and Valentin Magnan. "Inversion du sens génital." *Archives de neurologie: revue des maladies nerveuse et mentales*" Vol. 4, n. 10–12 (1882): 296–319. Accessed April 5, 2010. http://jubilotheque.upmc.fr/fonds-archneuro/CN_000032_004/document.pdf?name=CN_000032_004_pdf.pdf.

Chari, Hema. "Colonial Fantasies and Postcolonial Identities: Elaboration of Postcolonial Masculinity and Homoerotic Desire." In *Postcolonial, Queer: Theoretical Intersections*, edited by John C. Hawley, 277–304. Albany: State University of New York Press, 2001.

Chancer, Lynn S. "New Bedford, Massachusetts, March 6, 1983–March 22, 1984: The 'Before and After' of a Group Rape." *Gender & Society*, 1.3 (1987): 239–260

Cixous, Hélène and Catherine, Clément. *La Jeune Née*. Paris: Union Général de Éditions, 1975.

Cixous, Hélène and Catherine Clément. *The Newly Born Woman*. Translated by Betsy Wing. Minneapolis: University of Minnesota Press, 1986.

Clever, Eldridge. *Soul on Ice*. New York: McGraw-Hill, 1968.

Cohen, William B. "The Lure of Empire: Why Frenchmen Entered the Colonial Service." *Journal of Contemporary History*, 4.1 (Jan. 1969): 103–116.

Cole, Joshua. *The Power of Large Numbers: Population, Politics and Gender in Nineteenth-Century France*. Ithaca: Cornell University Press, 2000.

Connell, Raewyn. *Masculinities*. Cambridge: Polity Press, 1995.

Cousins, Helen. "Nothing Like Motherhood: Barrenness, Abortion and Infanticide in Yvonne Vera's Fiction." In *Rites of Passage in Postcolonial Women's Writing*, edited by Pauline Dodgson-Katiyo and Gina Wisker, 21–40. New York: Editions Rodopi, 2010.

Cousturier, Lucie. *Des inconnus chez moi*. Paris: Éditions de la Sirène, 1920.

Crompton, Louis. *Homosexuality and Civilization*. Cambridge: Harvard University Press, 2003. Accessed September 26, 2017. https://books.google.com/books?id=TfBYd9xVaXcC&lpg=PA66&dq=homosexuality%20stoics&pg=PA67#v=onepage&q=homosexuality%20stoics&f=false.

Dark Star Collective, eds. *Quiet Rumors: An Anarcha-Feminist Reader*. San Francisco: AK Press, 2002.

Davidis, Maria. "'Unarm, Eros!': Adventure, Homoeroticism, and Divine Order in *Prester John*," In *Imperial Desire: Dissident Sexualities and Colonial Literature*, edited by Philip Holden and Richard J. Ruppel, 223–240. Minneapolis: University of Minnesota Press, 2003.

Davis, Angela Y. *Women, Race, & Class*. New York: Random House, 1981.

Day, Patrick. "A comparative Study of Crime and Punishment in Ousmane Sembène's *Le Docker Noir* and Albert Camus's *L'Étranger*" *Africa Today*, 52. 3 (Spring 2006): 83–96.

De Lauretis, Teresa. "Sexual Indifference and Lesbian Representation." in *The Lesbian and Gay Studies Reader*, edited by Henry Abelove, Michèle Aina Barale and David M. Halperin, 141–158. New York: Routledge, 1993).

Delafosse, Maurice. *Broussard ou les états d'âme d'un colonial suivi de ses propos et ses opinions*. Paris: Comité de L'Afrique Française, 1923.

Desai, Gaurav. "Out in Africa." In *Post-Colonial Queer: Theoretical Intersections*, edited by John C. Hawley, 139–164. Albany: State University of New York Press, 2001.

Dewitte, Philippe. "Le 'Noir' dans l'imaginaire français." In *L'Autre et Nous "Scènes et Types,"* edited by Pascal Blanchard, Stéphane Blanchoin, Nicolas Bancel, Gilles Boëtsch, Hubert Gerbeau, 27–32. Paris: ACHAC and SYROS, 1995.

Diderot, Denis. *Indiscrete Jewels*. Translated by Sophie Hawkes. New York: Marsilio, 1993.

Diome, Fatou. *La Préférence Nationale*. Paris: Présence Africaine, 2001.

Doillon, Albert. *Le Dico du sexe*. Paris: Fayard, 2002.

Dowd Hall, Jacquelyn. "'The Mind that Burns in Each Body': Women, Rape and Racial Violence." In *Powers of Desire: The Politics of Sexuality*, edited by Ann Snitow, Christine Stansell and Sharon Thompson, 328–349. New York: Monthly Press Review, 1983.

Dreger, Alice Domurat. *Hermaphrodites and the Medical Invention of Sex*. Cambridge: Harvard University Press, 1998.

Dubois, W.E.B. *The Souls of black Folk*. Chicago: A.C. McClurg & Co., 1907.

Dunton, Chris. "'Wheything be Dat?' The Treatment of Homosexuality in African Literature." *Research in African Literatures*, 20. 3 (Autumn 1989): 422–448.

Dupuis, Joseph. *Journal of a Residence in Ashantee*. London: Frank Cass, 1966.

Dynes, Wayne R. "Orientation." In *Encyclopedia of Homosexuality, Volume II*, edited by Wayne R. Dynes, 552. Shrewsbury, MA: Garland Press, 1990.

Edmondson, Belinda. *Making Men: Gender, Literary Authority and Women's Writing in Caribbean Narrative*. Durham: Duke University Press, 1999.

Effa, Gaston-Paul. *Tout ce bleu*. Paris: Bernard Grasset, 1996.

Eilberg-Schwartz, Howard. *God's Phallus and Other Problems for Men and Monotheism*. Boston: Beacon Press, 1994.

Epprecht, Marc. *Heterosexual Africa? The History of an Idea from the Age of Exploration to the Age of AIDS*. Athens, OH: Ohio University Press, 2008.

Fanon, Frantz. *Peau noire, masques blancs*. Paris: Éditions du Seuil, 1952.

Fanon, Frantz. *Les damnés de la terre*. Paris: La Découverte, 2002.

Fanon, Frantz. *The Wretched of the Earth*. Translated by Richard Philcox. New York: Grove Press, 2004.

Fanon, Frantz. *Black Skin, white Masks*. Translated by Richard Philcox. New York: Grove Press, 2008.

Fanoudh-Siefer, Léon. *Le mythe du Nègre et de l'Afrique Noire dans la Littérature Française (de 1800 à la 2ᵉ Guerre Mondiale)*. Paris: Librairie C. Klincksieck, 1968.

Faure-Favier, Louise. *Blanche et Noir*. Paris: Ferenczi et Fils, 1928.

Fausto-Sterling, Anne. *Sexing the Body: Gender Politics and the Construction of Sexuality*. New York: Basic Books, 2000.

Feuser, W.F. "Richard Wright's *Native Son* and Sembène Ousmane's *Le Docker noir*" in *Essays in Comparative African Literature*, edited by Willfried F. Feuser and I.N.C. Aniebo, 252–267. Lagos: Center for black and African Arts and Civilization, 2001.

Féval, Paul. *Ton Corps est à moi*. Paris: Éditions Radot, 1927.

Fiber Luce, Louise. "Passages: The Women of Sony Labou Tansi." *The French Review*, 64. 5 (April 1991): 739–746.

Florian-Parmentier. *Pierre Mille*. Paris: Les Éditions G. Crès et Cie., 1923.

Foucault, Michel. *Discipline and Punish: The Birth of the Prison*. Translated by Alan Sheridan. New York: Vintage Books, 1979.

Foucault, Michel. *The History of Sexuality Volume 1: An Introduction*. Translated by Robert Hurley. New York: Vintage Books, 1990.

Fraiman, Susan. "Geometries of Race and Gender: Eve Sedgwick, Spike Lee, Charlayne Hunter-Gault." *Feminist Studies*, 20. 1 (Spring, 1994): 67–84.

Fraiture, Pierre-Philippe. "De l'influence du Goncourt sur le corpus colonial: le cas de *Batouala*." In *Prix Goncourt, 1903–2003: essais critiques*, edited by Katherine Ashley, 95–108. Bern: Peter Lang, 2003).

Freud, Sigmund. "Fetishism." In *The Standard Edition of the Complete Works of Sigmund Freud*. Vol. 22. Translated by James Strachey et al., 147–157. London: Hogarth Press and the Institute of Psychoanalysis, 1957.

Freud, Sigmund. *Three Essays of the Theory of Sexuality*. Translated by James Strachey. New York: Avon Books, 1962 [1905].

Freud, Sigmund. "The Economic Problem of Masochism" in *The Standard Edition of the Complete Psychological Works of Sigmund Freud*. Vol. 19 (1923–1925), Translated by James Strachey et al., 155–170. London: Hogarth Press and the Institute of Psychoanalysis, 1999.

Freud, Sigmund. *Three Contributions to the Theory of Sex.* Project Gutenberg, 2005, Accessed April 23, 2010. http://www.gutengerg.org/files/14969/14969-h/14969-h.htm.

Frye, Northrop. *The Secular Scripture: A Study of the Structure of Romance.* Cambridge, MA: Harvard University Press, 1976.

Fu-Kiau, Kimbwandende Kia Bunseki. *African Cosmology of the Bântu-Kôngo: Tying the Spiritual Knot: Principles of Life and Living.* New York: Athelia Henrietta Press, 2001.

Fuss, Diana. "Interior Colonies: Frantz Fanon and the Politics of Identification." *Diacritics,* 24. 2/3, Critical Crossings (Summer-Autumn, 1994): 20–42.

Garvey, Marcus. "Editorial." *Negro World* (11 September 1920). In *The Marcus Garvey and Universal Negro Improvement Association Papers* 3:9, edited by Robert A. Hill, 238–245. Berkeley: University of California Press, 1983.

Gauthier, Xavière. *Surréalisme et Sexualité.* Paris: Gallimard, 1971.

Gbouablé, Edwige. "Langage du corps et voix d'auteur dans le théâtre de Sony Labou Tansi: une écriture de l'alibi." *L'Esprit Créateur,* 48.3 (Fall 2008): 17–24.

Genet, Jean. *Querelle de Brest.* Paris: Gallimard, 1953.

Giddens, Anthony. *Modernity and Self-Identity: Self and Society in the Late Modern Age.* Stanford: Stanford University Press, 1991.

Gide, André. *L'Immoraliste.* Paris: Mercure de France, 1902.

Gide, André. *Corydon.* Paris: Éditions Gallimard, 1924.

Gide, André. *Voyage au Congo.* Paris: Éditions Gallimard, 1927.

Gide, André. *Les Cahiers de la Petite Dame* (I, II, III, IV). In *Cahiers André Gide.* Paris: Gallimard, 1992.

Girard, René. *Deceit, Desire and the Novel: Self and the Other in Literary Structure.* Translated by Yvonne Freccero. Baltimore: Johns Hopkins Press, 1965.

Girard, René. *Violence and the Sacred.* Translated by Patrick Gregory. Baltimore: Johns Hopkins University Press, 1977.

Goldie, Terry. "Saint Fanon and 'Homosexual Territory'." In *Frantz Fanon: Critical Perspectives,* edited by Anthony C. Alessandrini, 75–85. New York: Routledge, 1999.

Gondola, Ch. Didier. "The Search for Elegance among Congolese Youth." *African Studies Review,* 42.1 (April 1999): 23–48.

Gondola, Ch. Didier. *The History of Congo.* Westport, CT: Greenwood Publishing Group, 2002.

Gourmont, Remy de. *Physique de l'amour: essai sur l'instinct sexuel.* Paris: Société du Mercure de France, 1903.

Graves, Robert and Raphael Patai. *Hebrew Myths: The Book of Genesis.* New York, Doubleday and Company Inc., 1964.

Graziano, Frank. *Divine Violence: Spectacle, Psychosexuality & Radical Christianity in the Argentine "Dirty War."* San Francisco: Westview Press, 1992.

Grégoire, Herman. *Makako, singe d'Afrique.* Paris: La Renaissance du Livre, 1921.

Groth, A.N. and A.W. Burgess. "Male Rape: Offenders and Victims." *American Journal of Psychiatry* 137.7 (July 1980): 806–810.

Guex, Germaine. *La Névrose d'abandon.* Paris: Presses Universitaires de France, 1950.

Halen, Pierre. "Les fictions amoureuse et l'idéologie coloniale au Congo belge." In *L'Exotisme,* edited by Alain Buisine and Norbert Dodille, 247–258. Saint-Denis, Île de la Réunion: Cahiers C.R.L.H, 1988.

Halen, Pierre. *Le petit Belge avait vu Grand: Une Littérature Coloniale.* Brussels: Éditions Labor, 1993.

Hall, Stuart. "The After-life of Frantz Fanon: Why Fanon? Why Now? Why *black Skin, white Masks*?" in *The Fact of blackness: Frantz Fanon and Visual Representation,* edited by Alan Read, 12–37. Seattle: Bay Press, 1996.

Halley, Janet E. "The Construction of Heterosexuality." In *Fear of a Queer Planet: Queer Politics and Social Theory,* edited by Michael Warner, 82–104. Minneapolis: University of Minnesota Press, 1993.

Halperin, David. *One Hundred Years of Homosexuality: And other Essays on Greek Love.* New York: Manchester University Press, 1990.

Halperin, David. *How to Do the History of Homosexuality.* Chicago: University of Chicago Press, 2002.

Hargreaves, Alec. *The Colonial Experience in French Fiction: A Study of Pierre Loti, Ernest Psichari and Pierre Mille.* London: The Macmillan Press, Ltd., 1981.

Hargreaves, Alec. "An Emperor with No Clothes?" In *Riots in France,* Social Science Research Council. Nov. 28, 2005. Accessed April 24,2010. http://riotsfrance.ssrc.org/Hargreaves/.

Harvey, Penelope and Peter Gow. "Introduction." In *Sex and Violence: Issues in Representation and Experience,* edited by Harvey, Penelope and Peter Gow, 1–16. New York: Routledge, 1994.

Hayes, Jarrod. *Queer Nations: Marginalities in the Maghreb.* Chicago: University of Chicago Press, 2000.

Hayes, Jarrod. *Queer Roots for the Diaspora: Ghosts in the Family Tree.* Ann Arbor: University of Michigan Press, 2006.

Haynes, Stephen R. *Noah's Curse: The Biblical Justification of American Slavery.* New York: Oxford University Press, 2002.

Hegel, G.W.F. *The Phenomenology of Mind.* Translated by J.B. Baillie. New York: The Macmillan Company, 1931.

Hengehold, Laura. "An Immodest Proposal: Foucault, Hysterization, and the 'Second Rape'." *Hypatia,* 9.3 (Summer 1994): 88–107.

Hocquenghem, Guy. *Le désir homosexuel.* Paris: Fayard, 1993.

Hoffmann, Léon-François. *Le Nègre romantique: personnage littéraire et obsession collective.* Paris: Payot, 1973.

Horeck, Tanya. *Public Rape: Representing violation in fiction and film.* New York: Routledge, 2004.

Horkheimer, Max and Theodore Adorno. *The Dialectic of Enlightenment.* New York: Seabury Press, 1972.

Imperato, B.H. and P.J. Imperato. "Beliefs and Practices Concerning Twins, Hermaphrodites and Albinos Among the Bamana and Maninka of Mali." Department of Preventive Medicine and Community Health, State University of New York, Downstate Medical Center, Brooklyn, NY 11203, USA. Accessed May 1, 2016. http://www.ncbi.nlm.nih.gov/pubmed/16830507?itool=EntrezSystem2.PEntrez.Pubmed. Pubmed_ResultsPanel.Pubmed_RVDocSum&ordinalpos=5.

Irigaray, Luce. *This Sex Which is Not One.* Translated by Catherine Porter. Ithaca: Cornell University Press, 1985.

Jadot, Joseph-Marie. "La Littérature coloniale de Belgique, Conférence faite, le 2 mai 1922, aux Mardis des Lettres Belges." *La Revue Sincère,* No. 2 (Nov. 15, 1922): 71–79. Accessed June 1, 2016. http://gallica.bnf.fr/ark:/12148/bpt6k5741863c.image.hl.r= Grégoire.f14langEN.pagination.

JanMohamed, Abdul R. "The Economy of Manichean Allegory: The Function of Racial Difference in Colonialist Literature." *Critical Inquiry* 12. 1 (Autumn 1985): 59–87.

Julien, Eileen, "Rape, Repression, and Narrative Form in *Le Devoir de violence* and *La Vie et demie.*" In *Rape and Representation,* edited by Lynn A. Higgins and Brenda R. Silver, 160–181. New York: Columbia University Press, 1991.

Kaku, Michio. *Physics of the Impossible.* New York: Doubleday, 2008.

Kaplan, Ann E. "Is the Gaze Male?" In *Powers of Desire: The Politics of Sexuality,* edited by Ann Snitow, Christine Stansell and Sharon Thompson, 309–327. New York: Monthly Press Review, 1983.

Kappler, Susanne. *The Pornography of Representation.* Oxford: Polity Press, 1986.

Kelly, George. "The Language of Hypothesis: Man's Psychological Instrument." *Journal of Individual Psychology* 20 (1964): 137–152.

Kimmel, Michael. *Manhood in America.* New York: Free Press, 1996.

Kouakou, Jean-Marie. *La pensée de Sony Labou Tansi.* Paris: L'Harmattan, 2003.

Krafft-Ebing, Richard von. "Contribution à la psychopathie sexuelle." *Archives de neurologie,* 27. 83–88 (1894): 139. Accessed April 4, 2010. http://jubilotheque.upmc .fr/ead.html?id=CN_000055_027&c=CN_000055_027_e0009524&qid=sdx_q20 #!{"content":[CN_000055_027_e0009524",false,"sdx_q20"]}.

Kristeva, Julia. *Étrangers à nous-même.* Paris: Fayard, 1988.

Kritzman, Lawrence. "Ernaux's Testimony of Shame." *L'Esprit Créateur* 39.4 (Winter 1999): 139–148.

L'Arlequin: Caricaturiste. Accessed May 9, 2013. https://www.egaliteetreconciliation.fr/ Les-dessins-de-la-semaine-18511.html.

Lacan, Jacques. *Ecrits: A Selection*. Translated by Alan Sheridan. New York: W.W. Norton, 1977.

Lame, Danielle de, "Que sont mes amis devenus? Se Re-créer des rapports de genre." In *Changements au féminin en Afrique noire Vol 1.*, edited by Danielle de Lame and Chantal Zabus, 17–36. Paris: L'Harmattan, 1999.

Lane, Christopher. *The Ruling Passion: British Colonial Allegory and the Paradox of Homosexual Desire*. Durham: Duke University Press, 1995.

Lang, Andrew. *The Making of Religion*. London: Longman's Green and Co., 1900.

Lavodrama, Philippe. "Cham, le maudit de la Bible, Victime première." *Regards Africains*, 46/47 (Summer 2002): 47–48.

Lebel, Roland. *Le Livre du pays noir: Anthologie de Littérature Africaine*. Paris: Éditions du Monde Moderne, 1923.

Lejeune, Robert. "M. Pierre Mille, écrivain de droite." *Revue critique des idées et des livres* 36. 220 (1.25. 1924): 13–19.

Le Naour, Jean-Yves. *La Honte noire: L'Allemagne et les troupes coloniales françaises, 1914–1945*. Paris: Hachette Littérature, 2004.

Léonnec, Félix. *La Loi de la brousse*. Paris: Éditions Jules Tallandier, 1932.

Lévi-Strauss, Claude. *Les Structures élémentaires de la parenté*. Paris: La Haye, Mouton et Co., 1967.

Lévi-Strauss. *The Elementary Structures of Kinship*. Translated by James Harle Bell, John Richard von Sturmer, and Rodney Needham, edited by Rodney Needham. Boston: Beacon Press, 1969.

Lévy-Bruhl, Lucien. *La Mentalité primitive*. Paris: Presses Universitaires de France, 1960.

Lionnet, Françoise. *Postcolonial Representations: Women, Literature, Identity*. Ithaca: Cornell University Press, 1995.

Lionnet, Françoise and Shu-mei Shih. In "Introduction Thinking through the Minor, Transnationally." In *Minor Transnationalism*, edited by Françoise Lionnet and Shu-mei Shih, 1–26. Durham: Duke UP, 2005.

Little, Roger. "Blanche et Noir aux années vingt." In *Regards sur les littératures coloniales, Afrique Francophone: Approfondissements Tome II*, edited by Jean-François Durand, 7–50. Paris: L'Harmattan, 1999.

Little, Roger. *Between Totem and Taboo: Black Man, White Woman in Francographic Literature*. Exeter: University of Exeter Press, 2001.

Lorde, Audra. "Uses of the Erotic: The Erotic as Power." In *Black Feminist Cultural Criticism*, edited by Jacqueline Bobo Malden, 285–290. MA: Blackwell Publishers, 2001.

Loti, Pierre. *Le Roman d'un Spahi*. Paris: Calmann-Lévy, 1974.

Lucey, Michael. *Gide's Bent: Sexuality, Politics, Writing*. New York: Oxford University Press, 1995.

Mac an Ghaill, Máirtín. *The Making of Men: Masculinities, Sexualities and Schooling.* Buckingham: Open University Press, 1994.

MacGaffey, Wyatt. *Religion and Society in Central Africa: The BaKongo of Lower Zaire.* Chicago: University of Chicago Press, 1986.

MacKinnon, Catharine. *Only Words.* London: Harper Collins, 1993.

Mannheim, Karl. "The Problems of Generations." In *Essays on the Sociology of Knowledge,* edited by Paul Kecskmeti, 276–320. New York: Oxford University Press, 1952.

Mapplethorpe, Robert. *Black Males.* Amsterdam: Galerie Jurka, 1980.

Maran, René. *Un homme pareil aux autres.* Paris: Éditions Arc-en-Ciel, 1947.

Martinkus-Zemp, Ada. *Le Blanc et le Noir.* Paris: A.G. Nizet, 1975.

Mauss, Marcel. *The Gift: Forms and Functions of Exchange in Archaic Societies.* Translated by Ian Cunnison. London: Cohen & West, 1966.

Mbembe, Achille. *On the Postcolony.* Los Angeles: University of California Press, 2001.

McClintock, Anne. *Imperial Leather: Race, Gender, and Sexuality in the Colonial Contest.* New York: Routledge, 1995.

Mégevand, Martin. "Le corps et la pathologie du pouvoir dans le théâtre sonyien." In *Sony Labou Tansi à l'œuvre,* edited by Papa Samba Diop and Xavier Garnier, 77–86. Paris: L'Harmattan, 2007.

Memmi, Albert. "The Impossible Life of Frantz Fanon." Translated and edited by Thomas Cassirer and G. Michael Twomey. *The Massachusetts Review,* 14. 1 (Winter 1973): 9–39.

Memmi, Albert. *The Colonizer and the Colonized.* Translated by Howard Greenfeld. London: Earthscan Publications, 2003.

Memmi, Albert. *Decolonization and the Decolonized.* Translated by Robert Bononno. Minneapolis. University of Minnesota Press, 2006.

Mercer, Kobena. "Looking for Trouble." In *The Lesbian and Gay Studies Reader,* edited by Henry Abelove, Michèle Aina Barale, David M. Halperin, 350–359. New York: Routledge, 1993.

Mercer, Kobena. "Decolonisation and Disappointment: Reading Fanon's Sexual Politics." In *The Fact of blackness: Frantz Fanon and Visual Representation,* edited by Alan Read, 114–165. Seattle: Bay Press, 1996.

Metzger, Deena. "It is always the woman who is raped." *American Journal of Psychiatry* 133 (1976): 405–408.

Mille Pierre and André Demaison. *La Femme et l'homme nu.* Paris: Les Éditions de France, 1924.

Miller, Christopher L. *Blank Darkness: Africanist Discourse in French.* Chicago: University of Chicago Press, 1985.

Miller, Christopher L. *The French Atlantic Triangle: Literature and Culture of the Slave Trade*. Durham: Duke UP, 2008.

Miller, Monica L. *Slaves to Fashion: black Dandyism and the Styling of black Diasporic Identity*. Durham: Duke UP, 2009.

Miller, Nancy K. "Memory Stains: Annie Ernaux's *Shame*." In *a/b: Auto/Biography Studies* 14.1 (Summer 1999): 38–50.

Mills, C. Wright. *The Power Elite*. London: Oxford University Press, 1956.

Milon, Alain. *L'étranger dans la ville: du rap au graff mural*. Paris: PUF, 1999.

Monson-Rosen, Madeleine. "The Most Primeval of Passions: Incest in the Service of Women in Angela Carter's *The Magic Toyshop*." In *Straight Writ Queer: Non-Normative Expressions of Heterosexuality in Literature*, edited by Richard Fantina, 232–243. Jefferson, NC: McFarland and Company, 2006.

Monte, Christopher F. and Robert N. Sollod. *Beneath the Mask: An Introduction to Theories of Personality*. Hoboken, NJ: John Wiley & Sons, 2003.

Morand, Paul, *Magie noire*. Paris: Bernard Grasset, 1928.

Moudileno, Lydie. *Parades postcoloniales: la fabrication des identités dans le roman congolais*. Paris: Éditions Karthala, 2006.

Mudimbe, V.Y. *Entre Les Eaux*. Paris: Présence Africaine, 1973.

Mulvey, Laura. "Visual Pleasure and Narrative Cinema." *Screen* 16. 3 (Autumn 1975): 6–18.

Murphy, David. *Sembene: Imagining Alternatives in Film and Fiction*. Oxford: Oxford University Press, 2000.

Murphy, David. "La Danse et la parole: l'exil et l'identité chez les Noirs de Marseille dans *Banjo* de Claude McKay et *Le Docker noir* d'Ousmane Sembene." *Canadian Review of Comparative Literature* (September 2000): 462–479.

Nederveen Pieterse, Jan. *White on black: images of Africa and blacks in Western Popular Culture*. New Haven: Yale University Press, 1992.

Nicholson, Graeme. *Plato's Phaedrus: The Philosophy of Love*. West Lafayette, IN: Purdue UP, 1999.

Nkashama, Pius Ngandu. "The Golden Years of the Novel." In *European-language Writing in sub-Saharan Africa* Vol. 1, edited by Albert Gérard, 512–539. Budapest: UNESCO, 1986.

O'Connell Davidson, Julia. *Prostitution, Power and Freedom*. Ann Arbor: University of Michigan Press, 1998.

Ogborn, Miles. "Locating the Macaroni: Luxury, Sexuality, and Vision in Vauxhall Gardens." *Textual Practice* 11.3 (1997): 445–61.

Omgba, Richard Laurent. "Mythes et Fantasmes de la Littérature Coloniale." In *Regards sur les Littératures Coloniales, Afrique Francophone: Approfondissements*, Tome II, edited by Jean-François Durand, 125–137. Paris: L'Harmattan, 1999.

Patterson, Orlando. *Slavery and Social Death*. Cambridge, M.A.: Harvard University Press, 1982.

Plato. *The Phaedrus, Lysis and Protagoras of Plato: A New and Literal Translation mainly from the text of Bekker*. Translated by J. Wright. New York: Macmillan and Co., 1888.

Randau, Robert. *Des Blancs dans la cité des Noirs*. Paris: Albin Michel, 1935.

Ravet, Roger. "Sony Labou Tansi's 'violence engageante'." In *Postcolonial Violence, Culture and Identity in Francophone Africa and the Antilles*, edited by Lorna Milne, 59–82. New York: Peter Lang, 2007.

Rich, Adrienne. *Of Woman Born: Motherhood as Experience and Institution*. London: Virago, 1977.

Riesman, David, Nathan Glazer, and Rueul Denney. *The Lonely Crowd: A Study of the Changing American Character*. New York: Doubleday, 1955.

Riesz, János. *De la littérature coloniale à la littérature africaine: Prétextes, Contextes, Intertextes*. Paris: Éditions Karthala, 2007.

Ringdal, Nils Johan. *Love for Sale: A World History of Prostitution*. York: Grove Press, 2004.

Rosello, Mireille. *Declining the Stereotype: Ethnicity and Representation in French Cultures*. Hanover: University Press of New England, 1998.

Rosello, Mireille. *Postcolonial Hospitality: The Immigrant as Guest*. Stanford: Stanford University Press, 2001.

Rozat, Guy and Roger Bartra. "Racism and Capitalism." In *Sociological Theories: Race and Colonialism*, Unesco, 287–304. Paris: Bernan Associates, 1980.

Rubin, Gayle S. "Coconuts: Aspects of Male/Female Relationships in New Guinea." Unpublished Ms., 1974.

Rubin, Gayle S. "The Traffic in Women: Notes on the Political Economy of Sex." In *Toward an Anthropology of Women*, edited by Rayna Reiter, 157–210. New York: Monthly Review Press, 1975.

Rubin, Gayle S. "Thinking Sex: Notes for a Radical Theory of the Politics of Sexuality." In *The Lesbian and Gay Studies Reader*, edited by Henry Abelove, Michèle Aina Barale, David M. Halperin, 3–44. (New York: Routledge, 1993 [1984]).

Runciman, Walter Garrison. *Relative Deprivation and Social Justice: A Study of Attitudes to Social Inequality in Twentieth-Century England*. University of California Press, 1966.

Ruscio, Alain, ed. *Amours coloniales. Aventures et fantasmes exotiques, de Claire de Duras à Georges Simenon*. Brussels: Collection Bibliothèque Complexe, 1996.

Rutherford, Jonathan. *Forever England: Reflections on Race, Masculinity and Empire*. London: Lawrence & Wishart, 1997.

Rysselberghe, Maria Van. *Les Cahiers de la Petite Dame Tome I (1918–1929)*. Paris: Gallimard, 1973.

Rysselberghe, Maria Van. *Les Cahiers de la Petite Dame Tome II (1929–1937)*. Paris: Gallimard, 1974.

Rysselberghe, Maria Van. *Les Cahiers de la Petite Dame Tome III (1937–1945)*. Paris: Gallimard, 1975.

Rysselberghe, Maria Van. *Les Cahiers de la Petite Dame Tome IV (1945–1951)*. Paris: Gallimard, 1977.

Sadji, Abdoulaye. *Nini, mulâtresse du Sénégal*. Paris: Présence Africaine, 1954.

Sartre, Jean-Paul. *La Nausée*. Paris: Gallimard, 1938.

Sartre, Jean-Paul. "Orphée noir." In *Anthologie de la nouvelle poésie nègre et malgache de langue française*, edited by Léopold Sedar Senghor. Paris: Presses Universitaires de France, 1948.

Sartre, Jean-Paul. *Being and Nothingness: An Essay on Phenomenological Ontology*. Translated by Hazel E. Barnes. New York: Citadel Press, 1966.

Sassine, Williams. *Mémoire d'une peau*. Paris: Présence Africaine, 1998.

Sauvage, Marcel. *Les Secrets de l'Afrique noire*. Paris: Éditions Denoël, 1937.

Schipper-De Leeuw, Mineke. *Le blanc vu d'Afrique: le blanc et l'occident au miroir du roman négro-africain de langue française, des origines au Festival de Dakar, 1920–1966*. Yaoundé: Éditions CLE, 1973.

Séché, Alphonse. *Les Noirs (D'après des documents officiels)*. Paris: Payot & Cie, 1919.

Sedgwick, Eve Kosofsky. *Between Men: English Literature and Male Homosocial Desire*. New York: Columbia University Press, 1985.

Sedgwick, Eve Kosofsky. *Epistemology of the Closet*. Los Angeles: University of California Press, 1990.

Seltzer, Mark. *Serial Killers: Death and Life in America's Wound Culture*. New York: Routledge, 1998.

Sembene, Ousmane. *Le Docker Noir*. Paris: Présence Africaine, 1973.

Shakespeare, William. *The Tempest*. New York: St. Martin's Press, 1999.

Sheridan, Alan. *André Gide: Life in the Present*. London: Hamish Hamilton, 1999.

Shih, Shu-mei. "Global Literature and the Technologies of Recognition." *PMLA* 119.1, Special Topic: Literatures at Large (Jan. 2004): 16–30.

Sidikou, Aissata. *Recreating Words, Reshaping Worlds: The Verbal Art of Women from Niger, Mali, and Senegal*. Trenton: Africa World Press, 2001.

Silverman, Kaja. "White Skin, Brown Masks: With Lawrence in Arabia." *Differences*, no. 3 (1989): 3–54.

Simpson Fletcher, Yaël. "Catholics, Communists and Colonial Subjects: Working-Class Militancy and Racial Difference in Postwar Marseille." In *The Color of Liberty: Histories of Race in France*, edited by Sue Peabody and Tyler Edward Stovall, 338–350. Durham: Duke University Press, 2003.

Smart, Carol. *Feminism and the Power of Law*. London: Routledge, 1992.

Sony Labou Tansi. *La Vie et demie*. Paris: Éditions du Seuil, 1979.

Sony Labou Tansi. *Parenthèse de sang suivi de Je soussigné cardiaque*. Paris: Hatier, 1981.

Sony Labou Tansi. *L'Etat Honteux*. Paris: Seuil, 1981.

Sony Labou Tansi. *L'Anté-peuple*. Paris: Éditions du Seuil, 1983.

Sony Labou Tansi. "Lettre aux Africains sous couvert du parti punique." In *L'autre monde: écrits inédits*, 42–46. Paris: Revue Noire, 1997.

Sony Labou Tansi. "'An Open Letter to Africans' c/o The Punic One-Party State." Translated by John Conteh-Morgan. In *African Literature: An Anthology of Criticism and Theory*, edited by Tejumola Olaniyan and Ato Quayson, 271–273. Malden, MA: Blackwell, 2007.

Steady, Filomina. "African Feminism: A Worldwide Perspective." In *Women in Africa and the African Diaspora*, edited by Rosalyn Terborg-Penn, Sharon Harley & and Andrea Benton, pp. 18–19. Washington D.C.: Howard University Press, 1987.

Stoler, Ann-Laura. *Race and the Education of Desire: Foucault's History of Sexuality and the Colonial Order of Things*. Durham: Duke University Press, 1995.

Stovall, Tyler. *Paris Noir: African Americans in the City of Light*. Boston: Houghton Mifflin, 1996.

Summers, Martin. "'This Immoral Practice' The Prehistory of Homophobia in black Nationalist Thought." In *Gender Nonconformity, Race, and Sexuality: Charting the Connections*, edited by Toni Lester, 21–43. Madison: University of Wisconsin Press, 2002.

Surkis, Judith. *Sexing the Citizen: Morality and Masculinity in France, 1870–1920*. Ithaca: Cornell University Press, 2006.

Taussig, Michael. *Mimesis and Alterity: A Particular History of the Senses*. New York: Routledge, 1993.

Taylor, Edward B. *Primitive Culture: Researches into the Development of Mythology, Philosophy, Religion, Language, Art and Custom*. London: John Murry: 1871.

Thomas, Dominic. *Nation-Building, Propaganda, and Literature in Francophone Africa*. Bloomington: Indiana University Press, 2002.

Thomas, Dominic. *Black France: Colonialism, Immigration and Transnationalism*. Bloomington: Indiana University Press, 2007.

Tobner, Odile. *Du racisme français: Quatre siècles de négrophobie*. Paris: Editions des Arènes, 2007.

Todorov, Tzvetan and Bernard Pivot. "Le Choc des Cultures." *Apostrophes* (Feb. 24, 1989). Accessed April 24, 2010. http://www.ina.fr/art-et-culture/litterature/video/CPB89002559/le-choc-des-cultures.fr.html.

Tosh, John. *Manliness and Masculinities in Nineteenth-century Britain*. Harlow: Pearson/Longman, 2005.

Van Woerkens, Martine. "Guerre, 'Race' et Sexes dans *Le Masque d'or* de Charles Vidor." In *L'Autre et Nous: "Scènes et Types,"* edited by Pascal Blanchard, Stéphane Blanchoin, Nicolas Bancel, Gilles Boëtsch, Hubert Gerbeau, 171–174. Paris: ACHAC and SYROS, 1995.

Vergès, Françoise. "Creole Skin, black Masks: Fanon and Disavowal." *Critical Inquiry* 23 (Spring 1997): 578–595.

Vignal, Daniel. "Homophilie dans le roman négro-africain d'expression anglaise et française." *Peuple noir, peuple Africain*, no. 33 (May-June 1983): 63–81.

Voltaire. *Candide*. Paris: Librairie Larousse, 1970.

West, D.J. "Homophobia: Covert and Overt." In *Male Victims of Sexual Assault*, edited by G.C. Mezey and M.B. King, 17–34. Oxford: Oxford University Press, 1993.

Weulersse, Jacques. *Noirs et Blancs: A travers l'Afrique nouvelle: de Dakar au Cap*. Paris: Librairie Armand Colin, 1931.

Wittig, Monique. "One Is Not Born Woman." In *The Lesbian and Gay Studies Reader*, edited by Henry Abelove, Michèle Aina Barale, David M. Halperin, 103–109. New York: Routledge, 1993.

Woodward, Peter. *The Horn of Africa: Politics and International Relations*. New York: I.B. Tauris, 1996.

Young-Bruehl, Elisabeth. *Anatomy of Prejudice*. Cambridge: Harvard University Press, 1996.

Yewah, Emmanuel. "Sony Labou Tansi and his Unstable Political Figures," *The French Review*, 67.1 (Oct. 1993): 93–104.

Zabus, Chantal. "'Out' in Africa." *Gboungboun: The Ponal Magazine*, 1 (2) (November 2007). Accessed February 11, 2009. http://www.projectponal.com/newsletter/commentary/commentaryZabus.

Zabus, Chantal. *Out in Africa: Same-Sex Desire in Sub-Saharan Literatures and Cultures*. Suffolk, GB: James Curry, 2013.

Žižek, Slavoj. "Some politically incorrect reflections on violence in France." *Multitudes: revue politique, artistique, philosophique*. Nov. 21, 2005. Accessed April 24, 2010. http://multitudes.samizdat.net/Some-politically-incorecct.html.

Book of Jasher Referred to in Joshua and Second Samuel. (Salt Lake City: J.H. Parry & Co., 1887) Accessed May 27, 2016. http://www.ccel.org/a/anonymous/jasher/5.htm.

"Dévirginer." *Trésor de la langue française*. Accessed Sept. 10, 2012. http://stella.atilf.fr/Dendien/scripts/tlfiv5/advanced.exe?8;s=2222699085;.

"Fetish." Definitions 1a., and 1b. Accessed April 4, 2010. http://www.merriam-webster.com/dictionary/fetish.

The Holy Bible, King James Version. Harrisburg, V.A.: Meridian 1974.

"Imprégnable." Definition 2. *Trésor de la langue française*. Accessed Sept. 10, 2012. http://stella.atilf.fr/Dendien/scripts/tlfiv5/advanced.exe?8; s=2172564045;.

"Intimité." Definitions I.A.; IIA-1.; IIA-2a; IIA-2b, *Trésor de la langue française*. Accessed April 14, 2010. http://atilf.atilf.fr/dendien/scripts/tlfiv5/advanced.exe?35; s=2172564045;.

"Kermesse." *Dictionnaire Sexuelle: Lexique / Glossaire des Expressions Sexuelles.* Accessed March 1, 2010. http://www.dictionnaire-sexuel.com/definition-k.html.

"Viande." Definition 2. *Trésor de la Langue Française.* Accessed Sept. 10, 2012. http://stella.atilf.fr/Dendien/scripts/tlfiv5/visusel.exe?65;s=2172564045;r=3;nat=;sol=2;. Index.

Index